THE SECOND
INTERNATIONAL
1889-1914

THE SECOND INTERNATIONAL 1889-1914

James Joll

'C'est la lutte finale:
Groupons-nous, et demain,
L'Internationale
Sera le genre humain.'
EUGENE POTTIER, 1871

'It is not an easy job. It is easy to
go wrong. It is abominably easy
to mistake shams for realities.'
H. G. WELLS

Routledge & Kegan Paul
London and Boston

First published in 1955
by Weidenfeld & Nicolson
This revised and extended new edition
first published in 1974
by Routledge & Kegan Paul Ltd
Broadway House, 68–74 Carter Lane,
London EC4 5EL and
9 Park Street,
Boston, Mass. 02108, USA

Set in Plantin
and printed in Great Britain by
Alden & Mowbray Ltd at the Alden Press, Oxford

ISBN 0 7100 7966 4

CONTENTS

PREFACE TO THE SECOND EDITION

Since this book first appeared in 1955, there has been a great growth of interest in the history of international socialism before the First World War. Much important research has been done both on the international links and the ideological development of socialism as well as on the structure of individual parties and on the actual nature of their working-class support. In the Soviet Union, the period of the Second International is no longer dismissed as of no importance; and Lenin is now seen once more against the background from which he sprang. In France, M. Georges Haupt has done invaluable work both in establishing a bibliographical record of the printed sources for the study of the Second International, in publishing documents, and in giving an account of the situation and structure of the International at the outbreak of war in 1914.[1] Mme Annie Kriegel has examined the background from which the French Communist Party emerged and in so doing has thrown much light on the nature of the French socialist movement in 1914.[2] In Germany, the work of the *Historische Kommission zu Berlin* has contributed much to the development of systematic research into the history of the German working-class movement.[3] In

[1] Georges Haupt, *La Deuxième Internationale 1880–1914. Essai bibliographique* (Paris 1964); *Programm und Wirklichkeit* (Neuwied 1970); *Socialism and the Great War* (Oxford 1972); (ed.) Bureau Socialiste International, *Comptes rendus, manifestes et circulaires*, Vol. I, *1900–1907* (Paris—The Hague 1969); (ed.) *Correspondance entre Lénine et Camille Huysmans 1905–1914* (Paris—The Hague 1963).

[2] Annie Kriegel, *Aux origines du Communisme français* (2 vols, Paris—The Hague 1964).

[3] See their periodical publication *Internationale Wissenschaftliche Kor-*

East Germany, too, some detailed work of value is being carried out. The unique and invaluable collections of the International Institute for Social History in Amsterdam have become increasingly available to students, and have inspired a number of important research projects and monographs.[1] The late Julius Braunthal, drawing on a lifetime's personal experience of the international socialist movement which started in Vienna before 1914, published a three-volume summary of the activities of the various Internationals[2] which has taken its place alongside G. D. H. Cole's *History of Socialist Thought* as an indispensable handbook for students of the subject. Dr Dieter Groh has published a massive study of the German Social Democratic Party on the eve of the First World War.[3]

In revising my book for a new edition, I have tried to take account of some of this recent research by modifying, expanding and correcting some paragraphs. I have revised and re-written the Epilogue, and I have tried to bring the bibliography up to date. I have not however attempted to write a new book, and hope that this one may still serve as a brief introduction to a subject of growing complexity, interest and importance.

London, 1973   James Joll

respondenz zur Geschichte der deutschen Arbeiterbewegung, ed. by Henryk Skrzypczak.

[1] See especially their *International Review of Social History*.

[2] Julius Braunthal, *Geschichte der Internationale* (3 vols, Hanover 1961–71: Engl. tr. *History of the International* (2 vols, so far, London 1966–7).

[3] Dieter Groh, *Negative Integration und revolutionärer Attentismus* (Frankfurt-Main 1973).

ACKNOWLEDGMENTS

I am very grateful to those survivors from the pre-1914 socialist movement, many of whom have since died, who were kind enough to spare time to talk to me: the late President Karl Renner, Monsieur Bracke-Desrousseaux, and Dr Friedrich Adler. I should also like to thank, among others, Herr Willi Eichler, the late Dr Oskar Pollak and the late Herr Wenzel Jaksch for arousing my curiosity in European socialism: M. Etienne Weill-Raynal, M. Paul Louis, Herr Walter Hacker, the late Professor G. D. H. Cole, Sir Isaiah Berlin, Professor Asa Briggs, Mr Denis Healey MP, and Professor Carl Schorske for help on many points: and Mr Patrick Gardiner for reading the proofs. Dr Gerhard A. Ritter was good enough to read certain chapters and to let me see his work on the working-class movement in Wilhelmine Germany, before publication. Sir J. W. Wheeler-Bennett kindly allowed me to make use of an unpublished essay dealing with events in 1914. My chief debt is to those institutions of which I was a member while writing this book—the Institute for Advanced Study, Princeton, New Jersey, and St Antony's College, Oxford.

INTRODUCTION

There are a number of reasons why it seems worth while to attempt a history of the international aspects of Socialism between 1889, the year of the founding of the Second International, and 1914, when the unity of Socialists everywhere, in which so many hopes had been placed, was shown to be a sham. First of all, as in any historical episode, there is the interest of the personalities involved and their reaction to the problems presented to them. For at least fifty years international Socialism was one of the great intellectual forces in Europe; and the movement included at various times people as striking and as diverse as Lenin and Bernard Shaw, Rosa Luxemburg and William Morris, Jean Jaurès and Benito Mussolini, while no statesman or political thinker could avoid taking it into account.

Secondly, and it is from this angle that the question has most frequently been studied, it is in the Second International that the Third had its roots. Its weaknesses and mistakes contributed to the rise of Communism; its doctrinal discussions were the link between the original teachings of Marx and the 'Marxism-Leninism' which is the official creed of some nine hundred million people today.

Finally, Social Democracy was a genuinely international force. It was believed that certain problems were common to the parties which were members of the Second International and that they could be met by common solutions. Thus the tactical behaviour and the theoretical beliefs of one Socialist party often had a profound influence on other parties; and, indeed, one of the main themes of the history of the Second

International is the imposition by the strongest Socialist party of Europe, the German Social Democratic Party, of doctrines and tactics on other parties, notably the French, with, it may be thought, disastrous consequences to the whole subsequent development of French social and political life. Moreover, the Second International before 1914 represented large numbers of people all over Europe who believed that it would be possible to prevent war by international action against it; and the story of the failure of the Second International to do this is both pathetic and instructive.

This book does not set out to be a history of the Socialist parties of Europe. Nor is it a history of the development of Socialist political theory.[1] It attempts to be an account of European Socialism as it found organized expression in the Congresses and other activities of the Second International.[2] For this reason very little is said about the rise of the Labour Party in England, and still less about the socialist movement in the United States. The British Labour Party has always stood apart from the other European Socialist parties: it has been fortunate in that the concept of the class struggle has rarely been applicable to day to day English political life; and it has been mercifully free from the squabbles about doctrine that took up so much time at the conferences of the continental, and especially the German, parties. The British Labour movement was represented in the International; the 1896 International Congress was held in London; individuals, notably James Keir Hardie, played a big part in international discussions. But the Labour Party was never revolutionary and never Marxist, except for minorities like the Social Democratic Federation and its later offshoots which had, perhaps for that reason, an exaggerated importance in foreign eyes.

---

[1] For this aspect of the subject see John Plamenatz, *German Marxism and Russian Communism* (London 1954); G. D. H. Cole, *History of Socialist Thought* (Vols. I and II, London 1953–4. Further volumes to come).

[2] Even here it must be incomplete owing to the disappearance of the files of the Bureau of the International for this period.

Indeed, a study of the Second International must be mostly concerned with the French and German Socialist parties and their interaction. It is in part the story of the influence of German Socialism on the rest of Europe, of French attempts to resist it in the interest of a different tradition, and of the final powerlessness of the German Social Democrats to prevent a war against France in 1914. Just as the First International had collapsed because of Marx's attempts to dominate it and just as the Third International was to end as a tool of the government of the Soviet Union, so the Second International was to succumb to the efforts, however well intentioned, of the German Socialists to impose their theories and rules of action (or inaction) on the other member parties. In the First International the tyranny was only doctrinal: it could have little effect on practical politics. But once socialism began to be the creed of mass parties, decisions about doctrine and tactics affected political development more widely. The disastrous effects of the Russian Communist Party's intervention in the affairs of other members of the Third International are well-known; but it could perhaps be argued that the influence of German Socialism on other Social Democratic parties in the Second International was nearly as unfortunate, retarding, for example, the development of a specifically French Socialism, excluding some of the ablest men in the Third Republic from office for many years, and encouraging a rigid Marxism in the trammels of which an important section of the French Socialist Party remained caught until quite recently. For those who like to see political issues in personal terms, Jaurès and Bebel can be regarded as the protagonists not only of two rival forms of Socialism, but also of two different ways of looking at politics.

THE SOCIALIST WORLD
IN 1889

There are moments in history when ideas, long discussed by
intellectuals, begin to acquire political reality, when new forces
appear that are capable of upsetting the balance of power between classes, as between states, when old doctrines and prac-
tices have gradually to be abandoned, and existing society
strains itself to come to terms with a new age. Such a moment
was reached in Europe during the 1880s.

For the great depression of the previous decade had had many
effects. Free trade was no longer so widely regarded as the
natural goal of economic endeavour as it had been in the middle
of the century; in Germany the tariffs of 1879 marked the end,
politically as well as economically, of the brief liberal period;
the concessions which Napoleon III had made to Cobden's
arguments by lowering certain French tariffs in 1860 had been
revoked by the new republic; even in England, where free
trade was regarded as the axiomatic basis of Britain's prosperity,
some academic economists and the occasional politician on the
look out for a striking slogan began to appeal for 'Fair Trade'.
All over Europe landowners and peasants were beginning to
feel the effects of the development of North America: improved
methods of transport and farming enabled food from the vast
Middle West to be sold in Europe at prices below those that
were possible for the English or Prussian farmers, at a time
when a growing population provided an ever larger demand.
Like the industrialists, the farmers too began to want a protec-
tive tariff, and both groups were beginning to use political influence and organization to gain their economic ends.

The forces that were leading to the abandonment of the belief in free trade were also making people doubt other doctrines of the liberal political economy. In Germany, particularly, the phenomenally rapid development of heavy industry had created a new urban proletariat which had to be assimilated into the Bismarckian empire, if that empire was to survive. Professors and politicians began to preach doctrines for state action to deal with the problems of an industrial society. In England these problems were not new; but many people were beginning to think that the condition of the working class could not be improved by the natural laws of economics softened by voluntary charity. A new political theory, based on a belief in the necessity of state interference to secure a minimum standard of existence, was coming into being. Even in France and Italy, where the full force of the industrial revolution had yet to be felt, the 'Social Question' was being widely discussed. Moreover, with the spread of education and the growth of a popular press, more people were in a position to take part in these discussions than thirty or forty years earlier when intellectuals were first becoming aware that there was a 'social question'.

These changes in the climate of economic thought were accompanied by political changes. France had had universal manhood suffrage since 1848. In Germany, although many of the individual states obstinately maintained a restricted franchise, members of the Imperial Parliament were elected by all males over the age of twenty-five. The English Parliament in 1884 completed the work started in 1832 of enfranchising nearly all male citizens. Thus it was becoming possible for new political organizations to come into being and to send their representatives to parliament. Specifically working class parties began to emerge. Socialism, from being a doctrine of economic and political theorists, became the creed of mass parties. Along with this development of new political activity, industrial workers were beginning to be organized for other purposes; the depression of the 'seventies and its consequent unemployment made such organization an urgent necessity. Trade unions, for collective bargaining with employers, were replacing in Britain, France and Germany the old-fashioned workers' organizations, with their emphasis on the maintenance of professional standards and mutual help. And these new unions were able to show their economic power by mass stoppages of work, like the London dock strike of 1889, or the strike in the Ruhr coal mines in the same year.

These were international trends and regarded as such both by the leaders of the new parties and by the upholders of the existing order, although the size and forms of Socialist organization and the methods of its representation varied widely. Germany in the 1880s provided the most important and striking example of a mass Socialist movement and of the measures of a government to meet its challenge. Both the political traditions of Prussia and the economic and social conditions of the new empire favoured the development of Socialism. There was a tradition of state action in Prussia that had withstood and even counter-attacked *laisser-faire* political economy. There had been writers in Germany like Fichte who had preached the merits of state control of the economic life of the citizens long before the industrial revolution made such action practically necessary, and, indeed, one of the most intelligent French observers of German Socialism even went so far as to trace its ancestry back to Luther.[1] There had been since 1860 a great increase in the population and an enormous expansion in industry. And so, by the 1880s, Germany had the largest Socialist party in the world, while at the same time the government was embarking on the most advanced programme of social security yet seen, coupled

---

[1] Jean Jaurès, *De primis socialismi germanici lineamentis apud Lutherum, Kant, Fichte et Hegel* (Latin Thesis, Toulouse 1892). French translation *Les origines du socialisme allemand* reprinted in Jaurès, *Oeuvres*, ed. Max Bonnafous, *Etudes Socialistes*, I (Paris 1931).

with legislation intended to prevent the Socialist party from recruiting and organizing the working class.

By 1880 the German Social Democratic Party had a doctrine, a tradition of practical agitation, outstanding leaders and mass support. The doctrine was supplied by Marx and Engels, the tradition of agitation by Lassalle. In 1875, at the Gotha Congress, German Socialists had formed a united party with a programme that combined Marxist theory with some concessions to the followers of Lassalle; (because of these concessions the programme was subjected to typically ill-tempered criticism by the Master in London). Lassalle, who had been killed in a duel in 1864, had been more of an agitator than a theorist, and was not an original thinker like Marx; but he had appreciated the possibilities of creating a mass working class party under universal suffrage. He had been an advocate of Prussia's right to rule in a united Germany and had implied that the new order of society would come through the capture of the existing state machinery for collectivist ends. Thus the Gotha programme included, for instance, demands for producers' co-operative associations with state aid, as well as some of the Lassallean catch-phrases like 'the iron law of wages' and the assertion that all classes other than the working class are only 'one reactionary mass'. All of these demands and phrases were later dropped when the Erfurt Congress of 1891 produced a purely Marxist programme and statement of doctrine. Even by 1875, indeed, Lassalle's followers had no outstanding men among them and, since their leader's death, had been divided among themselves, so that the initiative had passed to their Marxist rivals. Yet the Lassallean and nationalist strain in German Socialism was an important one, and was to be revived later when the rigidity of Marxist orthodoxy began to break down.

The two leaders of the new party, which soon took the name by which it has been known ever since, the *Sozialdemokratische Partei Deutschlands* (SPD), were Wilhelm Liebknecht and

August Bebel. They were men of very different types. Liebknecht, the older of the two, was born in 1825. He came of an
old academic and professional family that could trace its family
history back to the time of the Reformation.[1] As a brilliant
young man, he soon broke away from the traditions of his
family and plunged into the romantic revolutionary activity
that preceded the revolution of 1848. He went to Paris when the
revolution broke out there and, because of sickness, could not
return to Germany till the autumn, when he took part in the
armed rising in Baden, and he spent the next months between
prison and the last desperate attempts to save something of the
revolution from collapse. From 1849 until 1863 he was in exile
in Switzerland and England, where he became a friend and
disciple of Karl Marx. He spoke fluent English and French, and
had acquired in his years abroad a real feeling for foreign
Socialism and international working-class movements. When he
returned to Germany, he settled in Leipzig (for he was rapidly
expelled from Prussia) and there met August Bebel, a carpenter
fourteen years younger than himself.

Bebel was of working class origin and upbringing. He had
had a hard childhood and little education. His father was a
Prussian NCO, his mother a domestic servant from Wetzlar.
He was born in a barracks outside Cologne. The father died
when August was three and the mother at once married her
brother-in-law, a prison warder, but he too died after three
years. Seven years later, when Bebel was thirteen, his mother
also died, worn out by the attempt to bring up her two sons.
The uncle and aunt into whose care August then came at once
apprenticed him to a carpenter. Five years later, as a skilled
journeyman, he started to wander round Germany until he
finally settled to practise his trade in Leipzig. There in 1861 he
began his political career in local working class politics.

[1] F. Mehring, *Geschichte der deutschen Sozialdemokratie* (Stuttgart 1897), I,
p.421.

It was his meeting with Liebknecht that converted him to Marxism. Liebknecht clearly made a great impression on him—'That is a man you can learn something from'[1] was his immediate, and typical, reaction. Both were elected to the North German Diet in 1867, and were from then on established political figures. Both had learnt their practical politics in the struggle not only with Bismarck but with Lassalle's followers, but Liebknecht was the more pliable of the two: his early romanticism was never fully quenched by his Marxist orthodoxy. Bebel, however, who lacked Liebknecht's wide international experience, volatile temperament and intellectual interests, was largely conditioned by these early years. He came into radical politics at a time when Lassalle's agitation had just launched the working class movement in Germany, and the years up to 1875 were dominated for him by the struggle with Lassalle's successors about doctrine and tactics. It was in these quarrels among what were still comparatively unimportant groups that Bebel's real political experience was gained. This is an important factor in his later development; from the Eisenach Congress of 1869, where he expelled his opponents skilfully and unscrupulously, he was never so much at home as in managing a congress, drafting agenda, expelling dissidents and hammering his points home in those three-hour speeches which have been the pattern for later Marxist oratory. By 1875 the Social Democratic Party emerged as a united body, and its increase in size, discipline and efficiency was largely Bebel's work.

Meanwhile Bebel and Liebknecht were gaining a reputation outside Germany. Unlike the Lassalleans, they were unremittingly opposed to the establishment of Prussian domination in Germany. They had opposed the war of 1866, and in 1870 were able to make a more striking protest. In July of that year they abstained from voting the credits demanded for the war against

---

[1] 'Donnerwetter, von dem kann man was lernen.' A. Bebel, *Aus Meinem Leben* (new ed. Berlin 1946), I, p.117.

France—abstained rather than opposed, because a vote against, they considered, would put them in a position of voting for Napoleon III; and in November 1870, with two of their colleagues in the North German Diet, they protested against the annexation of Alsace-Lorraine. Bebel indeed received a rather embarrassing letter of thanks from the French Consul in Vienna. These gestures in a moment of extreme national enthusiasm won Bebel and Liebknecht a deserved reputation as internationalists and explain some of the respect in which they were to be held abroad. In the following year, too, Bebel's activities led him to be sentenced to four years imprisonment for incitement to high treason. The imprisonment was not very rigorous, and it is characteristic that Bebel should have spent the time in serious study—he read Plato, Aristotle, Macchiavelli, Darwin, Ludwig Büchner and Liebig, while Liebknecht used to be allowed to visit him and give him lessons in English and French. It is during this period that he sketched his largest theoretical work, *Woman in the Past, Present and Future*; but he was never a political theorist, and was more concerned to make Marx's theories the basis of effective mass political action.

The extension of universal suffrage to the whole of Germany, at least as far as elections to the Reichstag were concerned, coupled with the increase of the urban proletariat and the breakneck economic development of the 1870s, soon gave the leaders of the Socialists the support they needed. From 1875 onwards they were a serious force in German politics. This was enough to make the government anxious, and in 1878 Bismarck used the pretext and atmosphere provided by two attempts to assassinate the Emperor to pass an anti-Socialist law, seriously restricting the activities of the new party. There is absolutely no evidence that the attempts at assassination had anything to do with the Social Democrats: but any terrorist outrages could be attributed to them by a public for whom the burning and looting of the Paris Commune of 1871 was still a vivid memory. Under the anti-Socialist law all the normal activities of a political party were made extremely difficult or impossible: meetings were forbidden, newspapers suppressed, local Socialist associations dissolved, while 'persons from whom danger to the public safety or order is feared'—the professional Socialist politicians in fact—could be expelled from the district in which they lived.[1] The anti-Socialist law was continuously in operation until 1890, when Bismarck fell without having succeeded in persuading the Reichstag to agree to its renewal. The main effect of these measures—like that of the comparable measures against the Roman Catholic Church a few years earlier—was to strengthen the will and organization of the victims, and provide them with a list of martyrs to their cause. In fact, neither the anti-Socialist Law nor the programme of social insurance on which Bismarck embarked soon after, checked the progress of the Social Democratic Party. Its members continued to be returned to the Reichstag in large numbers; its mass support increased. In 1890 it had thirty-five seats and nearly a million and a half votes: about a fifth of the votes cast were for Socialists.

This formidable mass party, with able leaders who had been in personal contact with Marx until his death in 1883, and who had the benefit of the continuous (if not always consistent) advice of Engels until he died in 1896, now had its prestige enhanced by the sufferings of its members under the anti-Socialist law, and was inevitably regarded with respect by Socialists in other countries. The small scattered groups which had been founded in the period of the First International began to amalgamate and form parties largely modelled on the German pattern: the *Parti Ouvrier Belge* for instance in 1885, or the Austrian and Swiss Social Democratic Parties in 1888. But countries like Switzerland and Belgium, though possessing the social and economic conditions for a mass working class party,

---

[1] The provisions of the anti-Socialist law are conveniently summarised in Bertrand Russell, *German Social Democracy* (London 1896), pp.100–2.

were too small for their Socialist parties to be equal in strength to that of Germany, while Austria and Hungary were too backward politically and industrially for the Socialists to have much part in internal politics (universal suffrage was not introduced into the Austrian half of the Monarchy until 1907 and, though promised in Hungary, never in fact came into effect till after 1918). These smaller parties therefore looked to Germany for a lead, and in many cases for financial assistance, although the Belgians, at least, were soon to show themselves a formidable force in internal politics and to develope on lines of their own. Only one country could produce a working class party and tradition that could compete with the German Social Democratic Party as an equal—France.

To the organizational gifts and achievements of the Germans the French could oppose a living tradition of violent revolution. The Commune of 1871 had taken its place as one of the great revolutionary acts of the century, and Marxist historians were already moulding the facts of that rising to fit their theories of what the nature of such an outbreak must be. However, the reaction after the Commune had shattered the French working class movement and it was only being slowly pieced together again. In the late 'seventies, as evidence in support of his case for the anti-Socialist laws, Bismarck was expressing the view that socialism was dead in France, while Germany was becoming its centre in Europe; and Thiers, shortly before his death in 1877, told his electors: 'Nobody talks of socialism any more, rightly. We are rid of it.'[1] The measures taken after the Commune—a law of 1872 made membership of the already disintegrating International a criminal offence, and over 9,000 people who had taken part in the insurrection were sentenced to death, deportation or prison—seemed to have been effective. 'The French

---

[1] 'On ne parle plus de socialisme, et l'on fait bien. Nous sommes débarrassés du socialisme,' quoted in A. Zévaès, *De l'introduction du Marxisme en France* (Paris 1947), p.70.

section of the International dissolved, the revolutionaries shot, sent to prison or condemned to exile; the clubs dispersed and meetings forbidden; the terror confining to obscure back rooms the few men who had escaped the massacre: such was the situation of the proletariat immediately after the Commune.'[1] However in 1879 most of the men condemned had been pardoned, and in the following year the Government, with an eye to popular support in the approaching elections, introduced a complete amnesty. The exiled leaders of the left returned to France and gave a new impetus to the workers' organizations which had been slowly growing in the past few years.

Yet there were many reasons why this revival of working class activity in France did not lead to the establishment of a powerful and united mass party on the German model. The differences between the conceptions of Socialist organization in the two countries were well, if idealistically, expressed by Lucien Herr, the librarian of the *Ecole Normale Supérieure* and the political confessor of several generations of French Socialists. He wrote in 1890:

'The German Socialist Party is above all a disciplined hierarchy; ours is a voluntary and free association of men bound together by confidence and not by obedience. Their disciplined cohesion is their strength; I am glad of it. But we neither can nor want to appropriate it. We cannot do so because we are differently made from them; because even politically militarism is repugnant to us. What is all powerful with us is the freedom and spontaneity of the formation of our groups; strong unity is that which results from this, not that which dominates the groups . . . . The Germans are an army and there lies their strength. It's perhaps also their weakness. For three dangers always threaten an army: flabbiness due to over-confidence, division among its leaders, and demoralisation caused by an initial defeat.'[2]

[1] F. Pelloutier, *Histoire des Bourses du Travail* (Paris 1921), p.69, quoted in Jean Maitron, *Histoire du Mouvement Anarchiste en France* (Paris 1951), p.78.
[2] Charles Andler, *Vie de Lucien Herr* (Paris 1932), p.102.

In fact unity of any kind was lacking in the French Socialist movement. Its traditions were diverse: the utopian idealism of Fourier, the plans for the economic reorganization of society of Saint-Simon or Louis Blanc, Proudhon's Anarchism and a tradition of insurrection unaccompanied by doctrine, represented by Auguste Blanqui, were now mingled, and sometimes conflicting, with ideas from abroad, such as those of Marx and Bakunin. The result was that in 1889 there were a number of groups competing for the allegiance of the French working class—and in any case that class, strictly considered, was not very numerous. (Only 35.9 per cent of the population were classed as urban in 1886.) Even by 1911, when the trade unions were making great efforts to assert their power, there were only 1,000,000 organized workers to compare with Britain's three million or Germany's formidable leap from 269,000 in 1895 to three million in 1909.

A Marxist Socialist party, the *Parti Ouvrier Français*, was founded at Marseilles in 1879, after a conference in which the other groups, notably the Anarchists, were outvoted. The new party and its programme were given the official blessing of Marx the following year when its most important member, Jules Guesde, went to London to visit the master. Guesde, who was born in 1845, was to be one of the most important figures in both the French and the international Socialist movement for the next forty years. He was a well-educated man from a poor middle-class family, and spent his life as a journalist, agitator and politician. He had been imprisoned for a short time under the Empire, exiled for five years after the Commune, during which time he associated with anarchists in Switzerland and Italy. But in spite of these early anarchist leanings and consequent differences of opinion with Marx, he had eventually emerged, with Marx's son-in-law Lafargue, as the main advocate of Marxism in France. He was a proud, honourable, bigoted man, lacking in personal charm, but with an energy, honesty and disinterestedness that gave him strength. Zola has left a description of him: 'His voice was warm, harsh and heartrending . . . . he had a whole range of passionate gesticulation with his arms . . . . rather hairy, stooping and with a perpetual cough.'[1]

But the Marxists' apparent successs in producing a united French Socialist Party did not last long. The French worker employed in a small workshop, often, and especially in Paris, on skilled work, had little sympathy with mass parties or mass trade unions. The ideals of Proudhon with their insistence on decentralization into small units were more attractive than Marxist or Lassallean conceptions of state Socialism. And, at the same time, with the amnesty for the Communards and the triumph of the republicans, Socialist leaders had a genuine interest in defending the bourgeois Republic, and in trying to gain such immediate reforms as were possible. Both the Anarchist refusal to accept Marxist dictation and a desire to influence practical politics as far as possible contributed to the first split in the new POF. In 1882 a man who embodied both the anarchist and what was coming to be called the 'Possibilist' trend, broke away and founded a new party, the *Fédération des Travailleurs Socialistes de France*. This was Paul Brousse (1844–1912), a doctor of medicine, who during his exile had been active as an Anarchist in Barcelona and Switzerland, where he had edited an Anarchist paper and had been imprisoned and expelled for publishing articles in defence of tyrannicide at the moment of the attempts of the life of the German Emperor in 1878.[2] Brousse had learnt to mistrust Marx's

[1] Quoted in Dolléans, *Histoire du Mouvement Ouvrier* (Paris 1946), II, p.21.
[2] At his trial Brousse tried to turn the tables on his Swiss accusers: 'Et Guillaume Tell, Messieurs, votre héros légendaire? Sa figure revit partout: sous la plume, le pinceau, le ciseau de vos artistes: sa flèche siffle dans la musique de Rossini, et son nom éclate dans vos chants et retentit dans vos discours officiels! Et pourquoi cette glorification? pour cette raison fort juste que Tell est réputé avoir tué Gessler.' Alain Sergent and Claude Harmel, *Histoire de l'Anarchie* (Paris 1949), Part I, p.444.

attempts to dictate to the international Socialist movement.
'There are two men of talent in London: Marx and Engels.
But these men have one unacceptable pretension: to keep
the whole Socialist movement within the limits of their
brains.'[1] This criticism reflects an attitude of suspicion and dislike of German control that was to recur constantly in the subsequent history of the French Socialist movement. The Possibilists, too, saw the advantages of the Republic; they were to
oppose General Boulanger's attempt to seize power; whereas
Guesde washed his hands of what he regarded as a bourgeois
struggle, just as he was to do in the Dreyfus affair. At the same
time the Broussists were prepared to adopt a policy of limited
co-operation with other parties, in municipal government, for
instance; here too their split with the Marxists was characteristic
of one of the perennial controversies of the International.

There were other groups that contributed to the disunity of
the French Socialist movement—though in many cases personal
antipathies and rivalries concealed themselves behind a screen
of political doctrine. In addition to anarchists and Possibilists,
there were, too, inheritors of an older, pre-Marxist revolutionary tradition. Auguste Blanqui, for instance, who spent some
two-thirds of his life in prison, lived on memories of the
glorious revolutionary days in Paris in 1848 and 1871, and
founded a Central Revolutionary Committee in 1881. On his
death shortly afterwards, at the age of seventy-six, the leadership
of this movement passed to Edouard Vaillant, and the party
took the name of *Parti Socialiste Révolutionnaire*. Vaillant was a
remarkable man; he had studied both medicine and engineer-
ing, had suffered the usual spell in exile and had been elected a
municipal councillor in Paris in 1884. '*Blanquisme*' was more the
expression of a political temperament than of a doctrine. It was
a method of revolutionary organization rather than a political

---

[1] Brousse, *Le Marxisme dans l'Internationale*, quoted in Zévaès, *De
l'introduction du Marxisme en France* (Paris 1947), p.127.

philosophy. It could be traced back to Babeuf, and combined a belief in direct revolutionary action with a belief in the importance of a small *élite* to lead the revolution, which has much in common with Leninist practice. Vaillant's insistence on the doctrine of the class struggle, however, and the necessity for planning and organizing revolutions, gave him in fact a natural sympathy with the Marxists, and his party was eventually to unite with theirs, although Vaillant himself continued to play an independent and courageous role in the international Socialist movement until his death in 1915.

The assets of the French Socialist and revolutionary movement—its traditions, the vigour and devotion of its members, outstanding leaders like Guesde, Brousse and Vaillant (the most remarkable of them, Jean Jaurès, was still a Radical deputy in 1889 and did not join the Socialists till four years later)—were outweighed by its disadvantages—the backwardness of French industry and political disunity (and further splits in the Socialist parties were still to occur). Therefore its practical importance was as yet small as far as French internal politics were concerned. In the elections of 1889 only seven members of various shades of Socialism were returned to parliament (as compared to the thirty-five seats the German Social Democrats were to win in 1890). Yet internationally the prestige of the French was great, and Paris still the natural place for an international Socialist congress, which in any case would have to be based on the French and German Socialists.

The parties founded on the German model in Belgium, Switzerland and Austria were too weak to be of international importance, though they were to contribute individual leaders to the international movement. In Italy and Spain the situation was comparable to that in France, but with the causes of working class weakness even stronger; economic backwardness and doctrinal disunity meant that as yet neither Italian nor Spanish Socialism was very important. In these two countries alone had the influence of Bakunin been really deep or lasting. The Anarchists captured the initiative in Spain and remained for many years the most powerful force in the Spanish working class. In Italy too, Marxism had not in Marx's lifetime been an important force. Marx himself had described the Italian section of the International as consisting of 'lawyers without clients, doctors without knowledge or patients, billiard-playing students, commercial travellers and various more or less unsavoury journalists of the gutter press'.[1] Yet by 1887 Socialism had attracted more distinguished supporters, and after many divisions and discussions on the same lines as those in France, in 1892 a vaguely Marxist, and definitely anti-Anarchist, Socialist party was founded which soon, in alliance with other parties of the left, won some parliamentary influence.

Although in the other European countries Socialism was of less international importance than in France or Germany, working class parties there developed on similar lines to those in one or other of those countries. Two countries alone remained largely outside this general movement—Russia and England. Russia was, of course, to all liberals everywhere in Europe the very pattern of an autocracy. Moreover, since the assassination of the Czar Alexander II in 1881, it had become even more difficult than before to organize any opposition to the Government. There could be no question of a mass movement there; the leaders of the revolutionary movement had been forced into exile, and it was abroad, especially in Switzerland, that the discussions about organization, doctrines and political activity were carried on. Thus it was not until the revolution of 1905 that the Russian revolutionary movement suddenly appeared to foreign Socialists as an example they themselves might profitably follow; it was only after October 1917 that the Russian Marxists captured the leadership of the international socialist movement. In the meantime, however, the Russian revolutionaries, when

[1] Quoted in W. Hilton-Young, *The Italian Left* (London 1949), p.9.

they appeared at international gatherings, were the object of particular sympathy and respect because of the dangers they had braved. One of them, moreover, George Valentinovitch Plekhanov, soon won an international reputation as expounder and interpreter of Marxist doctrine.

Plekhanov was born in 1856, the son of a minor landowner. From his childhood he was filled with sympathy for the lot of the peasant, and this gave the impulse to his revolutionary development. He was educated at the St. Petersburg Mining Institute; but his time was soon mainly devoted to theorising about the revolutionary movement. In 1880 these activities finally made life in Russia impossible for him, and he went to live abroad. He was to remain in exile until near the end of his life, for he died in 1918, and only returned with the Revolution. Plekhanov was a man of theory, a rationalist by temperament; and, as he thought about the Russian revolutionary movement, he became interested in the city worker as a possible revolutionary force in contrast to the peasant, on whom most of his original colleagues in the 'Land and Freedom' party based their hopes of revolution. His desire for rational theory and organization led him away both from that section of 'Land and Freedom' that broke off to form a terrorist organization (the 'People's Will'—*Narodnaya Volya*), and from the sentimental enthusiasts for the peasant and an idealized Russian past. The works of Marx had early been known in Russia; indeed, Russian was the first foreign language into which *Das Kapital* was translated. And Plekhanov, though he had disagreed with Marx and had grown up among people who sympathized with Bakunin, became more and more influenced by the writings of Marx and Engels. By 1882 he was producing an introduction to a translation of the Communist Manifesto that was wholly Marxist in tone. He had at length found a theoretical system to satisfy him.

The adoption of Marxism inevitably led Plekhanov into a

discussion of how the Marxist analysis could be adapted to Russian society. Could Russia, in fact, miss a step in the dialectical process, and pass straight from feudalism to the dictatorship of the proletariat without an intervening phase of bourgeois capitalism? Plekhanov thought that an industrial society must first emerge, and the industrial workers form the basis of a mass party. The debate was a long one; and it provided the Russian version of the Possibilist controversy in France, for, on Plekhanov's view, no attempt should be made to ameliorate existing conditions since this would only postpone unnecessarily the day when the masses would be ready for revolution. But these discussions were still in the future. In the 1880s the divisions in the Russian revolutionary movement—and especially among the political émigrés—were on the issue of whether revolution would come by the isolated action of individual heroes or by the patient awakening of the masses and formation of a mass party.

Plekhanov was largely responsible for the 'Europeanisation of Russian Socialism' and the formation of an embryo Marxist Social Democratic party. In 1883, Plekhanov, Vera Zasulich and Paul Borisovitch Axelrod formed, in Switzerland, a 'Group of the Liberation of Labour'. Vera Zasulich (1852–1919) brought her experience of militant revolutionary work and the reputation gained by a sensational acquittal after an attempt on the life of the chief of police in St. Petersburg. But if Plekhanov provided the theory for the new group and Vera Zasulich the glamour of practical revolutionary experience, its actual organization was perhaps mainly the work of Axelrod (1850–1928). He was a man who had known the bitterest poverty, for he was the son of Jewish paupers; in his periods of exile abroad he had visited Germany as well as attending Anarchist meetings in Switzerland, and had been influenced by the Lassallean wing of German Socialism: and there he learnt to admire the organizational strength of the SPD. This admiration the other members of the 'Liberation of Labour' were willing to share, now that German Social Democracy, under Bismarck's laws, appeared also to be becoming a party of persecuted martyrs. Thus both Axelrod and Plekhanov were in 1883 ready to found a Marxist party on the German model—even if it could not yet hope to win mass support in Russia. Marx's ideas were in fact gaining on those of Bakunin. Side by side with the older groups, therefore, which believed still in isolated acts of terrorism, in the need to treat the Russian character, institutions and situation as unique, and in the necessity of basing a revolutionary movement on the peasants, there now existed the nucleus of a Social Democratic party on the Western model that, in spite of all appearances to the contrary, would, it was hoped, bring Russian development into line with that predicted by Marx for Western Europe.

In Britain the situation was just the opposite. For there, in what, despite the rapid advances of Germany and the USA, was industrially still the most advanced state in the world, the predictions of Marx were being notoriously falsified. There was little sign of the class struggle; the ruling class had already shown itself capable of introducing radical social reforms. True, working class organizations were growing in strength; the new trade unions were becoming a formidable force. But as yet they were organs for collective bargaining with employers and were not concerned with independent political representation. A few middle class intellectuals, H. M. Hyndman and William Morris, for instance, were interested in Marxism and had founded parties whose internal feuds ran parallel to the schisms in continental Socialism, a fact which perhaps led foreign Socialists to take them more seriously than they deserved. Hyndman had founded the Democratic Federation in 1881 (to become the Social Democratic Federation in 1883); Morris (together with Marx's daughter Eleanor and her volatile companion Edward Aveling) split off in 1884 to form the Socialist League. Another group of intellectuals founded the Fabian Society in 1883, but it was more concerned with immediate improvements in British society than with an international working class movement. However, 'it was able to exert an influence on the British Socialist movement altogether out of proportion to its membership';[1] and it was thus largely responsible for giving the British working class a programme of practical reforms, and a philosophy, deriving from the English utilitarian tradition, that made the English labour movement different, both in theory and practice, from its largely Marxist European counterparts. In Scotland, James Keir Hardie, a coal miner, to whose lips phrases from the Bible were always to come more readily than sentences from the Communist Manifesto, started the Scottish Labour Party in 1888, in the hope of obtaining separate parliamentary representation for labour. He was to be one of the first three independent working class members to be elected to Parliament, and was an agitator of genius who, for all his distance from continental political thought, was almost alone among English Labour leaders of the period to win and hold a place of importance in the international Socialist movement. Yet even he, like some of his successors, as he advanced in international influence was losing in domestic prestige, and was never able to appear at an international conference like his European colleagues, the leader of a united party ready to play an international role.

2.

The International Working Men's Association (the 'First International') which Marx had founded in 1864 was formally dissolved at a meeting in Philadelphia in July 1876. It had in fact ceased to be an effective or coherent body at its Congress at The Hague in 1872 when the breach between Marx and the followers of Bakunin finally split the International, and the Marxist

[1] G. D. H. Cole, *British Working Class Politics 1832–1914* (London 1941), p.121.

rump decided to transfer its General Council to the United States. It had never been a serious force in practical politics; but it was nevertheless of enormous importance for the future. For not only had it provided an organ for the expression of the ideas and personalities of Marx and Bakunin, but also it had awakened all Europe to the possibilities of international working class action. There was at least this much justification for Engels' boast in 1877 that 'the International has completed its task, it has completely achieved its great aims, the union of the proletariat of the whole world against its oppressors'.[1] The Paris Commune became the symbol of the political power of the proletariat, as of the potential threat to the ruling class. Although in its origins this outbreak had nothing to do with the International, it was soon claimed by its adherents, in works like Marx's own address to the General Council of the International Working Men's Association on 30 May 1871,[2] or Lissagaray's *History of the Commune of 1871*, published in 1876. Equally it suited the French Government to lay the blame for the Commune on the intrigues of international adventurers rather than on the sufferings and exasperated patriotism of the Parisian population. And so, on the eve of its extinction, the International was endowed with a legendary power it had lacked in its lifetime, and acquired a largely spurious tradition of heroic international revolutionary action.

It was natural, therefore, that as the various working class movements began to win strength in the 1880s, they should think of creating an international organization to which their new mass support should give fresh vigour.[3] As soon as the survivors of the old International began to take practical steps

[1] In an article in the *Labor Standard* in 1877. Gustav Mayer, *Friedrich Engels* (The Hague 1934), II, p.382.
[2] Reprinted in 1892 as *The Civil War in France* with an introduction by Engels.
[3] For a detailed account see Leo Valiani, *Dalla prima alla seconda Internazionale* (*Movimento Operaio* VI no.2 March–April 1954).

to this end, however, they at once came up against two difficulties: the increased hostility of governments to any form of
international working class organization, and the fundamental
divisions between Marxists and Anarchists which had wrecked
the First International. The hostility of the Governments was
shown by acts like the anti-socialist laws in Germany or the
French Government's action in 1878 in banning a projected
international socialist congress in Paris. These difficulties could,
however, be overcome; Socialists could meet in traditionally
hospitable countries like England and Switzerland; after the
amnesty of the Communards the French government was
becoming more liberal. The controversy between Anarchists
and Marxists, however, was a graver obstacle and was to dominate the early years of the Second International as it had the
end of the First.

These differences were often genuine disagreements about
political tactics, and later the object of serious discussion at
Congresses of the Second International, while in some countries,
notably France and Spain, anarchism was to develop into a
whole system and philosophy of social and economic organization.
But behind these specific divisions there was a profound psycho-
logical difference, a contrast of types of political temperament.

For 'Anarchist' came to be a name to be applied to anybody
who rejected the Marxist ideas of a disciplined political party
with a rationalist 'scientific' philosophy. It was a term that later
was to become simply one of abuse. In a phrase foreshadowing
subsequent Marxist invective, for example, Victor Adler, the
Austrian Socialist leader, claimed proudly that the Austrian
delegation at the International Congress of 1893 had excluded
from its ranks a 'Czech-Nationalist-Chauvinist-Anarchist'.[1]

However, in 1889, the question of exactly who was an Anarchist was not yet settled: and the vague nature and wide range

[1] Proceedings of International Socialist Congress at Zurich, Wednesday
29 July 1893.

of Anarchist doctrine made it difficult to decide. Anarchism, indeed, was, in E. H. Carr's phrase, 'the logical conclusion of the romantic doctrine'.[1] It maintained the supreme importance of the individual, and much of its appeal was to those who disliked the irksome discipline of normal political activity and who liked, as Bakunin himself had, the drama of conspiratorial secret societies. This individualism was based on a hatred of all forms of political organization and a belief in the innate goodness and perfectibility of man, who only needed to be freed from the tyranny of existing institutions to emerge as his own noble self. 'Every state,' wrote Bakunin, 'like every theology, assumes men to be fundamentally bad and wicked,' or again, 'All exercise of power perverts and all submission to authority humiliates.'[2] It was a doctrine that could embrace, at the one extreme, a gentle, utopian belief in self-improvement, or, at the other, a conviction that any means, however violent (or indeed the more violent the better) were justified in order to shake the complacency of existing society. As far as political organization was concerned, Anarchism meant decentralization, a loose structure, and a belief in the effectiveness of '*le propagande par le fait*' in place of action by purely political means.

After the difficulties caused by the Commune and the split between Marxists and Anarchists at the Hague Congress of the International in 1872, the Anarchists survived largely because incoherence and decentralisation made it easier for them to exist as small clandestine groups. Even this was difficult; differences of doctrine divided Anarchists from each other as much as from Marxists. The Anarchist section of the International continued to meet only until 1877, and the last meeting of Bakunin's own loyal followers, the *Fédération Jurassienne*, was held in 1880. Yet the idea of an International had been kept alive, and in 1881 some of the leading Anarchists, Kropot-

[1] E. H. Carr, *Michael Bakunin* (London 1937), p.434.
[2] Carr, p.436.

kin, Elisée Reclus, Johann Most and Errico Malatesta organized an *Alliance Internationale Ouvrière*, (the 'Black International'), with branches in France, Italy and the United States. However both the nature of Anarchist doctrine and the memory of Marx's domination of the old International prevented the Anarchist International from ever being more than a loose association of independent federations; although an International Bureau was to be established for the exchange of information, it does not in fact ever seem to have come into existence.[1] In both France and Germany, too, many Anarchists had not given up hope of uniting with other revolutionary movements. In France they were defeated at the Marseilles Congress; in Germany they were formally expelled (it was to become almost a ritual at the early congresses of the SPD) at a Socialist congress in 1887, held, because of the anti-Socialist laws, at St. Gallen in Switzerland. Yet the influence of Anarchist ideas remained strong in the international Socialist movement and it was not until 1896 that they were finally purged and Marxist orthodoxy was triumphant.

The Marxists, too, had been renewing their international contacts as they recovered from the schisms and repressions of the early 'seventies. The very fact that their leaders had been exiled enabled them to get to know each other personally in the strange revolutionary life that went on in the tolerant atmosphere of Geneva and Zürich. Guesde founded a short-lived weekly paper, *L'Egalité*, in 1877 and began to get contributions from Socialist leaders abroad—among them Bebel, Liebknecht and César de Paepe, one of the leaders of the Belgian Socialist movement[2] and a veteran of the First International who had

---

[1] Maitron, pp.103–4; Dolléans, II, p.90.

[2] The Flemish Socialist Party and *Parti Socialiste Brabancon* were founded in 1877 and amalgamated into a Marxist party, the *Parti Socialiste Belge*, in 1879. A united working class party—*The Parti Ouvrier Belge*—was founded in 1885 by de Paepe, Volders and Anseele—'the first of those acts of realist opportunism so frequent in the history of the Belgian Socialist movement'. See E. Vandervelde, *Le cinquentenaire du POB* (Brussels 1936), p.28.

already made several vain proposals to heal the breach between the two sections. Elsewhere too, in Geneva, Zürich, London, Brussels, Milan,[1] Socialist newspapers encouraged correspondence from abroad and promoted the exchange of socialist ideas. On 9 June 1878 *L'Egalité* published an address of sympathy to the German Socialists at the moment of the introduction of the anti-Socialist laws: 'After the country of Babeuf, Fourier, Delescluze and Varlin[2], behold the country of Karl Marx and Lassalle becoming in its turn the battlefield of the social revolution.'[3] It was characteristic of the relations between French and German Socialism that the *Vorwärts* and the *Berliner Freie Presse*, the organs of the German Social Democratic Party, should have, in the sobriety imposed by the struggle with Bismarck, disavowed the revolutionary tone of the French article.[4]

The Germans were, in fact, very suspicious of any international initiative that did not come from themselves, an attitude in which they were encouraged by the intransigence of Marx and Engels. Both of them had learnt from the failure of the First International and were reluctant to start a new one too soon: what they were hoping for was a revolutionary outbreak in Germany, (now that persecution of Socialists was starting), or in Russia, (where the Emperor Alexander II was murdered by nihilists in 1881), which would provide them with an opportunity for asserting their leadership in a world revolutionary movement. 'We must save up any such demonstration until the moment when it can have a decisive effect,' Engels wrote in 1882, 'that is when European events provoke it.

---

[1] Mayer, *Friedrich Engels*, II, p.383.
[2] Charles Delescluze (1809–1871), one of the members of the Commune, who was killed on the barricades.
  Eugène Varlin (1834–1871), an anarchist, one of the founders of the First International and member of the Commune, executed in 1871.
[3] Zévaès, *Introduction du Marxisme*, p.84.
[4] Zévaès, p.86.

Otherwise we spoil the effect for the future and strike our blow in the air (*und tun einen Schlag ins Wasser*).'[1]

After Marx's death, Engels, perhaps more interested in theory than practice, and reluctant to become too involved in actual politics, while criticizing any action taken by anybody else, remained sceptical about international congresses. But the demand for the formal reconstitution of international links was growing; and Liebknecht, who was almost solely responsible for the international relations of the German Social Democratic Party, became convinced of its necessity. At the Party Congress at St. Gallen in October 1887 it was decided to take the initiative and make plans for an international Socialist congress.

However, the Germans were not alone in thinking that the time had come for such a step. Paul Brousse and the French Possibilists were seeking international contacts and turned naturally to those labour leaders abroad who were also working for such reforms as were possible in existing society, and especially to the English trade unionists. The initiative had in fact already come from the British. The Trades Union Congress at Swansea in September 1887 voted in favour of an international conference to urge claims for an eight-hour day. In November 1888 a meeting was held in London at the invitation of the Parliamentary Committee of the TUC. It was attended by a number of delegates from abroad—Brousse himself, and, among others, Anseele from Belgium. 'He has "done" his six months in jail for siding with the workers, but that has not daunted him any,' Keir Hardie wrote at the time. 'His power of speech is amazing, and, as he closes his lips with a snap at the end of each sentence, he seems to say "There! I have spoken and I mean it".'[2] It was Keir Hardie's first contact with foreign Socialists, and he was impressed: 'Certainly these foreigners

---

[1] Mayer, II, p.383.
[2] William Stewart, *James Keir Hardie* (new ed. London 1925), pp.50–1.

know what they are about.'[1] The Germans did not attend the London meeting, but thought it worth their while to issue a circular explaining and excusing their absence. The result of this meeting was a decision to summon a full dress international congress for the following year.

The fact that both the Germans and the British trade unionists with their French Possibilist friends had decided on an international congress independently and almost simultaneously, at once raised the question of what sort of congress it should be. Was it to be a meeting of political organizations or of trade unions? Was it going to embrace all sections of the working class movement—Guesdists and Broussists, British trade unionists, German Marxists, Anarchists and so on—and try to produce a united International that would at least mask their differences? Or was it to be a congress of Marxist Social Democrats which the Germans would inevitably dominate? The spirit of strife which attended the death of the First International already hovered round the birth of the Second.

[1] Stewart, p.49.

THE FOUNDING OF
THE SECOND INTERNATIONAL

1889 was a natural year for an international revolutionary congress, and Paris the natural place. For it was the centenary year of the French Revolution, and a great exhibition was being held in Paris to celebrate it. It was an opportunity for the French Republic to assert its stability, and for the French nation to demonstrate their recovery from the defeat of 1870. In these circumstances it was only to be expected that the French Socialists should act as hosts for an international Socialist congress: the only question was, which section of them?

Brousse and the Possibilists were the first to act, and, as a result of their meeting in London the previous autumn, issued on 11 March 1889 a public invitation to an international Socialist congress to be held in July. This brought to a head the negotiations that had been going on for some months about the nature of the proposed congress. The discussion was, in fact, the projection of the differences between the French socialist groups on to the international plane. Guesde and his supporters were irreconcilable with Brousse and the Possibilists; neither side were ready to allow the other the privilege of summoning and running an international congress. The Germans, on the other hand, especially Liebknecht, seem to have been genuinely anxious for the proposed congress to be as all-embracing as possible. When they heard of the British proposals for an international meeting, to be sponsored by the TUC and the French Possibilists, they postponed making any plans for the congress that had been decided on at St. Gallen, and started negotiations with the English trade unionists. Accordingly Bebel and Eduard

Bernstein were sent to London to discuss the whole question
both with the English committee and, more important, with
Engels.[1] It was at once clear that neither favoured German
collaboration in the projected congress. The British insisted
that only representatives of trades unions should attend; while
the Germans, whose strength lay rather in their political
organization, demanded that representatives of the German
and Austrian Social Democratic Parties should be present.
Engels viewed these discussions with scepticism, and was
pleased when they broke down. But Liebknecht did not immediately give up hope of reconciling the various Socialist groups
abroad, and on 28 February 1889 a meeting was held at The
Hague, at which the SPD was to make a last effort to unite
Marxists and Possibilists and ensure that the Socialists of
Europe did not display their divisions to the capitalist world by
holding two rival congresses simultaneously. The attempt was
a failure, for one of the main parties concerned, the Possibilists,
refused to attend, and went on with their preparations for their
own congress, so that the only delegates from France were
Marxists. But the smaller parties represented at the Hague,
the Swiss and the Belgians, were so anxious for a united front
that they succeeded in persuading their German colleagues to
postpone summoning a congress of their own in the hope that
a compromise might yet be reached. However, the terms proposed at the Hague meeting—that the Possibilists should
summon the congress, that workers and socialists should be free
to attend as far as the political situation in their countries
allowed, and that the congress as a whole and not the individual
national groups should decide who should be admitted[2]— were
rejected by the Possibilists, presumably (and justifiably) as an

[1] Mayer II, pp.392–3.
[2] Victor Adler, *Die Gründung der neuen Internationale* (Festschrift zum 10
Internationalen Sozialistenkongress, Wien 1914), reprinted in Victor Adler,
Aufsätze, Reden und Briefe (Vienna 1929), VII, p.60.

attempt to flood the congress with Marxists who would then impose their own discipline and rules of procedure.

Thus it was the Possibilists who were the first in the field with their proclamation of 11 March. The reaction of the Marxists was immediate and violent. Eduard Bernstein, the ex-bank clerk who had made his name in the Social Democratic Party as a journalist and one of the editors of the party's paper, published, at Engels' urgent insistence, a pamphlet attacking the Possibilists in terms that were to become only too common in Socialist controversy; the Possibilists, he said, were only agents of their Government; if they held a congress it would be under police protection, whereas a Marxist congress would be held under the suspicious gaze of a hostile police force.[1] It was now clear that if the Marxists wanted an international congress they must organize their own. Already, however, the first signs of future divisions inside the German Social Democratic Party began to appear, for two of its members, later to become prominent as 'Reformists'—the German equivalent of Possibilists—Ignaz Auer and Max Schippel, still wanted to attend the Paris conference. Engels, however, was adamant; an international congress should be held under Marxist auspices or not at all. Indeed, he welcomed the idea of two rival congresses: 'If the two congresses side by side only fulfilled the purpose of making the rival forces turn out—the Possibilists and the London clique on the one side, the European Socialists (who, thanks to the others, are reckoned as Marxists) on the other—and thus display before the world where the real movement is concentrated and where the swindle is, that will be enough.'[2]

Accordingly, the Guesdists set about organizing their congress, and the two rival meetings were both to open on the historic and exciting hundredth anniversary of the storming of

[1] Bernstein, *The International Working Men's Congress of 1889* (London 1889), Mayer, II, p.392.
[2] Engels to Sorge. Mayer, II, p.393.

the Bastille, 14 July. The Marxists met in the Salle Petrelle, rue Petrelle, while the Possibilists and trade unionists met in the rue de Lancry. At a time when, so it is said, there were no less than sixty-nine international congresses being held in Paris[1], the two rival congresses aroused little attention outside the world of organized socialists. The Possibilist Congress was briefly reported in *The Times*, the Marxist Congress scarcely mentioned, and the editor seems, in fact, to have been unaware that a second congress was held at all.[2] They were not even the only workers' congresses held that summer; for a small international printers' congress also met in Paris; it was attended by only seventeen delegates but it was the first of a series of loose links between trade unions of different countries that were to grow in importance over the next two decades.[3]

The passions aroused by the rivalry between the rue Petrelle and the rue de Lancry were considerable: there were rumours that wicked Possibilists lay in wait at the railway stations to lead unsuspecting delegates from the provinces off to the wrong congress.[4] Personal feuds decided in many cases who should attend which congress, and this in turn gave rise to fresh feuds. Thus Hyndman, for all his Marxist convictions, attended the Possibilist Congress, largely because his rivals of the Socialist League, William Morris and Eleanor Marx-Aveling, were at the rue Petrelle. It got him into trouble: the Italian socialist, Costa, 'meeting me by chance in the boulevards, and finding that the French language did not adequately express his socialist sentiments towards me, denounced me at the top of his voice, in the choicest Italian, as a renegade and betrayer. He

---

[1] Louis L. Lorwin, *Labor and Internationalism* (New York 1929), p. 69.
[2] See leading article in *The Times*, 18 July 1889.
[3] Dolléans, II, p.106.
[4] *Internationale Sozialisten Kongress zu Paris* (Nuremberg 1890). Report of proceedings for Wednesday 17 July. A summary of the proceedings, not a full stenographer's report, was published after the Congress both in French and German. The reports of the proceedings of this and later International Socialist Congresses are referred to as *Proc.*

collected a crowd, but, I rejoice to recall, did not upset my temper, and we parted in comparative peace to meet on excellent terms at a later date.'[1] Hyndman never forgot that he was a member of the English upper middle classes, who had been to Eton.

The situation was in fact chaotic. Delegates drifted from one congress to another; Anarchists disturbed both, though the Marxists alleged they deliberately caused more trouble to them than to the Possibilists,[2] while the Anarchists themselves claimed that they were at least accorded a 'courteous and patient hearing' at the Possibilists' meeting.[3] In fact, there were many people who still hoped that unity might be possible. Engels suspected Liebknecht of such treacherous desires, and rejoiced that he was staying with Edouard Vaillant who could be trusted to stop him flirting with Possibilists.[4] The question of unification largely occupied the first two days of the Congress in the Salle Petrelle, but it soon became clear that the Guesdists would only accept unification on their terms, and that these terms would have to enable them to exclude most of the Broussist delegates. Thus, on the second day, after French declarations that no collaboration was possible with bourgeois radicalism and opportunism, Liebknecht moved a motion regretting the failure to reach unification, and continuing 'We proclaim that unity is the indispensable condition for the liberation of the proletariat, and that it is therefore the duty of every Social Democrat to leave no step undone which could contribute to the removal of the division. The Congress declares that it even now is ready for agreement and unity provided that the groups of the other Congress pass a resolution in this sense which is acceptable to all members of our Congress.'[5] It was a vain hope,

[1] H. M. Hyndman, *Reminiscences of an Adventurous Life* (London 1911), p.442.
[2] *Proc.* 1889, Saturday 20 July.
[3] *The Times*, 19 July 1889.
[4] Mayer, II, pp. 394-5.
[5] *Proc.* 1889, Tuesday 16 July.

since what separated Brousse from Guesde was largely a dislike of Marxist dictation. And, on the other side, Guesde and his followers, like William Morris and his, were determined not to accept any conditions that would admit their rivals Brousse and Hyndman as equals, so that the Possibilists passed a similar motion reserving to themselves the right to scrutinise the mandates of any delegates who joined them from the other congress. The Liebknecht motion, as so often in international gatherings, by its acceptance effectively put a stop to the action which it professed to desire.

The Possibilist Congress, after a somewhat smug appeal to the foreign delegates to bear witness that they had avoided all personal attacks and done all they could for union, and this though they knew the Marxist Congress was composed in part of fictitious delegates, some representing fictitious nations, went on to discuss in an orderly way detailed measures for the improvement of labour conditions. They also planned to have another congress in 1891 and entrusted the Belgians with its organization. However, they were already losing delegates to the Marxist Congress: John Burns, for instance, the British trade union leader, still a revolutionary figure who was to play a leading part in the great dock strike a month later, and who was as yet far from being the inert Liberal Minister he was later to become, came over before the end of the Congress. And the next international congress was, in fact, to be called under Marxist auspices and to be attended by many who had been with the Possibilists in Paris, Hyndman among them.

Thus the Congress in the Salle Petrelle could claim to be the founding congress of the new International and was indeed genuinely and widely representative of organized Socialist parties from all over Europe as well as from the USA, and was attended by nearly 400 officially recognized delegates from twenty countries (including countries which as yet had no inde-

pendent existence like Poland and Bohemia).[1] Distance and
expense as well as the size of various Socialist parties, meant
that many delegations were very small and that the French delegation, 221 strong, was much the largest, with the German
group of eighty-one next in size.[2] The Germans were the most
solidly based and united delegation; but in spite of the divisions
in the French Socialist movements the Guesdists (POF), with
their Blanquist associates, were quite a substantial force. Other
delegations represented parties that were only just starting—the
Austrians, the Swiss, the Belgians, the Swedes; and others were
haphazard delegations from separate groups that had not yet
coalesced into a unified party—the British and the Dutch, and
the four delegates from American groups, for instance. Yet
others consisted of members of underground organizations, or
of such exiles as those unable to attend themselves could find to
represent them. The credentials of many of the delegates were
dubious. Other people, besides the 391 delegates recorded in the
official account of the proceedings, attended the Congress, interrupted, protested and demonstrated. Yet among those present
were nearly all the most important Socialist leaders of Europe,
and they were a varied and eminent collection.

Three members of the Marx family ensured the apostolic
succession and the continuity of this gathering with the meetings
of the first International—Eleanor Marx-Aveling and her two
brothers-in-law, Paul Lafargue and Charles Longuet. The leading Frenchman was undoubtedly Edouard Vaillant: Guesde was
already busy with his electoral campaign for the general election
in the autumn, and only made a brief appearance. Vaillant and
Wilhelm Liebknecht were elected joint presidents, and their
handshake amid stormy applause marked, it was felt, the soli-

---

[1] A Czech Social Democratic Party had been formed at a congress at
Brno in 1887.
[2] The difficulty of counting the number of delegates is shown by the fact
that the French and German official records of the Congress give slightly
differing figures for each national group.

darity of French and German Socialism, and the unity of the
proletariat as opposed to the enmities of the bourgeoisie. Liebknecht was, inevitably, the moving spirit of the Congress. His
linguistic ability, his eloquence, his experience both of the First
International and of the growth of the German Social Democratic Party, and, above all, the sincerity and depth of his international feeling, made him the chief figure at any such gathering,
and there is no reason to doubt that he meant what he said when
he declared, on his election as joint president of the Congress,
that it was the proudest moment of his life. With him in the
German delegation were Bebel, Bernstein, von Vollmar, the
Bavarian ex-officer who, two years later, was to sound the first
notes of discontent with the rigid tactics of the SPD, and Klara
Zetkin, the leader of the campaign for socialism among women,
and an energetic fighter for women's rights, who was to live to a
great age, and, as a Communist and the oldest member of the
Reichstag, to preside over the last freely elected German parliament in September 1932.

William Morris was the most distinguished British representative: he was a poet who saw in socialism the way back to a
lost imaginary mediaeval world, and a warm-hearted social
reformer with a belief in the value of individual craftsmanship
and of personal relationships. Yet as a politician he was ineffective, for his imaginative powers outstripped his administrative
ability while his sensitive nature made him dislike the personal
animosities so evident, for instance, at Paris. Of the other
British representatives Keir Hardie was not yet playing an
important international role; his one contribution on this occasion was to give a brief account of the trade union movement in
Britain and to complain of the competition with Scottish miners
caused by foreign immigrants; while Cunninghame Graham,
'the aristocratic socialist and cowboy dandy'[1] as *The Times*
called him, and the others who came as representatives of such

---

[1] Quoted in D. F. Tschiffely, *Don Roberto* (London 1937), p.212.

bodies as the East Finsbury Radical Club, did not contribute to the discussions. More important were some of the leaders of the smaller parties who, in many cases (like the representatives of small countries at the League of Nations and other international bodies later) sought in the international field a wider sphere of action than was open to them at home.

The leader of the Austrian delegation was Dr Victor Adler (1852–1918): he was a Doctor of Medicine, a member of the Viennese Jewish intelligentsia, a man of courage, intelligence and charm, whose writings and speeches have a clarity, and even a certain imaginative quality, rare among socialist leaders. In the words of one of his disciples:

> 'He saw the workers with the eyes of a doctor; he saw the injuries caused to their bodies by undernourishment, overwork, bad housing, the injuries caused to their souls by a life of dead mechanical work in another's service, the injuries of all the humiliations of proletarian existence. To lead these men in the struggle for another existence, in the struggle for health, culture, liberty, dignity: that was the task he set himself.'[1]

He was the architect of Socialism in Austria; and Austrian Socialism was inevitably German, for most of its supporters were from the industrial areas of Vienna, Lower Austria and Styria, while their relations with the growing Czech industrial working class in Bohemia and the Czech Social Democratic Party were to give rise to many tensions. Victor Adler, therefore, was both personally and by doctrine very close to the leaders of German Social Democracy to whom he inevitably looked for encouragement, support and example. Moreover, like Liebknecht, he regarded the war of 1866 as an unnatural and violent breach that cut off the Austrian Germans from their brothers in the Reich: there was always an undercurrent of *Grossdeutsch* feeling in Austrian Social Democracy. But Adler, perhaps from his own Viennese background, had a pliability and a humour

---

[1] Otto Bauer, Introduction to Adler, *Aufsätze*, VI, p.xxxiii.

that most of the German leaders lacked; he was the ideal man to pilot a young radical party through the legal labyrinths of a 'despotism tempered by sloppiness'[1], as he himself called the Austro-Hungarian monarchy. Moreover, especially after Liebknecht's death, he was to play an important part in international conferences as a constant worker for compromise and genuine understanding between the Socialist parties of different countries.

The leading Dutch delegate, Domela Nieuwenhuis, was a more startling and controversial figure. A Protestant pastor, from a family of theologians, he described his own career as 'From Christian to Anarchist'.[2] His clumsy speeches were impressive by their sincerity. His simplicity, though it could tend to sheer silliness, could yet enable him to utter unpleasant truths that nobody else would face. Examples of both can be found in his interventions in the 1889 Congress: he was ready to make a bad joke in support of his campaign against parliamentary activity by pointing out that the very meaning of the word parliament implied deceit (*parle-ment*), but he was also able, as an ardent supporter of unity between the two rival congresses, to exclaim that Marx had said 'Proletarians of all lands unite!' and not 'Socialists of all lands unite!'[3] His very Protestantism, transferred to the political plane, made him abhor all political parties and politics that came between the worker and his own better nature or ideal of what was good for him: and this was rapidly to lead him away from Socialism to Anarchism, though he continued to attend, and disrupt, international congresses for the next seven years.

It was not to be expected that the practical achievements of the Congress should be on a level with its symbolic value or the

---

[1] 'Despotismus gemildert durch Schlamperei.' *Proc.* 1889, p.43. Adler, *Aufsätze*, VI, p.18. It looks as though it was Adler who coined this famous phrase.

[2] *Van Christen tot Anarchist* (Amsterdam 1911).

[3] *Proc.* 1889, Saturday 20 July, Tuesday 16 July.

distinction of some of the individuals attending it. Indeed, its deliberations must have seemed very unimpressive; 'more than 400 delegates,' Victor Adler was to recall twenty-five years later, 'were crowded into the small hall and composed a polyglot and temporarily helpless chaos.'[1] The organizers were as yet unfamiliar with the technique of running an international congress: no adequate arrangements had been made for recording the proceedings or organizing the agenda. The interpreting was done by such members of the Congress as could manage it— Liebknecht, Lafargue, Eleanor Marx-Aveling, for instance: and they were always liable to interruption by others who thought their translation too free.[2] But what completed the confusion and caused most trouble was the question of who in fact had the right to attend, and to vote. Thus at this, and indeed many subsequent Congresses, as in all international meetings, questions of procedure—the scrutiny of delegates' mandates and the method of voting—occupied much time. On this occasion, after the opening demonstrations, the discussion of these two questions took up the first two days (Sunday 14 and Monday 15 July), and were further complicated by the existence of the rival congress. Apart from the question of dealing with Anarchist intruders who jumped on chairs, shouted, or displayed placards accusing the Socialist leaders of being enemies of the proletariat, there was the difficulty of deciding who should be officially recognized as delegates from countries which as yet had no unified Socialist movement. The Germans and Austrians presented no problems; nor, for once, did the French, since the opponents of the Guesdists were all safely out of the way in the rue de Lancry. But the Italians, especially, were a problem; and while some of their delegates were orthodox Social Democrats, another Italian, the dashing and temperamental Dr Saverio Merlino, at one moment appeared as a leader of the Anarchist interrupters

[1] Adler, *Aufsätze*, VII, p.60.
[2] See, e.g. Costa's interruption, *Proc.*, Tuesday 16 July.

and at the next as a reporter on the state of working class organization in Italy—an opportunity for a rousing Anarchist speech attacking most of the other delegates. (Merlino, indeed, repeated his performance at the rival congress the next day.)

These procedural difficulties were, for this first congress, overcome by not being too strict on the question of delegates' mandates and by permitting delegates to vote as individuals. Later Congresses were to be much stricter; and these discussions were to develop into arguments about the very nature of the Socialist movement. On this occasion, differences, except for the protests of the most violent of the Anarchists, were concealed by the atmosphere of international solidarity and the necessity of presenting a united front to the Possibilists—to say nothing of the capitalists. Moreover, such motions as were actually put to the vote were mostly of a general and innocuous nature and could be supported by everybody with at least a semblance of unanimity. Yet perhaps the most important function this Congress could perform was to complete the breakdown of the isolation in which Socialist leaders had lived after the Commune, and so provide an opportunity for the exchange of information about the state of the Socialist movement. Thus, once the procedural questions had been settled, the Congress devoted the next three days to hearing reports from the various countries represented.

These varied a great deal in interest. Bebel opened with a general account of the SPD's history and sufferings under the anti-Socialist law and was greeted with a 'veritable thunderstorm of salvoes of applause'. Guesde uttered a number of dull Marxist platitudes on behalf of the *Parti Ouvrier Français* and their allies, the Blanquist *Comité Revolutionnaire Centrale* and the *Fédération Nationale des Syndicats Ouvriers de France*. For Russia, reports were given both by Plekhanov, for the Marxists, and by Peter Lavrovitch Lavrov, for the *Narodnaya Volya*. Lavrov was a former teacher of mathematics in a military academy who had been in exile for twenty years and spent his time in leisured writing over a wide range of subjects. In spite of differences of opinion, however, he remained on good terms with the Marxists, and was on the distribution list for those annual Christmas puddings prepared with such care in Engels' London kitchen and sent to deserving revolutionaries each December.[1] On this occasion, Lavrov's speech was in fact a short history of Russia since Peter the Great, and its professorial tone so irritated some of the Anarchists that there was a free fight as they were thrown out by the French.

Plekhanov, who made a didactic Marxist speech, proclaimed amid great enthusiasm that 'the revolutionary movement in Russia will triumph as a workers' movement or it will never triumph'.[2] Both speakers, in fact, took little account of the bourgeois intelligentsia and the peasant dissatisfaction that were the real spur to revolution in Russia. For England, William Morris faced the truth about British Socialism: 'Socialism in England is a strong plant which produces lively sprouts, yet is young, so young that it has not yet produced flowers or fruit.'[3] The representatives of the suppressed nationalities were eager to proclaim their international faith: 'We want,' said a Polish delegate, 'especially to emphasize the solidarity which unites us to our comrades the Russian and German Socialists, our natural and nearest allies.'[4] This was, in fact, to disregard what was to be one of the main obstacles to the effective working of the International. For its was with increasing difficulty, in an age of growing popular national enthusiasm, that workers of subject nationalities could bring themselves to fraternize even with the poorer classes of their oppressors; while German Social Democrats, with the best will in the world (and this was sometimes

[1] See Eduard Bernstein, *My Years of Exile*, tr. by Bernard Miall (London 1921), pp.197–8.
[2] *Proc.* 1889, Thursday 18 July, p.63.
[3] *Proc.* 1889, Wednesday 17 July, p.43.
[4] *Proc.* 1889, Wednesday 17 July, p.52.

lacking), found it hard to treat people as equals who were genuinely more backward than themselves, both economically and culturally.

So the recital dragged on for three whole days; by the end the real substance had gone out of it, for the representatives of all the larger and more interesting groups had had their say—yet the Congress patiently listened to reports from such bodies as the German trade unions in New York and groups representing glass-workers and waiters, followed by accounts by individual delegates from the French provinces. By the Saturday morning it was clear that, with the Congress due to disperse the next day, there was very little time left to discuss the various topics originally proposed. (Things had been better managed in the rue de Lancry, for there a number of delegates had renounced their right to report in order to proceed with the items on the agenda.) However, after more Anarchist disturbances and some attempt to speed up the proceedings, the discussion turned to the question of international codes for the protection of labour. This was in fact a question of vital interest to the ordinary worker: hours of work, together with wages, were what interested him most. But it was clear that any improvements in this direction were only to be had from existing governments. With the discussion of this topic the Congress was already on the ground of practical political agitation within the present framework of society. The Anarchists were quick to spot this: and Merlino pointed out that the very fact of their discussing the question at all showed that they were not true Socialists. Most of the other delegates, however, realized the interest their supporters took in the question and the necessity of making some declaration on the subject, if only to forestall the action of would-be paternal capitalist governments.

For, with the growth of industry, nearly all the governments of civilized states had realized the necessity of legislation to regulate hours and conditions of labour in factories in order to prevent the worst excesses of exploitation that had grown up in the early years of the Industrial Revolution. In England for more than fifty years agitation had been going on, and resulted in a series of Factory Acts. Austria had legislation which, on paper at least, was among the most advanced in Europe; hours of work were legally limited to eleven a day. In the United States the great constitutional issue of the right of the Government to regulate hours of labour was soon to be joined.[1] France, however, reflected in the backwardness of her labour legislation the backwardness of her industrial structure; and, in spite of protests from social reformers both among Catholics and Socialists, it was not until 1900 that a legal ten-hour working day and an efficient factory-inspectorate were established. In Germany Bismarck had done much to improve the lot of the worker, though less by regulation of conditions of work than by other social benefits: and during the 1880s a whole programme of social insurance had been introduced in the hope of winning the industrial workers from the Social Democratic Party. The young Emperor William II seemed about to go still further: impressed by the effectiveness of the great coal strike in the Ruhr in the summer of 1889, he was about to make a bid for working class support by refusing to listen to Bismarck's suggestions for the abolition of universal suffrage, and by initiating an international movement for the regulation of labour conditions. In March 1890 he presided over an international congress in Berlin on social questions. It was an action both symptomatic of the preoccupation of contemporary politicians and typical of the Kaiser. For the past year the Swiss government had been trying to organize an international congress to discuss labour conditions, hours of work, factory legislation and so on, and at the beginning of 1890 it was awaiting answers to a

---

[1] From the case of *Holden* v. *Hardy* (1898) onwards, the Supreme Court was to give a series of conflicting rulings on the constitutionality of such regulation.

specific invitation. Suddenly, much to the irritation of the Swiss Federal Council, William II instructed Bismarck to issue invitations for an immediate congress in Berlin, and after some diplomatic pressure, the Swiss withdrew their own proposals.[1] It was part of William's attempt at the beginning of his reign to pose as the protector of the poor, the '*roi des gueux*'—the first of the many contradictory roles he was to assume—and it was a pose that did not last long. Yet the Berlin Conference served as a reminder that governments must pretend to take the 'social question' seriously if they were to meet the growing attacks from the new Socialist parties.

Equally, if the Socialist parties were not to be outdone in the eyes of their own supporters, they must lead a campaign for still further reforms, and demands for an eight-hour day had already begun to be made. On that last Saturday of the Paris Congress however, there was little time to discuss the campaign in detail. Moreover one thing led to another; a discussion on labour codes very easily slipped into one on the general profit or danger of existing parliamentary institutions and was only recalled by Liebknecht with difficulty to the original topic. At last, after more Anarchist disturbances and the ejection of the irrepressible Dr Merlino and two others, at the end of that afternoon resolutions on four topics were hastily passed before the Congress dispersed.

In spite of the fact that they were rushed through with little or no discussion, the resolutions voted almost unanimously at the end of the Congress were on the subjects that were to be vital both to individual Socialist parties and to the International as a whole, and most of the subsequent Congresses were to be devoted to talking about the same topics in one form or another. There were resolutions in favour of an eight-hour working day and improved conditions of labour; these, as we have seen, had

[1] For an account of the Berlin Conference see John W. Follows, *Antecedents of the International Labour Organization* (Oxford 1951), pp.120–43.

been hastily, if inconclusively, discussed, and were passed with some abstentions—those abstaining being people who rejected the whole idea of reforms within existing society and would only be satisfied with a revolutionary new start. Then a resolution about peace and war was passed unanimously. This condemned standing armies and called for national defence by means of the 'people in arms', stating too that the advent of socialism would of itself abolish war.

This resolution reveals two fundamental presuppositions of the Socialist leaders that were to influence all their subsequent discussions of means to prevent war as the international situation worsened over the next twenty-five years.[1] One was that the interests of the proletariat everywhere coincided and that the working class should not, and, in the end, would not, be divided by quarrels between capitalist governments. This very easily led to a comfortable belief that the spread of socialism and the existence of a Socialist International would prevent war without any further action—just as for many Marxists a belief in the inevitable historical necessity of the collapse of the capitalist system dispensed them from committing any immediate revolutionary acts. The second presupposition was that it was standing armies that were liable to provoke war, while some form of national militia would inevitably prevent it. Here socialist thought was derived from pre-socialist traditions. Both the armies of the French Revolution and the armies that were alleged to have expelled Napoleon from Germany (the two examples most frequently referred to) had, it was felt, been popular armies fighting for freedom and a just cause, unperverted by reactionary officers or bourgeois governments. A people in arms would know when a war was just, and would not fight in another cause. Just as Richard Cobden in England forty years before had seen in an aristocratic officer class the fomenters of wars which were against the interests of the international

---

[1] See Ch. VI below where the whole question is discussed at greater length.

and pacific middle-class, so socialists believed that the same professional officers would drive the working class to slaughter in the interest of capitalist rivalries. A national militia—and reference was constantly made to the Swiss model—would avoid this; and it would also save the sons of the working class from suffering the rigours of discipline imposed by a professional officer caste. Finally, a national militia would never be used, as a standing army could be, to shoot down the workers. However, at this stage, in 1889, the whole question of the Socialist parties' attitude to war was not yet an urgent one. In spite of Bismarck's and Boulanger's alarms, in spite of the first signs of imperialist rivalries among the great powers, the international situation was not yet, as it was to be later, the most urgent problem confronting the working class, or at least its leaders.

There were two ways in which the workers might influence governments and force them to introduce legislation protecting labour. They might win the vote and form mass parties, and thus use parliament as a means of righting wrongs; or they might attempt by direct action to intimidate the ruling class into taking notice of their demands. The first course was the one on which the German Social Democratic Party had in practice already embarked. And the French, or many of them, were, as the Congress was meeting, preparing for the approaching parliamentary elections—though they were to have little success. But in some countries, even where there was constitutional government, there was not yet universal suffrage—Belgium and Austria were obvious examples—and in many individual states of the German Empire, in spite of the existence of the Reichstag elected on universal manhood suffrage, the right to vote in elections to State Diets was limited, while these Diets still possessed much power to affect the life of their citizens by their control, for instance, of education or the police. Where constitutional development was at this stage, the question for Socialists then arose whether direct action—particularly action by means of mass strikes—was justified in order to win the vote. The Belgians had already tried it, unsuccessfully, in 1886, but they were to try again later with better luck. The question was one that was to occupy the minds of the Austrian leaders for many years until they too risked a mass strike on 28 November 1905. In these countries there was at least a hope of constitutional reform by peaceful means;[1] in Russia this was not a possibility, and direct revolutionary action was the only way open, and all attempts to pretend that social democracy there could develop along the same lines as in western Europe developed into stultifying dogmatism.

In the rush of that last day of the 1889 congress there was no time to discuss the methods by which universal suffrage might be won, or the complex and controversial question of the mass strike; these discussions were to come later and be repeated *ad nauseam*. Now—with only one Anarchist vote against this assumption that workers should play the parliamentary game— a resolution was passed, saying that in countries where the suffrage was not yet won Socialists should work for it, but remaining discreetly silent about the means. Elsewhere Socialists should participate in elections and aim at parliamentary power, but without compromising with any other parties. Once again many controversial points were left over for future discussion.

One last topic was the subject of a resolution; and it, too, not only raised the problem of the mass strike for political purposes, but also the question of how far an International Congress could produce and co-ordinate political action in different countries. This was the idea that May Day should be the occasion for a demonstration of the solidarity and effectiveness of the international working class movement. In 1888 the Congress of

[1] Universal manhood suffrage was introduced into the Austrian half of the Habsburg monarchy in 1907: but rather as the result of a Government initiative to deal with the national problem than as a result of Socialist agitation.

French trade unionists at Bordeaux had decided that the best way of displaying the strength of the working class was to have few but important and widespread demonstrations. Soon after, in December 1888, the American Federation of Labour at their congress at St. Louis had decided that they would make a mass demonstration on 1 May 1890, taking up an idea that had been proposed at their Congress of 1884 and had, in fact, led to some Anarchist outbreaks in Chicago on May Day of 1886. In 1888 at the trade union congress in London, Edouard Anseele, the Belgian leader, had suggested linking up the American date with the French syndicalist idea of a mass demonstration. As a result of these independent decisions a prominent French Socialist, the delegate from the Gironde, Raymond Lavigne, proposed that the Paris Congress should declare that all workers in every country should celebrate 1 May 1890 as a holiday, in order to give an international demonstration in favour of the eight-hour day and their other demands. As in the other cases there was no time for discussing this far-reaching proposal: and the Belgian delegates abstained from voting on this account. The Russians too abstained because, they said, any such demonstration was completely out of the question under existing conditions in Russia. Bebel and Liebknecht cautiously added a rider that the extent of the demonstration should be decided by the political conditions prevailing in particular countries. But even with this proviso, and even without specifying the nature of the action to be taken on May Day, the demand for a simultaneous international political demonstration was a formidable one and a real test of the effectiveness of the International.

It was a test that revealed only too clearly the difficulties of co-ordinated international action. No sooner was the resolution passed than disputes began about its interpretation. It was discussed and rephrased at the next Congresses of the International, in Brussels in 1891 and in Zürich in 1893, until it lost much of its original character. For most of the French and for the

Austrians, for instance, the aim of May Day was to demonstrate by as complete a stoppage of work as possible the real power of the proletariat that lay behind their demands for improved conditions. In both France and Austria, May Day 1890 was celebrated in this manner. In France these demonstrations led to serious clashes with the police; and in 1891 there was an episode at Fourmies, in the Department of the Nord, when ten people were killed, including some children, and new names were added to the list of martyrs in the socialist cause. This disaster was not without effect, for, as the Radical Clemenceau remarked in the Chamber of Deputies, 'It is the Fourth Estate which is rising up and arriving at the conquest of power.'[1] Moreover, Paul Lafargue was condemned to a year's imprisonment for instigating the manifestation, only to be released on his triumphant election to the Chamber as Deputy for Lille in a by-election in November 1891. And, doubtless as a result of this success, the Guesdists became firm partisans of the idea of a vigorous and actively revolutionary demonstration on May Day—so that their Anarchist rivals wrote ironically 'The fusillade of Fourmies will not have been vain since one of our good socialists has known how to make electoral propaganda from it . . . . Henceforth a few good people shot at the right moment will provide an excellent electoral college.'[2]

The Austrians, too, were determined to make the May Day demonstrations a serious symbol of working class needs and potentialities. They had fewer difficulties than either the French or the Germans; the number of holidays in the Austrian calendar was already numerous, and May Day was already regarded as a half-holiday in some areas. Austrian employers seem to have tolerated the cessation of work, while the unprovocative nature of the demonstrations caused little trouble with the police, in accordance with the slogan adopted for the occasion,

---

[1] *Journal Officiel*, 9 May 1891, quoted in Maitron, p.179.
[2] *La Revolte*, 27 November 1891, quoted in Maitron, p.184.

'We will not allow ourselves to be intimidated or provoked'.[1] The instructions issued by Victor Adler for the first May Day celebration were perhaps characteristic both of their author and of the temper of Austrian Socialism: 'All unions and groups shall hold meetings and where possible there should be popular meetings open to the public . . . . The afternoon may then be devoted to leisure and free enjoyment of Nature glad with spring (*dem freien Ergehen in der frühlingsfrohen Natur*).'[2] The success of these demonstrations in 1890 and 1891 made Victor Adler the great champion of celebrating May Day by a stoppage of work and mass meetings.

German experience was different: and it was on the Germans' initiative that May Day rapidly became merely an occasion for evening meetings and for leading articles in the Socialist Press instead of the great symbol of international solidarity it had been hoped to make it. As early as the Party Congress of October 1890 there were people urging that the celebrations should be held on the first Sunday in May to avoid difficulties (a view that was shared by some English trade unionists) and it was only at Liebknecht's insistence that a motion to this effect was dropped.[3] Experience during the next few years was to confirm in their opinion those who thought that any attempt to stop work on May Day would merely cause unnecessary suffering to the workers without any compensating advantages. Times were bad; and an economic recession meant that employers were quite ready to lock-out employees who took an unauthorized day off. The whole question came up for discussion at the Party Congress in November 1892. The reports of that year's May Day were discouraging; not only had it snowed in South Germany,

[1] 'Wir lassen uns nicht einschüchtern und nicht provozieren.' *Arbeiter Zeitung*, 11 April 1890.

[2] *Arbeiter Zeitung*, 11 April 1890; Adler, *Aufsätze*, VI, pp.180–1.

[3] *Protokoll über die Verhandlungen des Parteitages der Sozialdemokratischen Partei Deutschlands vom 12. bis 18. Oktober 1890* (Berlin 1890), p.213. The Proceedings of this and subsequent SPD Congresses are referred to as *Verhandlungen*.

but at Hamburg and elsewhere attempts to cease work had caused real hardship. It was clear that the majority of the delegates were prepared to support the Party Executive in recommending that the celebration be limited to evening meetings— in spite of the intervention of Victor Adler, present as a fraternal delegate from Austria, who took the unusual step for a delegate from abroad of speaking twice in the discussion to urge the Germans to reconsider their decision, since May Day was the only popular symbol of international solidarity there was.[1]

Victor Adler was not alone in his anxiety over the fact that the strongest Socialist party in the world should apparently be trying to minimize the one specific international action to which it was committed. Jules Guesde was equally worried; and he asked Charles Bonnier, a Frenchman who lived in Oxford and taught modern languages, to try to enlist Engels' support and his intervention with the Germans.[2] The old man was in a difficult position: he was anxious, as he wrote to Bebel, that the Germans should not promise more than they could perform, and realized the bad effect their action might have 'if the strongest party in the world suddenly sounds the retreat'.[3] At the same time Engels was always suspicious of French pretensions and of any hint that they might take the lead instead of the Germans; and the fact of Bonnier's intervention had irritated him: 'The idea of leading the European working class movement from Oxford—the last bit of the real middle ages that still exists in Europe—is incredible and I shall make a sharp protest in Paris against this intermediary.'[4] Therefore, in spite of his concern at the differences between the French and German Socialists, Engels' intervention was of little importance, and the German leaders had their way: the May Day celebrations would be relegated to the evening.

[1] *Verhandlungen* 1892, pp. 156–8, 166–7.
[2] Mayer, II, pp. 502ff.
[3] To Bebel, 3 December 1892. Mayer, II, p. 503.
[4] To Bebel, 5 December 1892. Mayer, II, p. 503.

The arguments were taken up again at the International Congress at Zürich in August 1893—a congress from which most of the French leaders were absent because of the French Elections. Victor Adler, therefore, was the main protagonist for the May Day demonstration, both because he was convinced of its emotional importance as a real symbol of international solidarity and because 'if we do not take a step forwards, the May Day celebrations will fall asleep'.[1] Eventually, after Bebel had reiterated the impossibility of a cessation of work in Germany, a motion proposed by Adler was adopted against the votes of most of the German delegation. This resolution urged that May Day should be marked by a stoppage of work and that each party should make all efforts to this end. Moreover, it was decided that the May Day demonstrations should be in favour of peace as well as of improved conditions of labour.

But any triumph Adler and his friends might have felt at the apparent decision to make something real of May Day was soon to be disappointed. Within three months the German Party, at their annual Congress at Cologne, were whittling down the international resolution, in such a way as to minimize the importance of a stoppage of work, by stating that only those organizations that felt able to undertake such a strike should do so. The grounds for this decision were sound; and Liebknecht presented them in an able speech, maintaining that the original Paris resolution had not said anything about a stoppage of work and that the discussion had mainly arisen from a verbal confusion about the two meanings of the German word 'Feier'—a 'holiday' or a 'festival'. A stoppage of work on May Day meant in fact a general strike; and 'a general strike is general nonsense',[2] as the Germans never tired of saying. There was much to be said for the German attitude: as Liebknecht said, echoing

---

[1] Proc., 1893, Friday 11 August, p.33; Adler, Aufsätze, VI, p.194.

[2] 'Generalstreik ist Generalunsinn'. For Liebknecht's speech on this occasion see Verhandlungen, 1893, pp.166ff.

Engels, a great party must not promise more than it can perform. And even Victor Adler made the best of the German resolution as voted,[1] since it did after all proclaim a stoppage of work
as desirable in the future, even if at present impossible.[2] Yet this
German realism, which in practice relegated the great May Day
celebration to an evening meeting, meant the end of May Day
as an effective demonstration of international solidarity. It was
still to remain an important date in the working class political
calendar; it was still to be the occasion of important demonstrations in individual countries; but after 1892 it ceased to be a
large-scale co-ordinated international manifestation. The imposing resolution carried by such a large majority at Paris, and
reaffirmed and strengthened at Zürich four years later, merely
meant in practice the holding of a number of political meetings
that might have occurred in the ordinary course of political agitation. A great symbolic gesture faded away when the practical
difficulties were explored and when the realism of the German
Party was brought to bear on them. It was, though in itself
unimportant, a depressing augury for the future of co-ordinated
international Socialist action.

Yet, although the one concrete recommendation of the Paris
Congress was to be shown over the next five years to have
amounted to very little in practice, it would be a mistake to
dismiss the Paris Congress as of no importance. As Vaillant

[1] The following is a translation of the resolution finally voted at Cologne:
'In accordance with the decisions of the International Working Men's
Congress of Paris (1889), Brussels (1891) and Zürich (1893) German Social
Democracy celebrates the First of May as a world festival of labour, dedicated
to the class demands of the proletariat, international fraternity, and world
peace. As a worthy celebration of the first of May we aim at a general stoppage of work (*erstreben wir die allgemeine Arbeitsruhe*). As however its
execution is not at present possible in the present economic situation of
Germany, the Party Congress recommends that only those workers and
workers' organizations which are in a position to do so without damaging
working class interests should celebrate May Day by a stoppage of work in
addition to the other manifestations.' See *Verhandlungen* p.163.
[2] *Arbeiter Zeitung*, 31 October 1893. *Aufsätze*, VI, pp.195 ff.

said at its opening, its most important achievement was the fact
of its meeting.[1] A Second International had come into being;
the isolation of the 1870s had been broken and the smaller
Socialist parties felt that they had the support of a powerful
international movement behind them. More important still, a
certain common pattern could be discerned in socialist development. There were certain problems that were shared by all
Socialist parties, and regular international congresses would
give an opportunity for discussing them. These questions had
only been posed by the Paris Conference: their discussion was
to fill the time of subsequent meetings.

So when, after laying wreaths on the graves of the 'martyrs'
of the Commune and attending an evening party, the delegates
went home to write up their speeches for the party press and
impose in recollection a little order on what must have been a
confusing experience, they were left with some challenging
problems to think about. What were the right tactics for a mass
party? Should it aim at revolution or at reform by parliamentary
means? How was universal suffrage to be won? How could
Socialists prevent wars? And, the most immediate question, who
was a true socialist and who an enemy of the working class?
How could the workers of the world unite when their leaders
still pointed down different roads, the one Marxist, the other
Anarchist?

[1] *Proc.* 1889, Sunday 14 July.

III

THE STRUGGLE
WITH THE ANARCHISTS

When ordinary people in Europe thought about international Socialists, it was not the disciplined mass-parties, the solid, bearded, self-improving working men of the German or Belgian Socialist Parties or the British trade unions that came to mind. The figure that had captured the popular imagination was the Anarchist with the smoking bomb in his pocket, whose outrages could be regarded either as the gallant defiance of an oppressive and materialist social system or as the senseless protest of a deranged individual. For such outrages were comparatively common in the 'eighties and 'nineties. Their most striking and obvious form was the assassination of the head of a state; the Czar of Russia was murdered in 1881, the President of the French Republic in 1894, the Empress of Austria in 1898, the King of Italy in 1900, the President of the United States in 1901; and there were numerous unsuccessful attempts on the lives of other sovereigns. On other occasions the Anarchist attacks were directed against the apparatus of bourgeois rule—as when, in 1877, Italian Anarchists went about attacking municipal offices and burning the archives, or when a bottle of vitriol was dropped from the galleries of the Paris stock exchange in 1886, or a bomb from the gallery of the French Chamber of Deputies in 1893. Most shocking of all were the indiscriminate attacks on casual and innocent victims: 'I shall not strike an innocent man if I strike the first bourgeois to come along', as one of the would-be assassins[1] put it. (The first bourgeois to appear

—————

[1] Léon-Jules Léauthier (1874–1894), who attacked and seriously wounded the Serbian Minister in a restaurant on 13 November 1894. See Maitron, p.211.

in this case happened to be the Serbian Minister in Paris.) And even the most disreputable of these murderers, like Ravachol, the most notorious of all, who was accused of six murders and three explosions, could go to his execution humming an anti-clerical doggerel and win a dubious martyrdom.

These were isolated acts; except in Russia, even the assassinations of an obviously political kind were undertaken by individuals or, at most, very small groups. But these dramatic and frightening actions inevitably had considerable effect; they are reflected in the literature of the day, in Conrad's *The Secret Agent* (published in 1907), for instance, and even, surprisingly, in Henry James.[1] And they provided the rulers with opportunities of attacking the whole working class movement, just as the Commune had. The Emperor William II was sufficiently impressed by the murder of President Carnot to try to reintroduce the anti-socialist legislation abandoned four years before; unsuccessfully, as it turned out, though nevertheless the officials and police, especially in Prussia, continued for many years to have considerable power to interfere with the ordinary activities of the Social Democratic Party. In Brussels, Elisée Reclus, the geographer and a leading theoretical Anarchist, was forbidden to lecture in the university after Auguste Vaillant's[2] bomb in the French Chamber; and it was as a result of this incident that the Free University of Brussels was founded. In France the terrorist acts of the early 'nineties provoked a crisis inside the working class parties rather than a struggle between them and the government. For the Government of the Republic acted with great restraint in face of the epidemic of terrorism between 1892 and 1894. (There were eleven bomb explosions in Paris, as well as the murder of Sadi Carnot and the attacks on

[1] *The Princess Casamassima* (1886). See Lionel Trilling, *The Liberal Imagination* (Cheap edition, New York 1953), pp.65–96.

[2] Auguste Vaillant, the Anarchist made notorious by the bomb outrage in the Chamber, must not be confused with Edouard Vaillant, the Socialist leader, who was no relation.

innocent private persons.)[1] A number of Anarchist suspects
were arrested—five were executed and three condemned to
hard labour for life—but no general repressive measures were
taken.

Indeed, the French Socialist parties were quick to see how
embarrassing to them this sort of anarchism could be: 'It is
monstrous, quite simply. It is the act of a lunatic. Those who do
this sort of thing are not only outside the law, they are outside
humanity,' Guesde wrote after the bomb in the Chamber of
Deputies.[2] Yet the appeal of direct action, even if not of futile
terrorism, was a strong one. Not only was there a theoretical
tradition in its favour, but also the vivid memory of the barricades of 1848 and the searing experience of the Commune.
The latter episode had shown, in fact, that street fighting was an
obsolete technique in an age of machine guns and town planning; but the romantic ideal of the insurrection was slow to
disappear: the followers of Blanqui, indeed, had little else to
believe in (and it is significant that their newspaper expressed
some sympathy with the attack on the Chamber of Deputies in
contrast to Guesde's indignant disavowal). Official Marxist
theory, too, was being revised to exclude insurrection: Engels
published a new preface to Marx's *Class Struggles in France* in
1895 in which, with his usual interest in military affairs, he
demonstrated the technical superiority of modern armies over
the revolutionaries: 'the revolutionary who of his own accord
provoked a barricade fight in the new workers' districts of Berlin
must be mad.' (It was characteristic, too, of the mood of the
German Socialist leaders that they, at the moment when proposals for new repressive measures were being discussed in the
Reichstag, suppressed in the German edition references to
Engels' belief that nevertheless in certain circumstances a violent revolution was justified and necessary.)

---

[1] Maitron, p.196.
[2] *Le Journal*, 10 December 1893, quoted in Maitron, p.217.

The difficulties of direct action and the growing possibilities of political life in the Third Republic both produced an effect on the French working class movement and provoked a crisis from which, in some senses, it has never recovered. The Socialist leaders were now in parliament—Guesde and Vaillant were both elected in 1893—and a number of hitherto Radical or Independent deputies began to vote with them; the Socialists could begin to exercise some influence on parliamentary life, and had to face all the problems of tactics that this involved. But this increase in importance was not accompanied by a growth in unity: the split among French Socialists that had been transferred to the international plane in 1889 continued to dominate the subsequent meetings of the International. Indeed, the situation had grown more complicated in the years since 1889; for in addition to the independent deputies now associated with the Socialists in the Chamber, there was a further split in the Possibilist party in 1890, when Jean Allemane, a printer and *Communard*, founded a new group, the *Parti Ouvrier Socialiste Révolutionnaire*. Allemane was protesting both against the Possibilists, who he felt had now become indistinguishable from a bourgeois political party like the Radicals, and against the Marxists' desire to dominate the working class movement and subject it to a rigid doctrine. Allemane, in fact, was appealing to the older Anarchist tradition. Political action was useless (though Allemane's followers continued to contest elections, and he himself was elected to the Chamber in 1902); only direct action by the working class outside parliament could achieve the revolution; and such action could only be undertaken by genuine workers, not by intellectuals: 'No white hands, only calloused ones!'[1] And the way in which such a movement could express itself was by means of the general strike.

These were ideas that appealed to French workmen of revo-

[1] A. Zévaès, *Histoire du Socialisme et du Communisme en France de 1871 à 1947* (Paris 1947), p.203.

lutionary temperament. But it was in the development of the
Syndicalist movement that they found expression rather than
in a comparatively unimportant political group like that of Allemane. In the 'seventies and 'eighties the organization of
Guesde's POF and the organization of trade unions (finally
allowed by law in 1884) had progressed together: but the Marxists failed to maintain their hold over the syndicates, while the
Anarchists and Allemanistes, realizing that neither isolated acts
of terrorism nor an old-fashioned insurrection would achieve
the revolution, were increasing their influence among the
workers' organizations.[1] As early as 1888 a congress of syndicates at Bordeaux had condemned political action and called for
direct action by means of the general strike. 'From that day the
alliance between the *Parti Ouvrier* and the federated syndicates
was to look precarious.'[2] And in 1894 the followers of Guesde
walked out of the Nantes Trade Union Congress. The breach
between syndicates and Socialists was never healed—at least
not until 1948 when it was too late. Although numerically this
was perhaps not important (by 1902 only seventeen per cent of
industrial workers were organized in syndicates),[3] it meant that
the French Socialists could never count on automatic mass
support, as the British Labour Party was soon to be able to do,
while they were constantly harassed by anti-parliamentary
demonstrations on the part of those very working men on whose
votes they inevitably depended for their election.

The leader and inspirer of this new 'anarcho-syndicalist'
movement was Fernand Pelloutier. A young man from a middle
class family, he was expelled from his Catholic school because

---

[1] There were two important groups of organizations, the *Fédération des
Syndicats* (Unions based on trades) and the *Fédération des Bourses du
Travail* (Labour Exchanges run by workers themselves for their own benefit
and mutual assistance). These groups amalgamated in 1902 to form the
Confédération Générale du Travail (CGT).
[2] Léon Blum, *Les Congrès ouvriers et socialistes français* (Paris 1901), p.113.
[3] Dolléans, II, p.31.

he was found to have written an anti-clerical novel. When he came to Paris from Brittany, he found there exactly the sort of working class ideas and organization that appealed to him— small groups of serious craftsmen, self-reliant and suspicious of all politicians. These were the men who he believed would make a revolution; their syndicates would serve as the model for a future state. 'Must even the transitory state to which we have to submit, necessarily and fatally be the collectivist jail?' he wrote in November, 1895. 'Can't it consist in a free organization limited exclusively to the needs of production and consumption, all political institutions having disappeared?'[1] And with inexhaustible energy he threw himself into the task of organizing the *Bourses du Travail*, centres not only of political action but of education and practical mutual assistance for the working men who joined them. The new Syndicalism was already well established when Pelloutier died of consumption in 1901 at the age of 34, leaving behind an indelible memory of energy, goodness and devotion.

But the Syndicalist movement was based on more than Pelloutier's sweetness of character: it contained militants who were prepared to go to considerable lengths in asserting the workers' claims by direct action—by organizing partial strikes that were alleged to be leading up to the moment when the general strike would place power in the workers' hands. Moreover, in spite of the anti-parliamentary doctrine of the Syndicalists, they still had personal links with the world of the political parties, and had among their number astute politicians like Aristide Briand, who, like Pierre Laval a generation later, was to make his political reputation as an enthusiastic advocate of the general strike. Thus in France the energies of the Anarchists were absorbed into the Syndicalist movement which was soon to find its philosopher in a retired civil engineer, Georges

[1] F. Pelloutier, 'L'Anarchisme et les syndicats ouvriers' in *Les Temps Nouveaux*, No. 27, November 1895; quoted in Maitron, p.251.

Sorel, who, if he did not directly influence the working class ('I read Alexandre Dumas,' one Syndicalist leader declared when asked if he had studied Sorel),[1] did display in a series of works that the movement was capable of producing a philosophy as wide-ranging and all-embracing, if not as coherent, as that of Marx himself. Thus, from the early 'nineties onwards, the French Marxists were always fighting on two fronts—against those Socialists on the Right who were ready to abandon dogmatic Marxism in the interests of practical politics, and against a revolutionary Syndicalism on the Left with a creed and programme in many ways more attractive to the French workers than Marxism.

The French Socialists therefore, although growing in strength and political importance were not able to produce a monolithic party on the German model—a fact of which the Germans were well aware:

'In spite of everything our French friends are again drunk with victory and crowing about the world and they would like to come to the forefront of the movement . . . .' Engels wrote in 1893. 'What the few Italians, who are a muddled bunch anyway, do, doesn't matter a jot; whether our Germans however will let themselves in this way simply be towed along in the wake of the French is doubtful. If one has won one's position by twenty-five years of hard struggle and has two million voters behind one, one has the right to look a little more closely at the "scratch lot" (*sic*) that suddenly wants to give orders . . . .'[2]

The divisions between Socialists and Anarchists were deeper in France than elsewhere, except for Spain and, to a lesser extent, Italy; but no Socialist party in Europe was entirely free from comparable anxieties. Both in Holland and Belgium groups split off from the Socialist parties because they believed

[1] Dolléans, II, p.127.
[2] Engels to Sorge, 30 December 1893. *Briefe und Auszüge aus Briefen von Joh. Phil. Becker, Jos. Dietzgen, Friedrich Engels, Karl Marx u. A. an F. A. Sorge und Andere* (Stuttgart 1906), p.405.

in direct action to bring about an immediate proletarian revolution. In both countries the orthodox Marxists received subsidies from the German Social Democratic Party to enable them to maintain their organization and publications.

In Holland the dissidents had a temporary importance because they were headed by the attractive and obviously sincere Domela Nieuwenhuis; but they failed to establish themselves—though a pacifist belief in the efficacy of direct action against war survived in Dutch Socialism for many years. The Belgian Socialists were too solidly rooted in the trade union and co-operative movement to be much affected, and with thirty deputies in parliament they were already a political force. Moreover, their party programme of 1893 allowed for one element at least in the Anarchist creed, since it coupled political development with 'a correlative transformation in morals by the development of altruistic feelings and the practice of solidarity'.[1] In any case they were themselves ready to adopt the tactics of the general strike to gain a political end; they had tried it in 1886 in the hope of winning an extension of the suffrage, but had been unsuccessful. However, in 1893 another attempt was made: workmen from all over Belgium poured into Brussels and the Government made considerable concessions. The success was repeated in 1913 when complete universal manhood suffrage was finally won; and the same tactics were to be used with equally good effect thirty-five years later to force the abdication of King Leopold III. With this record of effective action, the *Parti Ouvrier Belge* had little to fear from its Anarchist rivals.

Even the German Social Democratic Party was bothered by 'anarchising elements' (*anarchiselnde Elemente*), though not seriously. Once the anti-Socialist laws lapsed, the organization of a vast mass party called for administrative ability and moral leadership of the type Bebel so notably possessed, rather than the romantic and heroic qualities needed for an underground

[1] G. D. H. Cole, *Marxism and Anarchism 1850–1890* (London 1954), p.437.

struggle, even one whose difficulties were perhaps exaggerated.[1]
As a result a few younger men, mostly intellectuals, in some of
the larger cities, Dresden, Magdeburg and especially Berlin,
began to criticize the Party leadership and to accuse the party
of becoming a 'purely opportunist party' or a 'pure reform
party of petty-bourgeois leanings'.[2] Specific attacks were made
on the Party's policy towards the May Day celebrations and
the question of alliance with other parties for the second ballot
at Reichstag elections, but they were more the expression of
personal discontents and ambitions than a serious challenge to
the established leaders of the Party. Indeed in 1891 Bebel and
Liebknecht were able to carry the Party Congress with them
and expel two of the dissidents from membership: and most of
the others soon became respectable right-wing Socialists.
Although a few were to turn up again and demand admittance
to international congresses, only one of the real Anarchists
among them, a young student named Gustav Landauer, was to
have any political future—and his career was to culminate in
that embodiment of impractical romantic Anarchism, the Bavarian Soviet Republic of 1919. The Social Democratic Party
was in a strong position to discipline any such individualist
rebels. For it was becoming a solid mass party whose members
were bound by ties of loyalty so strong that they regarded party
unity and the preservation of the machinery so laboriously built
up over the past fifteen years as their most important aim.
Doubts and criticism that might threaten this unity could
always be dispelled by an appeal from Bebel or by a speech
combining revolutionary slogans with practical political sense
from one of the other Party leaders.

[1] 900 people had been expelled from their homes and 1,500 sentenced to
various terms of imprisonment in the twelve years during which the anti-
Socialist Law was in operation (Mehring, *Geschichte der Deutschen Sozialdemokratie*, (Stuttgart 1898), II, p.535).
[2] The phrases were used by Werner (Berlin) at the Erfurt Party Congress
in 1891. *Verhandlungen*, p.61.

Moreover, the SPD was the first all-embracing mass party in Europe and provided the working class with a doctrine that could take the place of a religion, and with opportunities for social and intellectual activity that no working men had hitherto known. For, both in Germany and in Austria, the Social Democratic Party was far more than an organization for conducting elections, winning votes or influencing legislation. It embraced the whole life of its members; it had a women's movement (and women like Klara Zetkin and Rosa Luxemburg were to be among its most intrepid leaders); it was soon to have a youth movement; its Congresses debated at length the question whether workers should drink spirits or—with a foretaste of future 'socialist realism'—the place of sex in modern art. Socialist composers wrote socialist songs which were sung with enthusiasm by socialist choral societies. A whole range of publications, daily, weekly, monthly, annually, all over Germany, provided instruction and entertainment for each section of the working class—from the high theoretical *Neue Zeit* in which Marxist first principles were discussed, to the comical *Wahre Jakob*, or the *Buch der Jugend* for proletarian children produced by Victor Adler's wife Emma. There was even money left over to make subsidies to periodicals in foreign countries—Belgium and Holland—where party splits had thrown native Marxists into financial embarrassment. More and more the Social Democratic Party formed a world of its own, a society within the state, which absorbed the interests, energies and imagination of its members, while its leaders acquired a mythological status usually reserved, in England at least, for the royal family.

These achievements of organization and propaganda were reflected in the party's electoral successes—nearly one-and-a-half million votes and thirty-five seats in 1890 and over two million votes and fifty-six seats in 1898—but the new mass movement perhaps also met a deeper need in German life, a need for some all-embracing creed and cause that would take the

place, at least for the intellectuals, which in the previous generation had been filled by the struggle for national unity. It had
therefore a unique position in international Socialism both politically and intellectually. 'This indeed is the great advantage of
our German movement,' Wilhelm Liebknecht wrote in 1892,
'an advantage which is not due to personal merit but to our
peculiar and in other respects disadvantageous historical development. It is that from the first moment on, it (the German
movement) had a programme founded on firm principles, a
scientific outlook and *realistic (realpolitische)* tactics.'[1] Moreover,
these realistic tactics were based on a close relationship with the
trade union movement: for, although there was never a formal
constitutional link between the Party and the socialist trade
unions, as there was to be later in the British Labour Party, the
members of the Free Trade Unions (the specifically socialist
unions, as opposed to the much less important Christian and
other non-socialist unions), did in fact vote Social Democrat
and their leaders played a big part in the party councils. As
Liebknecht said on another occasion:

'The working class movement with purely trade union organizations cannot reach its goal. A working class movement with purely
political organizations cannot reach its goal. The two forms of organization are indispensable to each other. If the English had our
political organization and if we had the trade union organization of
the English, in England and in Germany we would have gained the
victory and we would have power in our hands.'[2]

The very solidity of the German mass party was to produce
its own dangers: but they were not those produced by Anarchists or by too much free criticism of Party leadership and
tactics.

[1] W. Liebknecht, *Hochverrat und Revolution* (Berlin 1892); quoted in
Robert Michels 'Die deutsche Sozialdemokratie im internationalen Verbande' in *Archiv für Sozialwissenschaft und Sozialpolitik*, vol. xxv, 1 Heft
(1907), p.158.
[2] Speech at Bielefeld, 29 October 1893; quoted in Maurice Lair, *Jaurès et
l'Allemagne* (Paris 1935), p.18.

In these circumstances many of those who had quarrelled with their own parties or been expelled for Anarchist leanings inevitably tried to gain a hearing at international Socialist congresses and to find there the support they lacked at home. At the same time each branch of a divided party like the French tried to win foreign acceptance for its point of view. Slowly Socialists were creating in their congresses a sort of international public opinion. Thus once again the Germans were forced into a position of leadership: for they had a firm doctrine which could serve, so they thought, as a foundation for international action. They had, too, experience of organization that made them and the Belgians the natural organizers of the International. Gradually the Congresses of the International became more like Congresses of the German Social Democratic party, with their gaily decorated halls and their steamer excursions on the Rhine, their carefully prepared agenda and their orderly debates and records. But it was to take time; and the next three International Congresses after that of 1889 were nearly as confused as the first.

The Brussels Congress in August 1891 represented in fact an attempt to heal the breach between the two congresses of 1889, and delegates who had attended each of them came. The Belgians, under the leadership of Anseele (for César de Paepe had just died) organized the Congress with considerably more efficiency than the French: (they even gave the delegates an outing to Ghent and a '*dîner démocratique*'). But the Anarchists were soon knocking at the doors of the hall. At the opening session it was pointed out that they had not been invited, and they were formally excluded. But the next day, Dr Saverio Merlino appeared, rather inadequately disguised under the name of Levi for fear of the Belgian police, and obtained admission, though after considerable hesitation and discussion. In fact he was not present long; for, on the next day he was arrested during the lunch interval and deported to England; and there were several voices raised to say that it was the orthodox Socialists who had revealed his identity to the police. Indeed, although the Belgian Anarchists had been formally excluded from the start, and the Spanish Anarchists were ejected on the second day (leaving as sole Spanish delegate the Marxist Pablo Iglesias), their point of view was still represented by some members of the French delegation and by Domela Nieuwenhuis, who had retained the support of a considerable section of the Dutch working class movement.

As a result of these arguments about membership and the Anarchist interruptions, the Brussels Congress did not in fact achieve any very remarkable resolutions or statements of policy. But there was at least more time for discussion of some of the problems which were preoccupying working class leaders. The need for legislation about working class conditions was accepted unanimously; for, as Bebel pointed out, the workers could and did vote for a Socialist party that aimed at improving conditions. An American group raised the question of the position of the Jews—a point of some concern at a moment when anti-Semitism in Germany and Austria was beginning to be a serious popular movement. The Congress, in fact, adopted what was to be the orthodox socialist attitude (and one which the French Marxists were to maintain at the time of the Dreyfus case).

'The Congress, considering that the Socialist and workers' parties of all lands have always maintained that there could not be for them any antagonism or struggle of race or nationality, but only the class struggle between proletarians of all races and capitalists of all races, ... while condemning anti-semitic and philosemitic agitation as one of the manoeuvres by which the capitalist class and reactionary governments try to make the Socialist movement deviate and to divide the workers, decides that there is no need to discuss the question raised by the delegation of American Socialist groups of Jewish language and passes to the order of the day.'[1]

[1] *Proc.* 1891, Wednesday 19 August, pp.43–4.

It was the attitude that was to be maintained about all national problems and not just about the Jewish question, and it was one, in an age of growing national consciousness, that was to lose the socialist movement the support of many Czech and Polish workers. In fact, it was only the Jews, whose national consciousness as yet lacked a territorial basis, who could reasonably follow such a line; and indeed they did so, providing the socialist movement with some of its most outstanding leaders.

Apart from a discussion of May Day, which has been treated in the previous chapter, the Congress dealt with the problems of organizing international trade union activity to parallel the international activity of the Socialist parties. Here they were forced to recognize all manner of difficulties: the average member of a trade union was even less interested in international action than the average member of a Socialist party; not all unions were socialist unions, and even the socialist Free Trade Unions in Germany were opposed to the establishment of any central organization. At length a compromise resolution was accepted, urging each country to create a secretariat, 'so that as soon as a conflict arises somewhere between capital and labour the workers of different nationalities could be warned of it and given the opportunity of consultation'.[1] In practice this was to mean very little. Certain trades (notably the builders and the transport workers) established international links and even contributed money to each other during strikes or lockouts. But although in 1901 an international trade union secretariat was established (in Germany) and organized a number of congresses, it never got beyond being an 'international letter box', and such international influence as the trade unions were able to exercise was through the channel of the Socialist International—or rather, perhaps, the activities of the political International were constantly hampered by their dependence on the trade unions of the member countries and the lack of any

[1] *Proc.* 1891, Thursday 20 August, p.61.

solid international links among rank and file trade unionists.

It was in fact this dependence on the unions for mass support and thus for mass political action that, as we have seen, made the international May Day demonstrations less impressive than they might otherwise have been. The same factor was to influence still more any effective international action against war, the remaining topic discussed at Brussels, and one which was to be brought before every subsequent Congress with increasing urgency until it became almost the reason for existence of a Socialist International. For the moment the question served mainly to allow the utopian Anarchists a final opportunity of getting in some sharp blows at their opponents. At Brussels, for example, Liebknecht had a lively exchange with Domela Nieuwenhuis who complained of the innocuousness of a motion introduced by Liebknecht and Vaillant. Even the Pope could accept it, Nieuwenhuis said, if the word Christianity were substituted for the word socialism throughout. And then he went on to urge that a war between nations should be turned into a civil war between classes, and to introduce a motion to this effect. In the course of his speech, however, he let fall a shocking heretical prophetic remark: 'The international sentiments presupposed by socialism do not exist among our German brothers.'[1] It was a suspicion that was to be voiced and as promptly suppressed several times subsequently. And on this occasion Liebknecht, whose own international sentiments no one could call in question, had little difficulty in rebuffing the charges by a reference to his behaviour in 1870, and expressed the basic difference between his practical position and that of idealists like Nieuwenhuis: 'Instead of talking ceaselessly of revolution, it is more valuable to work for the improvement of the lot of the proletariat and to strengthen working class organization; that is the way to serve the popular cause effectively.'[2]

[1] *Proc.* 1891, Friday 21 August.
[2] *Proc.* 1891, Friday 21 August.

These arguments were hard to answer; and Nieuwenhuis' motion was rejected by a large majority, only some of his Dutch and Danish friends and a number of French delegates, ever eager to support a revolutionary cause, voting with him.

The Anarchists and their fellow-members returned to the attack two years later at the next Congress of the International, held at Zürich in the second week of August 1893. Indeed, the proceedings opened with a tremendous row about who should be admitted, that belied (or did it confirm?) the words of the Swiss chairman, who declared in the opening session that the Congress was 'a little blueprint (*Vorbild*) of the United States of Europe and the future world republic'. For the Germans who had been expelled from the SPD, notably Werner and Land-auer, appeared and demanded admission, winning unexpected support from some of the British trade unionists who were anxious that there should not be too much emphasis on ortho-dox Socialist political activity. Bebel, annoyed at the reappear-ance of people whom he had successfully dealt with at his own Party Congress, made a slashing attack on them amid such an uproar that the Swiss comrades had to be asked to restore order. The substance of Bebel's attack, apart from general abuse, was that it was essential in the existing situation for Socialists to take political, as opposed to direct, action—they must 'use political rights and the legislative machinery as much as they can or seek to conquer them in order to enhance the interests of the pro-letariat and win political power'.[1] A motion was accordingly carried limiting membership to groups and parties who ac-cepted political action. There was incredible commotion: Werner and Landauer were hustled from the room shouting 'We protest!'; the Spanish Marxist Pablo Iglesias found himself voting with the Anarchists by mistake; the French delegation began to wrangle among themselves.

Nor were the next day's proceedings any better. The French

[1] *Proc.* 1893, Monday 7 August.

delegate Argyriadès, who was acting as president for the day,
(none of the leading Frenchmen, including Vaillant and Guesde,
were present) set the tone by remarking at the beginning that
he wished that the hall was decorated with pictures of Blanqui,
Fourier and Saint-Simon as well as with those of Marx. After
an hour and a half of wrangling, one of the English delegates,
Sydney Olivier, pointed out, in his best Fabian Society committee manner, that the time had been spent in discussing questions already dealt with on the previous day. But he did not
succeed in hurrying up the proceedings much, and the rest of
the day was spent arguing about mandates. Finally, after Plekhanov had explained that because his organization was secret it
must not be thought that he was in any way an Anarchist, fifteen
delegates were excluded, including a twenty-two year old Polish
Jewish girl, Rosa Luxemburg, who had been studying political
science, history and economics at the University of Zürich, and
was being increasingly drawn into the conspiratorial life of the
emigré political groups, and thus starting a remarkable career
of unremitting revolutionary zeal. On the next day she and her
colleagues were joined by one more Italian, Amilcare Cipriani,
who resigned his mandate with the words: 'I go with those you
have banished, with the victims of your intolerance and brutality.'[1]

The Congress was able to get down to business, under the
competent chairmanship for the day of an English trade unionist, Hodge, who was determined to get on with the discussions.
These in fact were on familiar topics—the eight-hour day, May
Day, political activity and war. And the discussion followed
familiar lines too, with Nieuwenhuis once again attacking the
Germans by recalling embarrassing statements of Bebel's about

[1] *Proc.* Wednesday 9 August. The final figures of delegates admitted were:
Australia 1, Austria 34 (incl. 7 Czechs), Belgium 17, Bulgaria 2, Denmark 2,
France 39, Germany 92, Great Britain 65, Holland 6, Hungary 9 (incl.
Croatia), Italy 21, Norway 1, Poland 11, Rumania 5, Russia 1, Serbia 1,
Switzerland 101, U.S.A. 3.

his readiness to fight Russia. Indeed Bebel had proclaimed his
position in unequivocal terms at the SPD Congress at Erfurt
two years before: 'If Russia, the champion of cruelty and bar-
barity, the enemy of all human culture were to attack Germany . . . . we are as much and more interested than those who
stand at the head of Germany, and we would resist Russia, for
a Russian victory means the defeat of social democracy.'[1] Nieuwenhuis' motion, calling for a general strike on the outbreak of
war and refusal of service by conscripts, was rejected by a large
majority, only the Australian, Dutch, Norwegian and some of
the French delegates voting with him. Once again the claims of
practical political organization proved stronger than the hopes
of large scale direct action of a kind that could be dismissed by
Liebknecht as just a pious wish.

The Zürich Congress, for all its squabbles, did in fact mark
an increasing community of opinion among the Socialist leaders
who attended it. For while the dogmas of Marxism were repeated—and Engels himself appeared in person to give the conference's last session his blessing and flirt with the girl comrades during a steamer excursion on the lake—there was a growing feeling that, while waiting for the contradictions in the
capitalist system to lead to its downfall, there was yet much to
be done by normal political means within the existing state. The
inherent contrast between such a policy in practice and the
revolutionary slogans of Marxist theory had not yet begun to
cause trouble. The revolutionary slogans satisfied for the
moment those people on the left who were later to demand
revolutionary action, like, for example, the Bulgarian Rakovsky
who appeared at Zürich, while the possibility of practical political action was what attracted to the Socialist movement men
like Emile Vandervelde, a young lawyer from Brussels and the
son of a judge, whose education and common sense soon made
him a leader of the Belgian Party and a prominent member of

[1] *Verhandlungen*, 1891, p.285.

the International from his first appearance at the Brussels Congress at the age of twenty-five.

However, in spite of the formal exclusion of the Anarchists at Zürich and Nieuwenhuis' lack of support, there were still enough adherents of direct revolutionary action inside the French parties to enable them to raise the question again at the next International Congress, held in London during the last week of July 1896. It was the noisiest meeting so far, but its English setting gave it a particular flavour, from the very first day when a demonstration in Hyde Park was dispersed by a sudden deluge of rain. The contrast between English and foreign socialists had never been more clearly marked, for the English representatives included people like Mr and Mrs Sidney Webb and George Lansbury, who were far removed from Marxist theorists like Plekhanov or political bosses like Bebel. The British delegation also contained a shrewd and sardonic observer who recorded his impressions of the proceedings—George Bernard Shaw. The difference between Britain and the Continent was not only marked by the views of the delegates. At no point was the difference between the British and Continental administration clearer than at the moment on the first day when 'the Anarchists made such a disturbance in the hall and corridors, shouting and stamping, that the president (an English trade unionist) threatened to call the police to eject the makers of the disturbance.'[1]

Most of those who had previously been expelled reappeared in the public galleries of the Queen's Hall, where the Congress was sitting. Gustav Landauer, Errico Malatesta, the Italian Anarchist who was living in London at the time, and the Dutchman Cornelissen were now finally joined by Nieuwenhuis. He had been growing increasingly irritated by parliamentary practice and compromises. (His enemies attributed it to his own lack of success in the Dutch parliament to which he had been elected

[1] *Proc.* 1896, p.6.

in 1888.) And in London, when a discussion on political action began, he and the majority of the Dutch delegation withdrew and did not return. In addition to the Dutch withdrawal and the isolated Anarchist interruptions (Landauer had taken over the role of Saverio Merlino in appearing unexpectedly, jumping on chairs and shouting), the French divisions were obviously causing more and more trouble; the Congress was late starting because they were unable to constitute themselves into a single delegation and eventually appeared as two opposed groups. Under these circumstances the efforts of the British delegation to discuss such questions as universal suffrage, national self-determination, the emancipation of women, and education, did not meet with much success (they were rebuked at one moment by the Germans for thinking it was an English and not an international congress). In fact, therefore, the Congress added little to the development of socialist theory or practice. Still, perhaps, as Shaw remarked, 'An International Socialist Congress that everybody laughs at and nobody fears is a gratifying step in advance.'[1]

The London Congress, then, not only served to point the differences between British and foreign socialists. It also showed how far international socialists had gone towards becoming respectable and uniform, and how consistently they had expelled revolutionary dissidents. However the French still obstinately refused to conform to the pattern of the Marxist mass party set by the Germans—for the British were never seriously expected to do so. The search for a basis for French Socialist unity was, in fact, to dominate the next two International Congresses and to raise fundamental questions about the nature of socialist activity. Above all, the London Congress had brought out the paradoxes inherent in German Social Democracy and its relation to German society—paradoxes that Bernard Shaw was, as

---

[1] G. B. Shaw, 'Socialism at the International Congress' in *Cosmopolis*, September 1896, vol. III, p.658.

ever, quick to note. 'The Germans with their compact Social Democratic Party in the Reichstag,' he wrote, 'are apparently far ahead of us. But then their leader, Herr Liebknecht, is going to prison for a speech which Mr Arthur Balfour might make to the Primrose League with the approbation of England tomorrow.'[1] And of Liebknecht himself he said: 'He has become . . . . a parliamentarian, but his Marxism has prevented him from becoming a statesman . . . . He still covers every compromise by a declaration that the Social Democrats never compromise.'[2]

The International Congresses of the 'nineties had shown that most of the leaders of European Socialism had accepted the necessity of political action inside existing bourgeois society, even though that society was in fact doomed by the inexorable process of the Dialectic. They had also shown how far the Socialist parties had advanced in common sense and practical political knowledge. The Socialist parties of western Europe, if not in practice revolutionary, were at least satisfying many of the social, political and cultural needs of the members of the industrial working class. But this very success had its own dangers, as the crisis that was about to shake the German Social Democratic Party showed, for there were many Social Democrats who were beginning to wonder whether, now that practical agitation for measures of immediate reform had taken its place alongside the reiteration of Marxist slogans, the Marxist analysis was wholly appropriate to contemporary society. Moreover, the contrast between the strength of the Social Democrats in Germany and their political weakness, and the weakness of the French Socialist parties and their political strength in alliance with a liberal middle class, was soon to be demonstrated in the internal crisis in France caused by the Dreyfus case. The real test of the relations between socialists and existing political society was at hand.

---

[1] Shaw, p.662. Liebknecht had been prosecuted for *lèse-majesté* ('*Majestäts-beleidigung*').
[2] Shaw, p.667.

IV

REFORMISM AND
REVISIONISM

By the end of the nineteenth century no Socialist party could escape the difficulties presented by its own existence as a mass party, forced, for the moment at least, to function within a political system which at the same time it was seeking to destroy. All the Socialist parties in Europe had to face the problems, practical and theoretical, raised by the organizational and parliamentary successes of the 'nineties: but, as always, it was in France and Germany that the crisis was clearest and had the most far-reaching consequences. In the German Social Democratic Party the crisis primarily took a theoretical form. Although the decisions taken about Marxist doctrine were to have practical effects of great importance, it was as a theoretical controversy that the issue was presented. In France, on the other hand, Socialist politicians had to face problems of immediate action to deal with a specific crisis and of day-to-day political behaviour. The Third Republic offered plenty of opportunities for parliamentary activity. France's social legislation was behind that of Germany or England; but a genuine democratic system and universal suffrage could give scope for reformers, anxious to deal with a growing industrial society. Moreover, by the 1890s, the Republic had established itself; and, as a result, those political groups that twenty years earlier had been on the extreme left now found themselves with a stake in the existing state of affairs. Even extreme radicals like Clemenceau, once they became involved in financial scandals like the Panama affair, could be denounced by their new rivals on the left as hypocritical bourgeois involved in the maintenance of the capitalist order. And, at the same time, the very agitation which the Radicals of the previous generation had started led to increased demands by those still underprivileged: 'You have finally torn the people away from the protection of the church and its dogma . . . . You have interrupted the old song which lulled human misery, and human misery has awoken and is crying out, it has risen before you and is now demanding its place,'[1] Jaurès called to the Radicals; and it was the Socialists who benefited from this awakening. For it was becoming clear that a new left wing was now important in the Chamber of Deputies. Some Radicals were beginning to advocate reforms of a kind which brought them nearer to the newly-elected representatives of the organized Socialist movement, Guesde and Lafargue and Edouard Vaillant. Ambitious lawyers like René Viviani or Alexandre Millerand began to make a political reputation, defending Socialist militants accused of breaches of the peace, or advocating social reforms in the Chamber. Others, like Aristide Briand, another lawyer, who left Saint Nazaire to live down a personal scandal, came into parliament through the extreme wing of the Syndicalist movement, but once there began to move to the right.

Thus, side by side with the representatives of the organized but often quarrelling groups like the POF, the *Parti Ouvrier Socialiste Révolutionnaire* (Allemanistes), the *Fédération des Travailleurs Socialistes de France* (Possibilists), and the *Comité Central Révolutionnaire* (Blanquists), a number of deputies calling themselves Independent Socialists began to vote as a group in the Chamber in favour of mild reforms, and against colonial adventures and infringements of individual liberty. They were joined by Radicals, and were in almost constant alliance with a small number of independents who had been elected as Boulangists—foremost among them Maurice Barrès.

[1] In Chamber of Deputies, 21 November 1893. Jean Jaurès, *Etudes Socialistes, Oeuvres*, I, p.236.

Socialism, in France as in Germany and Italy, was becoming one of the great intellectual forces in the 'nineties. The students in Paris were turning to the discussion of socialist ideas as they were to a rediscovery of German idealism and to the symbolist aesthetic proclaimed by Jean Moréas—sometimes to all these at once. One of the remarkable things about the Third Republic was the intimacy of its intellectual and political life. Clemenceau wrote novels and was the friend of Monet and Debussy: a young socialist intellectual like Alexandre Zévaès, later to become one of the main historians of the French working class movement, could drink in cafés with Paul Verlaine; even the austere and dedicated Jules Guesde could write feeble Baudelairian verse. Maurice Barrès, soon to be the main theorist of reaction, was in the 'nineties on good terms with the socialist intellectuals. And the Socialist movement itself could include, for a time at least, men as different as Charles Péguy and the young aesthete Léon Blum. The centre of this intellectual influence was the *Ecole Normale Supérieure*, where Lucien Herr, for many years its Librarian, produced a group of devoted socialists in each generation of students.

By far the most remarkable of the new converts to socialism was Jean Jaurès. He was born in 1859 and he came from a middle class family in Castres in south west France: his father's cousin had been an admiral and Ambassador at St. Petersburg; Jean's brother also became an admiral. It was a family, therefore, of professional and business people, but the father owned a small estate where Jean Jaurès was brought up and where he acquired a feeling for the French countryside and French peasant society that influenced his whole political outlook. He was a man of outstanding intellectual ability and passed third out of the *Ecole Normale* in 1881, with Bergson second and a M. Lesbazeille first. He became a teacher of philosophy at the Lycée at Albi, and then at the University of Toulouse. All his life he retained an unaffected simplicity of manner, and his

political success never changed the untidiness of his appearance
or habits.

Jaurès was drawn to politics by a deep feeling of sympathy
for the oppressed and underprivileged, and by an equally profound optimism about the possibility of improving their lot. He
was never a Marxist, although he acknowledged his debt to
Marx—and his *Histoire Socialiste de la révolution française*
shows it—and even defended Marx's theory of surplus value
against Bernstein. He was an orator in the great tradition of
French revolutionary speakers—there are moments, indeed,
when he recalls Gambetta whom he himself describes 'with his
burning, highly coloured imagination, his lively feeling for
nature and art, his many-sided ever-alert curiosity'.[1] But for all
his oratorical power, he was too much of an intellectual to
become a demagogue: 'You must know how to be popular,' he
once said, 'but you must know how to spend your popularity.'[2]
It was his irrepressible optimism that gave him strength, but
also produced his greatest mistakes. Everything was going to be
all right—every point that marked an improvement in the international situation, every turn for the better in the domestic politics of foreign countries, was seized on: the Americans were
supporting arbitration, Alsace-Lorraine will be given autonomy,
Ireland is to have home rule, women in England will be given
the vote. As one reads his speeches and articles one is reminded
of Puck's 'Jack shall have Jill, nought shall go ill: the man shall
have his maid again, and all shall be well'.

Jaurès was first elected a deputy in 1885, and for the next
four years was a moderate Radical: he lost his seat in 1889, but
when he was returned in a by-election in 1892 he started voting
with the Socialist group in the Chamber. During the next few
years he was working out his political position—in a series of

---

[1] Jean Jaurès, 'A propos de Gambetta' in *Revue de l'enseignement primaire et
primaire superieur*, Feb. 1909; reprinted in Jaurès, *Pour la Paix Oeuvres*,
IV, p.83.
[2] C. Andler, *Vie de Lucien Herr* (Paris 1932), p.149.

articles, in conversations with Lucien Herr, or in public discussion with Paul Lafargue on the Marxist theory of history.
Socialism was for him the logical culmination of republicanism,
collectivism the natural end of radical reform. His intelligence,
political skill and rhetorical gifts soon made him a leader of the
Socialist movement, perhaps its greatest, though he was as yet
uncommitted to any specific Socialist organization. Indeed, the
independent Socialists in the Chamber—Jaurès, Millerand,
Clovis Hugues, Viviani, and others, added to the complication
of the relationships between the various Socialist groups. They
were more effective parliamentarians than Guesde or Vaillant,
and Jaurès especially had a wide popular appeal. Guesde's election at Roubaix in 1893 had been regarded as a triumph for the
international Socialist cause, and he had startled the Chamber
in one of his first speeches by giving a complete exposé of collectivist principles that had little to do with the motion on hand.
But he was more effective at mass meetings, where his emaciated
appearance and his air of burning sincerity coupled with a
beard and hair 'with which he looks like either Jesus or Alphonse
Daudet',[1] contributed to make him the 'apostle of socialism',
the chosen expounder of socialist doctrine to the masses. Guesde
was perhaps the only member of the organized Socialist movement in France who could compete with the fervour and eloquence of a Jaurès or a Viviani, or the legal and parliamentary
skill of a Millerand. The other leaders were less remarkable.
Edouard Vaillant, for all his courage and honesty, was an unimpressive speaker. Lafargue, a creole from the West Indies,
gained his leading position in the POF by his marriage with
Marx's daughter. He soon lost the seat in the Chamber that he
had won so dramatically while in prison after the fusillade of
Fourmies, and although he remained Secretary of the POF for
some years, he soon retired from active politics, preferring to
use the fortune he had inherited from Engels for private ends,

[1] A. Zévaès, *Notes et souvenirs d'un militant* (Paris 1913), p.198.

until in 1911, appalled, so it is said, by the prospect of old age and the end of his pleasures, he poisoned both himself and his wife—the second of Marx's three daughters to meet a violent end, for her sister Eleanor had killed herself in 1898 after years of wretched life with the unsatisfactory Edward Aveling.

There were plenty of issues in which the Socialist deputies of all shades could attack the governments of the 1890s without raising difficulties about the proper aim of socialist activities, or theoretical problems concerning the nature of contemporary bourgeois society. And, on occasion, Socialist deputies could help to overthrow the government, as Millerand and Jaurès did in November 1893, when their interpellation forced the fall of the Dupuy administration. Socialists of all kinds had considerable successes in the municipal elections of 1896; and at a banquet to celebrate these victories, Millerand made a famous speech which attempted to define a minimum common programme to which all socialists could subscribe. The 'Saint-Mandé programme', as it came to be called, was extremely vague: 'No one is a socialist who does not accept the necessary and progressive substitution of social property for capitalist property.' But the emphasis was on gradual progress: 'No socialist has ever in fact dreamed of transforming the capitalist régime by a stroke of a magic wand or of creating a completely new society as a *tabula rasa* . . . . If we are looking ever higher we are not losing our feet; we are keeping contact with the solid earth.' And, above all, Millerand renounced force and placed his hopes in universal suffrage and the persuasion of the electorate. Moreover, taking care to avoid the charge of being pro-German that was too readily levelled at Guesde, 'We shall at no moment forget that at the same time as being internationalists we are Frenchmen and patriots. Patriots and internationalists, these are two titles which our ancestors of the French Revolution knew how to link nobly.'[1] The leaders of all the Socialist groups

[1] Quoted in Albert Orry, *Les Socialistes indépendants* (Paris 1911), pp.28–9.

except the unbending Allemane were there to listen to this mild
stuff. And before Millerand rose to speak Vaillant had paid
tribute to his 'eminent and incomparable' services to socialism,
while Guesde had urged unity for the attainment of immediate
goals. In the enthusiasm of practical success, theoretical differences were temporarily forgotten, and in the following months
alliances were struck for the senatorial elections and the next
general elections, to be held in 1898. So, although no nearer
formal unification, and although their differences shocked
foreign socialists at international congresses, some sort of practical co-operation was established between the leaders of the
various groups, and the need for unity was stressed in many of
their speeches. But the theoretical and practical differences
between Jaurès and Guesde were bound to make such co-operation rather precarious, and it was inevitable that the Dreyfus
case, which revealed all the lines of cleavage in French society,
should have shown too how deep were the splits in French
Socialism.

When the campaign for the reversal of the verdict on Captain
Dreyfus was started in the summer of 1897 it was sponsored by
a group of intellectuals and individual politicians on purely
humanitarian grounds: it was not at first a major political issue
on which the political groups necessarily had to take a stand. It
was only with the publication of Zola's article *J'Accuse* in Janu-
ary 1898 that the extent of the political crisis caused by the
affair became clear. Several socialists had already become involved in the campaign for revision, largely at the instigation of
Lucien Herr. 'During the month of September,' Léon Blum,
who had been on holiday in the country at the time near where
Herr was staying, later recalled, 'Lucien Herr got on his bi-
cycle and came to see me nearly every afternoon. He suddenly
said one day: "Do you know that Dreyfus is innocent?" '[1] Herr,
supported by Lucien Lévy-Bruhl, succeeded in convincing

[1] Léon Blum, *Souvenirs sur L'Affaire* (Paris 1935), p.17.

Jaurès of Dreyfus' innocence and winning the active support of the great orator. Jaurès characteristically threw himself into the struggle with all his fervour. He soon found himself going much further than many other socialists were prepared to go. Guesde and the Marxists had been delighted by the confusion caused among the bourgeois by the *Affaire*; they would have been pleased to see justice done; but they were not prepared to embark on a joint campaign with bourgeois parties to save somebody who, after all, was only a bourgeois himself. It was this view that Jaurès especially attacked. All his instincts were against it, for he believed that the existing state could be expanded so as to give equal rights to every citizen. He once quoted with approval a remark of Michelet: 'If every being, even the humblest, does not enter the city, I am staying outside.'[1] And now he was writing about Dreyfus. 'He is no longer an officer or a bourgeois: he is despoiled by the very excess of misfortune of all class characteristics; he is nothing but humanity itself in the deepest misery and despair that one can imagine.'[2] Guesde's anxiety about Jaurès' and his friends' enthusiasm for the Dreyfus case was not entirely due to a doctrinaire desire to avoid an association with bourgeois parties. He felt that too much energy was being devoted to what, to him, was a personal controversy, and that Socialists, while remaining, if not pro-Dreyfus, at least anti-anti-Dreyfusard, should not allow this passing quarrel to distract them from pursuing the class struggle in which a Clemenceau was as great an enemy as a Déroulède.

In fact, both Jaurès and Guesde lost their seats in the general election of May, 1898, and some Socialists were ready to blame this on Jaurès' absorption in the Dreyfus case; Jaurès, however, remained confident that sooner or later the elections would show that he was right, that no socialist could remain indifferent to a struggle both for human rights and the preservation of the

[1] L. Lévy-Bruhl, *Jaurès* (Paris 1924), p.61.
[2] Jean Jaurès, *Les Preuves* (Paris 1898), p.12.

Republic, for him a necessary and desirable stage on the road to the socialist state. However, those socialists who had allied themselves with the bourgeois supporters of Dreyfus soon found themselves in an even more difficult position, which was, in fact, the logical conclusion of their policy. In June 1899 a new ministry was formed by René Waldeck-Rousseau in a chamber whose composition had been little changed by the elections of the previous year; but this was a ministry generally looking to the Left for support, and avowedly intending to defend the Republic. For the first time the Socialists in the Chamber were confronted with a Government whose immediate aims were the same as theirs. One at least of the independent Socialists, Alexandre Millerand, as soon as the previous Government had fallen, made it quite clear where he stood; 'No one among the republicans will think of quibbling with the statesmen who take power about the details of their declaration of policy. Whatever be the name of the Prime Minister, he is sure of support from the republican party.'[1] He was soon to profit from this declaration of the ideal of republican solidarity, for when Waldeck-Rousseau formed his Government he was offered the post of Minister of Commerce, which he promptly accepted.

It is hard now to imagine the stir that this created in the international Socialist world. Millerand, for all his moderation and parliamentary success, was universally regarded as a socialist: his Saint-Mandé speech had laid down the minimum programme on which French socialists might be able to agree; as a lawyer he was famous for his defence of the workers' interests. It was astounding that anyone calling himself a socialist should suddenly find himself a minister; and the news was received in very different ways. For some people it was yet another sign of the progress that socialism had made in the past ten years; for others it was a great betrayal of socialist principles by a treacherous opportunist. Millerand did not consult any of his col-

[1] Quoted in Georges Suarez, *Briand* (Paris 1938), I, p.255.

leagues before accepting Waldeck-Rousseau's offer, though he
had discussed with Jaurès what might happen if an offer were
made, and had told the parliamentary group of Socialists that
discussions were going on, but that he had not committed the
Socialists as a group. What really shocked his Socialist colleagues when the news became known, was that Millerand's
colleague at the Ministry of War was to be General Gallifet, the
man who had suppressed the Commune in 1871 and one of the
most hated figures on the socialist black list. 'They say that you
will form part of a ministerial combination with Gallifet,'
Edouard Vaillant wrote. 'That would wipe out what was said
yesterday to the Socialist (parliamentary) group. If there is one
name which must not appear because it expresses for us all the
crimes of Versailles, it is that of Gallifet . . . . This seems to me
so odious and so ignoble that I cannot believe it and I hope to
be reassured as soon as possible.'[1]

Millerand's appointment at once became the symbol of all
the conflicts inside the French Socialist movement; and indeed
the 'Millerand case' was to have international repercussions of
enormous importance, and influence Socialist tactics for a
generation. The Dreyfus affair had, of course, aroused much
interest and anxiety outside France, not only among socialists;
and the general discussions involved questions of socialist
theory that the Germans at least could not leave alone. Wilhelm
Liebknecht, 'the general secretary of all foreign parties in Berlin',[2] took the same line as Guesde; indeed, he went further and
at one moment even wrote that he did not believe in Dreyfus's
innocence and that the only use of the Affair was that it exposed
the dangers of military espionage.[3] The old man, indeed, realized that he had gone a bit far when the *Action Française* trans-

[1] A. Zévaès, *Histoire du Socialisme et du Communisme en France* (Paris
1947), p.280.
[2] V. Adler, *Aufsätze*, VI, p.297.
[3] W. Liebknecht, 'Nachträgliches zur "Affaire"', *Die Fackel* vol. I, Nos.
18–19 (Vienna) Sept.–Oct. 1899.

lated and reprinted the article, and he hastened to assure the French Socialist Dreyfusards that he was not criticizing them but only their supporters in Germany who were falling into bourgeois traps. But if the Dreyfus affair aroused international controversy about co-operation with other parties for specific and immediate aims, the Millerand case caused even more violent discussion.

The form this discussion took inside each Socialist party of Europe was determined mainly by the possibility or impossibility of any of its own leaders being placed in the same situation as Millerand, or of its being able to intervene effectively in a campaign such as that of the Dreyfusards. The Italian Socialists, for instance, were rent by divisions about practical tactics as well as by controversies about theory; and they were just emerging from a political crisis not entirely unlike the Dreyfus case. Between 1898 and 1900 constitutional government in Italy was in danger. Bad harvests and rising prices had led to sporadic rioting in the South, in which people were killed. Then a young student, the son of a radical deputy for Milan, was killed in disturbances at Pavia. When the news reached the workers at the Pirelli factory in Milan, they, and especially their wives and children, started demonstrations of a harmless kind, although Filippo Turati, a leading socialist intellectual and himself a deputy for Milan advised against it: 'The days for street fighting are past . . . . because everything is ready for the most final repression . . . . we must not allow the authorities to determine the day of battle . . . . As your deputy I call on you to be calm and patient.'[1] The Government at once became alarmed and took the demonstrations more seriously than they deserved, perhaps as an excuse for acting against the Socialists; for there were many influential people anxious to use the opportunity for a revision of the constitution and a curtail-

[1] Filippo Turati — Anna Kuliscioff. *Carteggio I. Maggio 1898—Giugno 1899* (Milan 1949), p. xxvi.

ment of democracy in Bismarckian fashion. Artillery was moved into Milan, and a state of siege proclaimed there, as it was in Naples and Florence. Filippo Turati, Anna Kuliscioff, his friend and colleague in the editing of *La Critica Sociale,* and other Socialist leaders, were arrested and condemned to prison. Shortly afterwards a new Government was formed under General Pelloux, and in February 1899 laws were introduced in parliament limiting the freedom of speech and assembly on lines similar to those of the German anti-Socialist laws.

However, in contrast to Germany in 1879, the Liberals and Radicals at this point saw what was in danger; and by the end of 1899 their opposition had prevented Pelloux's scheme from being successful. Elections in June 1900 returned a Liberal majority, and constitutional government was safe. Turati had been released from prison in the summer of 1899 and drew many lessons from the events of the past year. His mistrust of open battles with the power of the state was confirmed; his rejection of Anarchist methods had been justified. The Socialist Party was increasing its strength as a parliamentary force. In 1897 it had fifteen deputies and in 1904 it was to have thirty, so that, with direct action discredited by the Milan days of June 1898, it was obliged to ally itself with other groups of the left if it was to attain its ends; and, like Jaurès at the time of the Dreyfus affair, Turati and his friends felt that in the present crisis the interests of Socialists coincided with those of Liberals and Radicals in order to save the constitutional system within which a Socialist party could exist at all. The debate was by no means over; right up until 1915 discussions were to continue about the question of co-operation and electoral alliances with other parties and about the advantages of direct action over parliamentary inaction, and in 1912 a small group split off on this issue to form an unsuccessful Reformist Party under Bissolati and Bonomi. However, a precarious balance was maintained inside the PSI behind a screen of compromise resolutions adopted at each party congress—a resolution adopted in 1902 is a good example: 'The Congress declares that the existence of two distinct tendencies based on substantial differences is intolerable, and that what has been termed such in the recent discussions are only differences depending on a natural and fruitful variety of views.'[1] Indeed, the use that the liberals under Giolitti made of their success in the crisis of 1898–1900 justified many of the criticisms of the most intransigent Marxists and Syndicalists. However, the crisis showed that Turati and his friends, like Jaurès and his, were not ready to reject out of hand practical co-operation with other parties and alliances for specific purposes with the bourgeoisie; and they had learnt that such alliances could be successful.

While in France and Italy Socialists were being driven into effective co-operation with other parties in order to defend political liberties and human rights, and while in Belgium Socialists were allied with Liberals in the struggle for universal suffrage, the situation in Germany was different. The Social Democratic Party had been growing in strength without any corresponding growth in the power of parliament. The Imperial Chancellor and his state secretaries needed the approval of the Reichstag for any actual legislation introduced; they also needed the Reichstag to vote the budget annually, although many of the most important credits, such as those for the army and navy, were voted for several years at a stretch. The Government could not be overthrown by a vote of the Reichstag; it was only when a chancellor lost the confidence of the Emperor, like Bismarck in 1890 or Bülow in 1909, that he felt obliged to resign. The Social Democratic Party was in fact the only continuous opposition in the Imperial Parliament, and the Socialists used their votes against the credits demanded by the Government as a symbol of their hostility to the whole system. Indeed this

---

[1] Filippo Meda, 'Attraverso i Congressi socialisti italiani' in *Nuova Antologia*, Dec. 1920, vol. 293, p.251.

hostility was carried further, and they did their best to dissociate themselves from parliament so far as possible: in 1895, for example, they refused to attend the ceremonial laying of the last stone of the new Reichstag building out of disapproval of a 'military and dynastic festival'; at the opening they ostentatiously remained seated when called on to cheer the Kaiser; they refused to submit candidates for parliamentary offices until 1912, when after some discussion they permitted Scheidemann to become Vice-President of the house, an election that did in fact involve them in complicated negotiations with other parties.

Right up to 1914 the Social Democrats regarded themselves as set apart from bourgeois society: 'Social Democracy differs from all other parties through its fundamental opposition to the social and governmental system of capitalism;'[1] and bourgeois society reciprocated. From time to time in the 'nineties the Government had tried to reintroduce some form of anti-Socialist law, though this time, unlike 1879, they failed to get a majority in the Reichstag, since the Independent Liberals and the Centre Party were not prepared to support them. Equally, the Socialists were prepared to vote with liberals and join them in parliamentary obstruction against laws affecting individual liberty like the notorious *Lex Heinze*, which would have imposed a literary and artistic censorship, but these parliamentary alignments were not a sign of any alliance with other parties; each party acted independently and happened to have the same immediate aim. The Government, too, discriminated against the Socialists, so that there was some justification for their regarding themselves as different from other parties and for concentrating on the building up of their own vast and all-embracing organization. Their meetings were interfered with; it was decided not to hold the 1900 International Socialist Congress in Germany because it was uncertain whether the delegates would have

[1] Report of Parliamentary Party to the Party Congress 1912. *Verhandlungen*, p.100.

sufficient freedom of speech. Indeed, Wilhelm Liebknecht had been imprisoned for *lèse-majesté* after his speech at the 1895 party congress.

Moreover, Social Democrats found themselves in different situations according to which state of the Empire they lived in; and it was in the South and West that they began to be less strictly exclusive. While in Prussia the restricted franchise made it doubtful whether it was ever worth while fighting elections to the Diet, in Baden and Bavaria and Württemberg a more liberal tradition prevailed, and in the cosier atmosphere of the *Land* Diets members of different parties could co-operate in a manner that would have been unthinkable in the colder and more rigorous atmosphere of Berlin. The electors, too, in the West and South were less concerned with the class struggle than the industrial masses of Prussia or Saxony. Georg von Vollmar in Bavaria was the first to point out the necessity of an immediate practical programme in the interest of electoral success: 'If you want to win the people and educate them politically your political behaviour must be understandable to them,'[1] he said at the Party Congress of 1894. And three years earlier he had made a series of speeches in Munich advocating a more pragmatic and flexible form of socialism, and 'tactics of practical reforming political action which tries to achieve the object desired by the only possible means, practical partial success.'[2] Above all, if you wanted to win the support of the Bavarian peasant, it was no good going and telling him that he was doomed to expropriation by the inevitable laws of history; and, as a result of this pressure, Karl Kautsky, the official party theorist and 'Pope of socialism', was trying to devise in the 1890s an ingenious agrarian programme that would appeal to the peasant while not departing too far from Marxist orthodoxy.

---

[1] *Verhandlungen* 1894, p.111.
[2] G. von. Vollmar, *Über die nächsten Aufgaben der deutschen Sozialdemokratie* (Munich 1891), p.19.

This 'reformism' was the reaction of experienced practical politicians to the situation caused by the growth of a mass party. It led its exponents into compromises with other parties which were systematically condemned by the Social Democratic leadership. Vollmar and his friends voted for the Bavarian budget in 1894. In spite of official condemnation by the Party Congresses of 1907, 1908 and 1910, such action continued, particularly in Baden, and was defended on the grounds that local budgets often contained measures of benefit to the workers.

If there was a certain latitude in political practice in the SPD, there was no latitude in political theory, and it was on the theoretical line that the struggle was most bitterly engaged. It took the form of a movement to revise Marxist doctrine; and the name Revisionism was thus applied to the whole trend. The theoretical spokesman of this movement was Eduard Bernstein. Bernstein had lived for many years abroad, in Switzerland, and in England, and was perhaps the only one among the Socialist leaders of Germany who was really pro-British, and did not look at England with the eyes of Engels in 1845 and regard England as the typical capitalist state and the natural enemy of the working class. (He was also one of the few Socialists prepared after 1918 to accept unequivocally Germany's guilt for the war.)[1] In London he had got to know and respect the early Fabians; the practical conclusion of his doctrine was not very different from theirs, but he started from a theoretical rather than an empirical basis. He stated his views in a series of articles in the late 'nineties, and summed them up in his *Die Voraussetzungen des Sozialismus und die Aufgaben der Sozialdemokratie* (*The Presuppositions of Socialism and the Tasks of Social Democracy*) published in 1899.[2] There is no need to follow the details of the theoretical controversy which occupied hundreds of pages of

---

[1] See Peter Gay, *The Dilemma of Democratic Socialism* (New York 1952) for detailed and critical discussion of Bernstein's views.

[2] An English translation *Evolutionary Socialism* was published in 1901.

the Socialist periodicals and hours of time at party conferences. Briefly, Bernstein attacked some of Marx's general theories such as the labour theory of value and a too rigid insistence on the economic interpretation of history, while he was ready to modify Marx's materialism by the introduction of neo-Kantian ethics. Above all, he maintained that Marx was wrong in his predictions about the future development and impending collapse of the capitalist order. In spite of the growth of trusts and cartels, capitalism was not becoming exclusively a system of large concerns, the members of the lower middle class were not everywhere being forced to become members of the proletariat; there was no absolute and rigid division between classes, and therefore it was false to interpret the political situation solely in terms of a class struggle; the standard of living of the working class was in fact rising and they were not being forced into the ever increasing misery which Marx had prophesied. For these reasons, according to Bernstein, the revolution in the sense of the total overthrow of the existing system might well be not only impossible but unnecessary. Instead, changes would come by evolution not by revolution. The total transformation of society would remain as an ultimate goal towards which the socialist movement might strive. In the meantime, there was much to be done; and what was important was the day-to-day struggle to win improvements in the world as it was. As Bernstein put it, in a much-quoted and much criticized phrase, 'The movement is everything: the final goal of socialism is nothing.'[1]

Bernstein's criticisms of Marx were answered by Karl Kautsky in a doctrinal duel worthy of the early Church. For Kautsky and the orthodox Marxists, the acceptance of Bernstein's ideas would mean the abandonment of the essential elements in Marx's teaching—the class struggle and the materialist conception of history, as well as much of Marx's economic analysis

[1] *Neue Zeit 1897–1898*, I. p.556, q. Erika Rikli, *Der Revisionismus* (Zürich 1936), p.87.

of the capitalist system. Moreover, if, as Bernstein argued, capitalism was not about to collapse and the revolution therefore had to be postponed indefinitely, one of the great attractions of the Social Democratic Party programme would disappear, and it would be in danger of becoming a reformist party indistinguishable, it might seem, from some of its bour-geois counterparts. Kautsky was supported by most of the party leaders, such as Bebel, anxious not to see the orthodoxy on which their position was based eroded by new theories, what-ever they might be doing in practice. At the same time it was in these discussions that the young Rosa Luxemburg, soon to be Kautsky's most formidable critic on the left, first made her reputation as a theorist and controversialist. Bernstein was formally condemned by the Social Democratic Party at its annual congress at Hanover in 1899, and the condemnation was even more expressly repeated at the Dresden Congress of 1903 with much interpretation and reinterpretation of the last works and writings of Engels and of Wilhelm Liebknecht (who had died in August 1900), and with many personal accusations and counter-accusations. (There were even rumours that Bernstein was in the pay of the German government!)[1] The result of these disputations was to make it more difficult for the reformist wing of the party to carry out a practical change of tactics without at once being accused of treacherous heresy; the cause of reform was hindered, not helped, by general theoretical discussions. As Ignaz Auer, an old, shrewd and experienced Bavarian Socialist wrote to Bernstein:

'Do you think it is really possible that a party which has a literature going back fifty years, an organization going back forty years and a still older tradition, can change its direction like this in the twinkling of an eye? For the most influential members of the party to behave as you demand would simply mean splitting the party and throwing decades of work to the winds. My dear Ede, one doesn't formally

---

[1] Turati—Kuliscioff, *Carteggio* (3 April 1899), p.387.

decide to do what you ask, one doesn't say it, one *does* it. Our whole activity—even under the shameful anti-Socialist law—was the activity of a Social Democratic reforming party. A party which reckons with the masses simply cannot be anything else.'[1]

This was quite true; but the tragedy of the Hanover and Dresden Congresses was that the German Social Democratic Party asserted its allegiance to a rigid doctrine which did not wholly correspond to its own practice, but which it proceeded to impose on other member parties of the Socialist International.

2.

Revisionism and Reformism were international trends which resulted from the success of mass social democracy in Europe. Millerand's acceptance of office in France and Bernstein's condemnation in Germany meant that the next two Congresses of the International were concerned with these problems in an immediate practical form. Moreover, the Dreyfus affair and the Millerand case had emphasized once more the division among the French Socialist groups. When the International Congress assembled in Paris in September 1900, the Germans arrived in strength, confident after their electoral successes and the triumph of orthodox Marxism at the Hanover Congress. Yet there were a few among them, and still more among some of the other delegations who looked with envy on the French and regarded Millerand not as a renegade but as a symbol of the influence socialists might hope to win. 'For the moment the leaders of our party for whom such a question could present itself were nearer a prison cell than a ministerial post,'[2] Ignaz Auer remarked, regretfully. And as Jaurès walked with the veteran German leader, Singer, to pay the routine visit to lay a wreath on the Mur

[1] E. Bernstein, 'Ignaz Auer der Führer, Freund und Berater' in *Sozialistische Monatshefte*, 1907, I, pp.845–6.
[2] *Proc.* 1900, p. 85.

des Féderes, where the Communards had been shot, the latter remarked, 'One cannot approve the entry of a socialist in a bourgeois ministry; but I cannot help saying that whereas thirty years ago the bourgeoisie were shooting proletarians here, now the Socialist Party has so grown that in an hour of peril the bourgeoisie is obliged to call on one of us to save elementary liberties.'[1]

However, the French were well aware that their disunity made them rather ridiculous in the eyes of their foreign comrades. The opening of the proceedings of the Congress had once more been held up by their wrangling, and they were again forced in fact to act as two separate delegations. But Jaurès opened the Congress with a passionate plea for unity: and Vandervelde responded with the cry, '*Socialistes français, unissez-vous !*' Inevitably the issue dividing the French—that of co-operation with bourgeois parties—was the main subject of debate; and even after two days of discussion the question was not finally decided. While the Marxists from countries where there was a strong reformist wing—Guesde and the Italian, Ferri—wanted an unequivocal veto on any participation in bourgeois governments or co-operation with non-socialist parties, there were many who wanted a more elastic policy. Vandervelde put the case with his usual clarity and common sense: 'A coalition is legitimate in the case where liberty is threatened as in Italy: it is legitimate again when it is a question of defending the rights of the human personality, as recently in France. It is legitimate finally when it is a question of winning universal suffrage as in Belgium.'[2] He criticized Millerand, but less for what he had done than for the way he did it, without prior consultation with his party. Above all, the question of tactics must be left to individual parties to decide. Vandervelde was supported by Jaurès, who reminded the Germans of what had been achieved by an *ad hoc* alignment with bourgeois parties in rejecting the *Lex Heinze* in

[1] Jean Jaurès, *Les Deux Méthodes. Oeuvres*, VI, pp.199–200.
[2] *Proc.* 1900, Wednesday 26 September.

the Reichstag: 'It is to their credit, for thanks to them Germany
has not become the country of Attila, it has remained the country of Goethe.'[1] And he went on to say that a Millerand situation
might occur in Switzerland or Belgium.

Ferri and Guesde repeated the orthodox Marxist arguments:
and on this occasion Guesde added another one which, indeed,
his own actions in 1914 were paradoxically to support. Ministers, he argued, must support the military budgets of their
Governments, even Socialist ministers, and thus one of the
main reasons for the International would disappear: 'With an
Italian Millerand, a German Millerand, an English Millerand,
there would be no International possible any more.'[2]

But on this occasion the main Marxist forces, the German
delegation, were not prepared to go into action. Presumably
from a desire not to make the divisions between their French
hosts worse, they were ready for compromise; and Kautsky introduced the motion which was ultimately adopted, allowing that
socialists might, as an exceptional measure of a temporary kind,
enter a bourgeois government, but implicitly condemning Millerand by saying that such action must be approved by the
party. This indeed was the line that Wilhelm Liebknecht had
already taken shortly before his sudden death.

'We must remain *strictissime* neutral,' he wrote to Victor Adler.
'The entry of Millerand into the ministry was a serious tactical mistake but the logical result of Jaurès' campaign which subordinated
everything else to the *Affaire*. Jaurès however is certainly no fool,
while Millerand in my opinion is one of those over clever people
whom one still cannot class as traitors. We are now mediating: my
friend Deville and others are at work and I too am the confidential
agent of both parties.'[3]

[1] *Proc.* 1900, Wednesday 26 September.
[2] *Proc.* 1900, Thursday 27 September.
[3] Victor Adler, 'Wilhelm Liebknecht zum Gedächtnis' in *Der Wahre
Jakob*, August 1901, printed in *Aufsätze*, VI, p.294ff. Adler, *Briefwechsel mit
August Bebel und Karl Kautsky* (ed. Friedrich Adler) (Vienna 1954), p.319.

It was this sort of genuine mediation and understanding that made Liebknecht's death a loss for the International, even if his romantic inconsistencies and intellectual pretentions had lost him some of his popularity with some of the younger German theoreticians like Kautsky. The decision taken at the Congress seemed to be a triumph for the reformists: but the issue still had to be fought out within the French Socialist groups. What had been established was the right of the International to discuss these problems of tactics and lay down a common line for all member parties to follow. The other important practical step taken in Paris was a further sign of the increased efficiency and the growing claims of the International: an International Bureau was appointed of representatives of the leading parties and provided with its own secretariat and offices in Brussels. Emile Vandervelde was its first president; and great hopes were placed on this headquarters of the International Socialist Movement.

The first secretary, a Belgian, Victor Serwy, who served until 1905, took a limited view of his functions and seems to have been mainly occupied in organizing the international congress held at Amsterdam in 1904. However, his successor, Camille Huysmans, rapidly became an influential figure in the international Socialist movement and later in Belgian political life, until his death in 1968 aged 96. A man of considerable intellectual as well as linguistic gifts, he was also a skilful diplomat and an efficient administrator. Under his direction, the secretariat produced a large amount of documentary material, which is only beginning to be utilized by historians, and assumed increasing importance in providing a link between the member parties and even, on occasions, in attempting to resolve their internal disputes. As the secretariat became more active and seemed to be about to play a more important part in the life of the International, some people hoped that the International Socialist Bureau, the permanent executive committee whose periodical meetings were attended by the leading Socialist politicians of Europe, would become a real general staff of the revolution. It soon became clear, however, that in practice the functions of the Bureau were strictly limited and that it could do little to co-ordinate the activities of the individual parties which belonged to the International. Thus, for all the hopes which continued to be placed in it, the job of the Bureau and its Secretariat remained primarily that of disseminating information, organizing congresses and providing the opportunity for the maintenance of regular contacts between the Socialist leaders.

Once the Paris congress dispersed, the debates about the Millerand case were immediately taken up again by the French Socialists. They had already held, in the preceding year, a conference between Guesdists and Jaurèsists at which the latter had been outvoted and any attempt at unification about tactical and theoretical problems made more difficult. The great event of the autumn of 1900 was a full scale public debate in Lille between Jaurès and Guesde; but it added little except a certain oratorical *éclat* to the arguments that had been advanced at the Congress the previous year (which had led Aristide Briand to remark that the party was going to meet in 'annual scissions').[1] What is noticeable, however, about the controversy is the way in which both participants constantly cite German precedents and quote German pronouncements to justify their position. In spite of interruptions from hecklers, this debate at least rose above the personal animosities that were becoming keener as the crisis in French socialism dragged on. The group of intellectuals, for example, who had founded the *Cahiers de la Quinzaine* began to break up, with Lucien Herr remaining an orthodox Socialist and Charles Péguy turning into a mystical Catholic patriot. It was typical of the atmosphere, too, that at the moment when he was engaged in vigorous prosecution of the campaign for the disestablishment of the Church, Jaurès should

[1] 'Scissions annuelles'. Suarez, I, p.294.

have been viciously attacked by his rivals in the Socialist parties for allowing, so it was alleged, his daughter to be brought up as a Catholic and to make her first communion. If the story is true, it is perhaps not surprising; Jaurès' anti-clericalism stopped short of private life. And it is shortly after this episode that he was writing to Briand about a proposed resolution: 'Renaudel wants the party to declare itself "materialist and anti-clerical". It is absurd. We are not metaphysicians. I will never abandon my freedom of thought.'[1]

The feuds between socialists aroused by the Millerand case were as bitter as those aroused in the French middle class by Dreyfus. Millerand's conduct while minister was continuously discussed and criticized: he had introduced bills about trade unions and compulsory arbitration and was alternately praised and blamed for them. He had arranged for a pension to be paid to Fernand Pelloutier who was a dying man; and Pelloutier was attacked for accepting. M. and Mme Millerand were mocked for sending engraved cards to working men to invite them to a democratic reception by the Minister. (Millerand was not formally expelled from the Socialist group until after 1904; he was to be later one of the most reactionary Presidents of the Republic.) With these constant discussions of fundamental principles and immediate tactics mixed up with personal denunciations and abuse, it is not surprising that the joint committee set up in 1899 to try and keep the Socialist groups together failed in its purpose. By 1902 the split was formalized and two separate parties had come into being, the *Parti Socialiste de France* composed of Guesdistes and Blanquists, and the *Parti Socialiste Français* composed of the supporters of Jaurès, the remnants of the old Possibilists and a certain number of independent local Socialist parties. Jaurès' group was stronger in parliament after the elections of 1902, with thirty-two seats compared with the Guesdists' dozen. But the position of both groups was a little

[1] Suarez, I, p.373.

insecure in the face of the growing syndicalist agitation and the increased industrial unrest that accompanied their endless internecine discussions.

While the splits in the French parties were growing, German Social Democracy was increasing in strength; and French Marxists began to look more than ever to it for support. The elections of 1903 gave the SPD its biggest electoral victory yet— eighty-one seats and over three million votes. This success aroused hopes that the final triumph of socialism was not far off, that electoral organization and the inevitable laws of history would combine to overthrow the existing order and bring the proletariat into power without any further action on their part. Thus, while success encouraged reformist practice, and the question of voting for the budget in the individual states had to be fought out all over again, it also gave new strength to rigorous Marxist theorizing. And the Dresden Congress of 1903 produced the strongest condemnation so far both of revisionist theory and of reformist practice, with bitter personal discussions (in the course of which Vollmar was called the German Miller-and) ending in a great triumph for Bebel, Kautsky and the orthodox. In fact, however, a new group was emerging inside the party, who, while ready to side with the Party leadership against the Revisionists, were nevertheless as aware as practical politicians like Auer and Vollmar of the gap between official Party theory and day-to-day practice. But whereas Bernstein had drawn the conclusion that the theory needed to be amended to fit the practice, the younger people on the left were urging that the Party's practice should fit its theory. The most notable figures in this group were Karl Liebknecht, Wilhelm's son, who had inherited his father's political romanticism without his common sense, and Rosa Luxemburg. The latter was a courageous and tireless agitator, and a formidable theorist; one of her enemies referred to her after her death as 'that pedantic and quarrelsome person with her mechanistic interpretation of

Marxism.'[1] But her political rigour and intellectual achievements were accompanied by a warmth, charm and sensibility,
(she even used to sing songs by Hugo Wolf), rare in the socialist
world, and made her one of the most fascinating figures produced by the International. For the moment Karl Liebknecht,
Rosa Luxemburg and their friends were rather embarrassing
allies of the Party leadership in their struggle against the
Revisionists; but it was not to be long before they started attacking the leaders too, and they were to be a crucial link between
the Second and Third Internationals.

When the next International Congress met, at Amsterdam in
August 1904, the Germans and their allies were determined to
settle the revisionist controversy on the international plane as
they had dealt with it at home the previous year. At the same
time they were anxions to see the French parties united; and
Guesde and his friends were eager for German support to help
them impose unity on their terms. This was to be the main
issue at the Congress; and the two greatest leaders of European
social democracy, Bebel and Jaurès, met and argued for their
respective views of the nature of socialism. The discussions took
place on a motion by Guesde which simply repeated, word for
word, the motion accepted by the German Party at Dresden the
previous year:

'The Congress condemns in the most decisive fashion revisionist
efforts to change the victorious tactics we have hitherto followed
based on the class struggle, in such a way that instead of conquering
political power by defeating our opponents, a policy of coming to
terms with the existing order is followed. The result of such revisionist tactics would be that instead of being a party which works for
the most rapid transformation possible of existing bourgeois society
into the socialist social order, i.e. revolutionary in the best sense of
the word, the party would become one which is content with reforming bourgeois society.

[1] Paul Frölich, *Rosa Luxemburg* (London 1940), p.53. The phrase is
Dazhinsky's.

Therefore the Congress is convinced, in contradiction to present revisionist efforts, that class conflicts are not growing weaker but are continually becoming more acute, and declares:

1. That the Party disclaims responsibility for political and economic circumstances based on the capitalist modes of production, and that it therefore refuses to support any measures calculated to keep the ruling classes in power;

2. That Social Democracy, in accordance with the Kautsky resolution of the International Socialist Congress in Paris, 1900, cannot *aim at* participating in governmental power within capitalist society. The Congress furthermore condemns any attempt to disguise existing class conflicts in order to facilitate support of bourgeois parties.

The Congress expects that the Social Democratic parties will use the increased power resulting from the increased number of their members and the powerful increase of the electoral masses behind them, so as primarily to explain the goal of Social Democracy and the corresponding principles of our programme, to preserve vigorously and explicitly the interests of the working class, to extend and secure political liberty and equal rights and to wage the battle against militarism and navalism, against colonial and world power politics, against injustice, oppression and exploitation in every form, even more energetically than has hitherto been possible, and to work energetically for the building up of social legislation and the fulfilling of the political and cultural tasks of the working class.'

This was at once taken up and supported by Bebel and his disciplined German contingent. He had made it a question of confidence within his own delegation (one of the Revisionist members complained afterwards that the delegates had never been given a chance to express an opinion), and could be certain of their support. The argument took four days—three in committee and one in the full congress, when Vandervelde opened the discussion as *rapporteur* of the committee. Vandervelde's own sympathies were with Jaurès, and he and Victor Adler had failed to get the committee to agree on a compromise resolution that would leave the position much as it had been under the Paris resolution of 1900. But the committee had, after what Vandervelde called a wonderful struggle of minds and ideas notable for its lack of personal animosity (though it is uncertain whether this was true of Guesde's contributions), rejected the Adler-Vandervelde motion by twenty-four votes to sixteen; and thus it was the Dresden resolution that was now before the Congress. Kautsky was furious in spite of this success. Even his friendship with Victor Adler, his closest personal friend in the Socialist movement (he was himself Austrian), was temporarily troubled. He was a fanatic who did not believe in compromise, and Adler's attempts to reach an agreed solution were treachery in his eyes. He believed that the French Party would only be unified 'against Jaurès and without Jaurès',[1] and that to display him to the international Socialist world as an isolated figure would undermine his prestige, and so even the limited support for his views expressed by Adler and Vandervelde was extremely disagreeable.

Jaurès opened the debate with a long and brilliant defence of his conduct during the Dreyfus case—he and his friends had saved the republic and it was worth saving: socialists must be trusted to know when co-operation with the bourgeoisie was becoming dangerous—and so on. But the most notable feature of his speech was a direct attack on the German Social Democrats who wanted to impose their tactics on all other countries. 'What at present most weighs on Europe and the world, on the guarantee of peace, the safeguarding of political liberties, the progress of socialism and the working class, what presses hard on the political and social progress of Europe, is not the alleged compromises, the dangerous enterprises of the French Socialists who had allied themselves with democracy in order to save the liberty, progress and peace of the world, but it is the political powerlessness of German Social Democracy.'[2] The report adds that at this point there was 'great sensation' (*grosse Bewegung*).

[1] Letter to Victor Adler, 18 October 1904. Adler, *Briefwechsel*, p.432.
[2] *Proc.* 1904, Friday 19 August, p.37.

Indeed nobody (except some of the Anarchists in the early days of the International) had ever spoken to the Germans like this before, and Jaurès went on to ram home his point. 'The essential vice of the Dresden resolution was that it tried to apply the rules of action, or rather of inaction, which are at present imposed on the German Party, which had no revolutionary tradition but only one of receiving benefits—universal suffrage, for instance,—from above.' Even if the German Socialists were to win a majority in the Reichstag they would still be impotent, for parliament itself was without power. It was a disaster that this impotence should be masked by theoretical intransigence. 'Behind the inflexibility of theoretical formulas which your excellent Comrade Kautsky will supply you with till the end of his days, you concealed from your own proletariat, from the international proletariat, your inability to act.'

When Bebel rose to reply amid loud applause he merely reiterated his usual position. Capitalism was capitalism wherever it was to be found, in monarchies or republics: 'However much we may envy you French your republic, and wish we had one, we don't intend to get our heads smashed in for its sake. Monarchy or republic—both are class states, both are a form of state to maintain the class rule of the bourgeoisie, both are designed to protect the capitalist order of society.' French opportunism only led to splits and disintegration of the working class movement. After speeches by Adler, Ferri, who attacked revisionism in the Italian party, and Anseele, who praised its advantages for the Belgians, the Adler-Vandervelde amendment that allowed for local variations in different countries was again rejected, by twenty-one votes to nineteen. And then the Dresden resolution was passed by twenty-five votes to four with twelve abstentions. At the same time the Congress passed unanimously a resolution calling on the French to settle their differences and unite. It is significant that the people who opposed the Dresden motion, or who abstained, were representatives of those countries where liberal parliamentary institutions were strongest—England, France, Scandinavia, Belgium, Switzerland—while, with the exception of the Italians, those who supported it (including the solitary delegate from Japan), came from countries where political power was unlikely to be offered to them.

It was a great victory for Bebel and a great personal defeat for Jaurès. Many of his French supporters went away in a bitter mood. 'Genossen, Genossen, j'en ai assez de ces genosseries,'[1] Briand remarked. And Briand was to be one of those French Socialists who, like Viviani, rather than face a future in which there were to be no ministerial posts, left the party never to return. Jaurès himself accepted the decisions of the Congress in the interests of international solidarity and from a genuine desire to see the French Socialists united. In April of the following year the two French groups met in conference in Paris and formed themselves into a united party as recommended by the International Congress and on the basis of the principles accepted at Amsterdam. The new party acknowledged its origins by taking the name of *Section Française de l'Internationale Ouvrière* (SFIO).

The price paid by Jaurès in the interests of socialist unity was a heavy one, both personally and politically. 'My personal situation in the unified party is becoming more difficult and is a painful one,' he wrote to Briand a year later. 'But I am fiercely determined to stay and to work in it. Alas! Divergent currents are going to carry us far away from each other for many years . . . .'[2] Moreover, he was condemned to the same impotence as the German Party. (Indeed, Kautsky himself had admitted that it would be 'political castration' for Jaurès to unite with Guesde.)[3] It is a measure of his greatness that, although excluded from the possibility of power and responsibility, Jaurès should have yet retained a considerable parliamentary position and reputation. Vandervelde relates that as they left the confer-

[1] Suarez, I, p.463.   [2] Suarez, II, p.58.   [3] Adler, *Briefwechsel*, p.433.

ence room Jaurès said, 'I am going to study military questions',[1] and he implies that this was a result of momentary despair of ever co-operating with the Germans. But it is more likely that Jaurès saw that if the sacrifices he was ready to make in the interests of international Socialist unity were to be justified, the International must be made an effective instrument for the fighting of militarism and the prevention of war. It was to this cause that he was to devote the rest of his life.

The Amsterdam Congress marks the highest point in the influence of the International. For here it was laying down general rules of political behaviour and persuading one of its most important member parties to accept them (though one Belgian delegate was overheard to say that he would take no notice of them). The dangers of this success are obvious: the Germans in fact were able to impose their policy on the other Socialist parties of Europe, showing in their disregard of the circumstances in other countries a blind insistence on doctrinal uniformity. And when the moment of decision came, in 1914 and again in 1918, they were to be the first to abandon their own rules. Yet this effective demonstration of the solidarity and loyalty of the members of the International was impressive, and it gave good grounds for hope that the movement might be equally solid and loyal in the execution of what was coming to be seen, with increasing insistency and anxiety, as its main task, the prevention of war.

[1] E. Vandervelde (ed.), *Jaurès* (Paris 1929), p.25.

SOCIALISM AND
NATIONALISM

At the opening of the Amsterdam Congress there was a touching
scene: Plekhanov and Katayama, whose countries had been at
war for the past six months, rose and shook hands amid the loud
applause of the assembled delegates. It was felt to be an encouraging symbol of the solidarity between socialists of all lands
that transcended the rivalries of their governments; and perhaps those present at the conference forgot that Plekhanov had
been an exile for nearly a quarter of a century and that Katayama
represented a diminutive party which at no stage was to influence the policies of Japan.

The Russo-Japanese War was the first important war between
countries represented in the Second International (for the
Spanish-American War had not caused much anxiety in
Europe); it was the first war of major concern to the great
powers since the Russo-Turkish War of 1877; and it coincided
with a growth of international tension that was to be demonstrated in the spring of 1905 with the Kaiser's landing at Tangier
and the consequent talk of war between France and Germany.
For the past decade the colonial rivalries between all the great
powers, except Austria-Hungary, had led to recurrent crises and
to a general increase in armies and navies. The British were just
beginning to be aware that Germany was preparing a serious
challenge to their supremacy at sea. The question of international action to prevent war, which had been discussed in a somewhat desultory and academic fashion at the early Congresses of
the International, thus became of increasing urgency; and new
hopes were placed in the international Socialist movement as a

possible means of stopping a war which, as Engels had foreseen as early as 1887, might well become a world war of the most disastrous kind:

'Eight to ten million soldiers will swallow each other up and in doing so eat all Europe more bare than any swarm of locusts. The devastation of the Thirty Years' War compressed into the space of three or four years and extending over the whole continent; famine, sickness, want, brutalizing the army and the mass of the population; irrevocable confusion of our artificial structure of trade, industry and credit, ending in general bankruptcy; collapse of the old states and their traditional statecraft, so that crowns will roll by dozens in the gutter and no one be found to pick them up; it is absolutely impossible to predict where it will all end and who will emerge from the struggle as victor. Only *one* result is absolutely certain: general exhaustion and the establishment of the conditions for the final victory of the working class.'[1]

Socialists shared a desire to avoid such horrors with members of other political movements. The growing preparations for war were accompanied by attempts to provide international organizations to control them. The two Hague Conferences of 1899 and 1907, which attempted to regulate armaments and establish rules of war, and the development of arbitration agreements between individual states, were all signs that liberal ideals of a previous generation were beginning to be adopted, however cynically, by the governments of the great powers. Much that socialists demanded for the improvement of international relations was the same as liberals had been urging for fifty years or more—disarmament, arbitration, no secret treaties. But, on the other hand, for those socialists who stressed their separation from the whole bourgeois ideology, there was also the feeling, expressed at the end of Engels' remarkable prophecy, that in spite of everything war would produce the conditions for the

[1] Fr. Engels, Introduction to Sigismund Borkheim's pamphlet *Zur Erinnerung für die deutschen Mordspatrioten 1806–12* (1887), quoted in K. Kautsky, *Sozialisten und Krieg* (Prague 1937), pp.250–1.

final victory of the working class; and others, convinced that
capitalist rivalries would necessarily end in war, believed that
the only way to prevent such a catastrophe was through the
winning of power by socialists before it was too late. There were
still other influences to increase the confusion into which a
socialist was liable to be thrown when he thought about these
problems: he was a citizen of a state in which he had a home and
a part; he did not feel himself to be without a fatherland. If he
were French, the ideas of revolution and the ideas of patriotism
were closely connected. In Germany the memory of the War
of Liberation was bound up with that of liberal reform. And in
Italy the struggle for unity and national greatness was one to
which people on the left had been recently devoting themselves.

It is not surprising that the discussions of socialist action to
prevent war, arising as they did out of such conflicting attitudes,
should be often confused and contradictory.[1] Moreover, the
problems led back to the fundamental ones over which so much
time and so many words had already been spent—the nature of
contemporary society itself and the socialist attitude towards it,
the problem of effective tactics, the relation between political
parties and trade unions, and the value of the political mass
strike. The discussions also led on to a study of the causes of
imperialist rivalries and the attitude socialists ought to adopt to
colonial questions as well as to those nationalist emotions that
were, in the minds of many workers, more potent than the sense
of proletarian solidarity and the feeling of class struggle. Just as
the problem of war became one to which socialists, with increasing anxiety and insistence, were forced to devote their attention,
so it revealed more clearly than any other the dilemmas, equivo-

[1] The theoretical side of this problem is fully discussed and documented
in Karl Kautsky, *Sozialisten und Krieg* (Prague 1937), See also Louis L.
Lorwin, *Labor and Internationalism* (New York 1929) and the interesting
study by Milorad M. Drachkovitch, *Les Socialismes français et allemand et
le problème de la guerre* (Geneva 1953).

cations and difficulties in which the members of the Socialist International found themselves.

There were two immediate questions which socialists had to face: what was their attitude to be to the military arrangements of their present Governments? What action could they take to prevent war? The answers were by no means simple. Nearly every country of continental Europe had a system of universal compulsory military service. Therefore, however much socialists may have disapproved of the whole system, they could not remain indifferent to the conditions under which they themselves, their sons, brothers and comrades passed some two years of their life, any more than they could remain indifferent to the conditions under which they were working in the factories. The Socialist parties were forced to discuss immediate remedies for the abuses of the existing system as well as the transformation of that system into something quite different. The German Social Democratic Party, for example, accompanied its regular vote in the Reichstag against army credits with criticism of such things as excessive punishments, and gambling and 'other orgies' in officers' messes. Sometimes this criticism was positive; there was a famous occasion when Bebel urged the abandonment of the blue Prussian uniform and the change to something less conspicuous so that 'in the next war thousands of our own comrades are not mown down through the inefficiency of our military administration'. (Perhaps he was not the son of a Prussian NCO for nothing.)

The most cherished aim of the Socialists. however, was the abolition of standing armies and the creation of a militia. It was a concept that was full of romantic memories of the victorious revolutionary armies of 1793 and of the myth of the rising of the German people against their foreign oppressors in 1813. And, indeed, in an age of conscription under professional officers, it was felt that it was only in a country like Switzerland, where there was a popular militia, that personal liberty was safe.

In France the Dreyfus case renewed suspicion of the professional officer class: in Germany there were constant reminders
of the danger. The Prussian officers had long believed that
through the discipline instilled into the young conscript during
his military service they could keep him loyal for the rest of his
days. And the Emperor William II, in one of his many rash and
ill-judged speeches, had called on newly-recruited conscripts
to be ready to shoot their fathers and mothers if necessary. It
was because they realized the strength of the Prussian military
machine that the Social Democrat leaders were in practice so
much less revolutionary than in theory. For this very reason
the chances of ever being able to put into practice the annual
motions for recommending the transformation of a standing
army into a militia were negligible.

The most interesting and extensive study of how such a militia would work was provided by Jaurès. In 1910 he published
L'Armée Nouvelle; and at the same time he tabled a bill in the
Chamber for the remodelling of the French army on the lines
he recommended. The bill never reached the floor of the house,
but *L'Armée Nouvelle* throws much light on Jaurès' political
ideas and presuppositions. The book had as its sub-title
'National defence and international peace', thus assuming that
the abolition of a professional army would instantly remove one
of the causes of war, and taking for granted that a popular militia would be free from the sinister passions that stirred the
existing ruling class. The book itself was intended to be the
first of a series of volumes in which each aspect of the new
socialist France would be described; and Jaurès was going to
follow it with a work on 'The New Diplomacy'. The plan was
never carried further, for Jaurès' political activity, to say nothing of his activities as a historian writing a *Histoire Socialiste de
la Révolution Française*[1] and organizing a *Histoire Socialiste de*

---

[1] For an excellent discussion of this aspect of Jaurès' thought see Franco
Venturi, *Jean Jaurès e altri storici della Rivoluzione francese* (Turin 1948).

France, left him with many uncompleted projects. The fact, however, that he should have begun with a study of defence and of international relations shows what were his chief preoccupations from 1904 onwards.

The technical recommendations in *L'Armée Nouvelle* make curiously naïve reading now. And even at the time of publication they were not really appropriate to existing military conditions. As Max Schippel, one of the intellectuals in the German Socialist Party who had moved over to the Revisionist wing, wrote in a discussion of the similar proposals that were the official doctrine of the SPD: 'You can't put a cannon in the bed of every former gunner and give each old sea dog a little warship to put in his farmyard trough or wash tub'.[1] The idea of a popular army of trained soldiers, each with his rifle at home ready to join the colours in an emergency, was as out of date as the idea of the revolution made on the barricades. What is important about all these discussions is that they presuppose the necessity of national defence in certain circumstances. In fact *L'Armée Nouvelle* is a deeply patriotic book, full of the rhetorical ardour of the revolutionary tradition and of scholarly references to past military successes. And the object of the proposed military reforms is quite simply 'the protection of national independence for the free evolution of social justice'.[2] The emphasis is, militarily, on the defensive; for Jaurès excludes the possibility that a true social democracy could ever want to wage an offensive war. Jaurès believed, indeed, that if a system of international relations based on arbitration between states could be established, then it would be easy to designate the state which refused arbitration as the aggressor, and thus determine whether the people of the country attacked were justified or not in taking up arms.

Jaurès was making it quite clear that, for all his belief in in-

[1] *Neue Zeit*, 1898–99, vol. XVII, p.784.
[2] Jaurès, *L'Armée Nouvelle. Oeuvres*, IV, p.181.

ternational solidarity, the French Socialists would be justified in resisting a German attack.

'Those Frenchmen, if there are any left,' Jaurès wrote, 'who say that it is all the same to them whether they live under the German troopers or the French troopers . . . . commit a sophism which by its very absurdity makes refutation difficult. And when we answer, as we often do, invoking France's particular claims, exalting the generosity of her history and her services to the human race, the answer is also sophistical, for this only justifies French patriotism and it looks as though the other European countries have not an equal right to the independence and devotion of their citizens. The truth is that wherever there are countries, that is historical groups having a consciousness of their continuity and their unity, any attack on the freedom and integrity of these countries is an attack against civilization, a reaction into barbarism.'[1]

And on the German side Bebel was even more explicit about the German Socialists' attitude to their neighbour, Russia. 'The soil of Germany, the German fatherland belongs to us the masses as much and more than to the others. If Russia, the champion of terror and barbarism went to attack Germany to break and destroy it . . . . we are as much concerned as those who stand at the head of Germany,' he said in 1891[2].

This was a natural attitude for socialists to adopt when they realized that the workers in fact had a good deal more to lose than their chains. It was also an attitude that was much criticized by those people on the left who attacked revisionist practice, whether avowed or concealed, and insisted that there was nothing worth preserving in the existing bourgeois world and that under no circumstances should socialists be ready to sacrifice themselves for the defence of any part of it. The Anarchists had always pointed out the inconsistencies of the attitude of the German Party leadership: Domela Nieuwenhuis had attacked Bebel at Zürich in 1893 on strictly pacifist grounds. 'I have not

[1] Jaurès, L'Armée Nouvelle, p.303.
[2] Verhandlungen 1891, p.285.

forgotten', he said, 'how people in Germany have preached war against the "hereditary enemy" Russia, how Bebel himself has passed a sponge over all the misdeeds of his own bourgeoisie if it was a question of the hereditary foe .... One cannot help laughing when Russia is called the champion of atrocities and barbarism, as if Germany were a protector of enlightenment and gentleness.'[1] And, after the turn of the century, a new anti-militarism was becoming important among people who believed that the outbreak of a war would offer a splendid chance of overthrowing the whole capitalist system, or who thought, as the international situation grew worse, that drastic measures would be needed to prevent the horrors that would otherwise follow.

In France the revelations of the Dreyfus case had given some excuse for an anti-militarist campaign, and there was inside the French Socialist movement a very vociferous group prepared to conduct it. Its leader was Gustave Hervé, a hysterical schoolmaster who seems to have been taken more seriously by those who did not know him than by those who did. Jaurès once said that Hervé and Bebel agreed on one thing—their overestimation of Hervé. Certainly the violence of his anti-patriotism and the subversive nature of his propaganda was of considerable embarrassment to the party leaders who did not hesitate to point out his inconsistencies. 'Hervé has a genius for misunderstandings,' Jaurès wrote. 'When he wants to glorify the flag of Valmy he behaves as if he is planting it on the dunghill. His incoherent doctrine includes two contradictory elements: passive resignation in the face of foreign invasion and the idea of a necessary social revolution in the case of an international conflict. But a revolution is necessarily active. And it could only be so if it defends the national existence which serves as its base.'[2] However, Hervé's campaign was important be-

---

[1] *Proc.* 1893, Thursday 10 August, p.22.
[2] Quoted in Maurice Lair, *Jaurès et l'Allemagne* (Paris 1935), p.114. The reference is to a notorious speech of Hervé's about planting the French flag on the dunghill.

cause it provided the enemies of socialism with new weapons: in
their eyes every school was staffed by men like Hervé corrupting
the native patriotism of the young. It was also important not
because of what it achieved outside France (though Bebel once
said that Hervé's propaganda encouraged the German General
Staff as providing a sign of French military weakness), but because the campaign helped to force the French Socialist Party,
the syndicates, and thus the International to discuss once more
what action could in fact be taken to prevent war.

2.

It is notoriously difficult to interest the members of the public in international affairs except at moments of acute and startling crisis. So it was inevitable that the internationalism of the
Socialist movement, however deeply felt by individual leaders
like Wilhelm Liebknecht or Jean Jaurès, should have remained
a question of speeches and resolutions for the majority of the
party members, who had more immediate problems to worry
about. 'I know,' Bebel said at the Erfurt Congress of the SPD
in 1891, 'that a great number of our comrades if they so much as
hear about foreign policy prefer to shrug their shoulders. With
some justification.'[1] Even when the international situation grew
worse it was still hard to arouse an interest except among a
minority. But there were a few areas where the question of international co-operation was not just theoretical, and where some
socialists had a day-to-day national struggle always before their
eyes. It was here that practical co-operation between members
of different nationalities proved hardest, and provided a real
test of the ability of socialists to work together in spite of national
differences. In Posen and Silesia German and Polish workers
lived side by side; and, indeed, increasing numbers of Poles
were finding their way into the other industrial areas of the
Reich. In Austria-Hungary the national struggle was the daily

[1] *Verhandlungen* 1891, p.283.

stuff of politics for all parties. And even in Western Europe the question of Alsace-Lorraine was one which both French and German Socialists had to face, although all that this meant on the French side was a hope that if the German Socialists came to power they would restore the two provinces, while the Germans talked vaguely about plebiscites and autonomy.

The restoration of Polish independence had been a cause dear to all the liberals of Europe throughout the nineteenth century. But in Germany the liberals had not always carried their theoretical enthusiasm into practice and had, in the revolution of 1848, for instance, shown themselves insensitive to Polish claims; and this was an attitude inherited by the Social Democrats. There was, in fact, some justification for anti-Polish sentiment among the German working class. The Polish provinces provided a reservoir of cheap labour that competed with Germans in agriculture and in industry, and both in the mixed areas of Eastern Germany and in the industrial areas of the West local friction could easily arise. The official Marxist answer to this problem was in effect to deny that it existed. The interests of the proletariat were the same whatever their nationality; and those interests could best be served by a uniform centralized social democratic party. 'We recognize only one German Social Democracy in our organization,' one speaker said unequivocally in 1897[1] 'in which our Polish brothers are comrades with equal rights . . . .' This policy inevitably led to arguments: some of the Polish socialists complained that candidates in their constituencies did not know Polish, and the party leaders retorted by quoting the sums they had spent on propaganda and newspapers in the Polish language. But the official attitude was, in fact, to refuse to give the Poles separate treatment; a remark of Bebel about political agitators is typical: 'A good comrade who

[1] *Verhandlungen* 1897, p.97. The speaker is Wilhelm Pfannkuch from Berlin, for many years a member of the Party Executive.

only knows German is more use than an incompetent Polish speaking one.'[1]

One of the most active proponents of this view was Rosa Luxemburg. She had begun her political career in the exiled Socialist Party of Russian Poland; and when, by a formal marriage with a German, she came to Germany and the SPD, she spoke with her usual self-confidence as an expert both on Poland (she prepared a doctoral thesis on industrialization in Poland), and on Marxist theory. Between 1898 and 1905 she was making her name in the German party; and if, as her first biographer maintained, the older generation at first despised this frail ugly young woman because of her sex,[2] they soon learnt to respect her intelligence and fire, and to fear her sharp tongue, (for she was always a controversialist of the rudest kind in the tradition established by Marx himself), although Bebel and Adler, at least, never overcame their dislike of her. Her intransigence on the national question, which during the First World War was to lead her into one of her celebrated controversies with Lenin, was already causing differences between her and other members of the left wing of the party, notably Georg Ledebour, who declared frankly in 1901: 'We are in Germany very backward in respect of understanding the needs of foreign nationalities within our territory.'[3] Thus by 1905 there were a number of splits among Polish Social Democrats to which Rosa Luxemburg had contributed much; and in spite of long discussions a number of Polish Socialists in Prussian Poland established themselves as an independent party, though with little success since they lacked the support of the vast German organization which was at the disposal of their rivals.

However, recalcitrant Polish Socialists who disliked German dictation and wanted to see an independent Poland did not cause

[1] *Verhandlungen* 1897, p.152.
[2] Frölich, p.56.
[3] *Verhandlungen* 1901, p.125.

much anxiety to the great German mass party, although they produced an interesting and significant example of the difficulties of effective international co-operation in an age of nationalist rivalries. The Germans congratulated themselves: 'We are glad that we are not obliged to labour under the confusion of languages which our comrades in Austria have to deal with.'[1]

Social Democracy in Austria was German in its doctrine and origins. Its original strength was in the German speaking areas. Its links with the German Social Democratic Party were of the closest kind, and its leaders continued to regret the Bismarckian solution of the German problem which had severed them from the rest of the German working class movement. But Austrian Social Democracy could not remain just German. The number of industrial workers of other nationalities was increasing, especially among the Czechs of Bohemia and Moravia, and the organized Czech workers were, it was claimed in 1910,[2] stronger in proportion to the total Czech population than the Germans in the German provinces, and had twenty-four deputies in the Reichsrat side by side with the Germans. Among the other nationalities too socialism was growing—in parts of Galicia, in the cities of South Tirol and the Küstenland, in Slovenia, while in the Hungarian half of the monarchy a small party had come into being, mainly in Budapest, which co-operated with, though it never formed part of, the Austrian Social Democratic Party.

The leaders of Austrian Social Democracy were well aware of the responsibilities and opportunities presented by this situation. Indeed, some of them began to see that they might find a solution to the predicament into which German Austrians had been thrown by the severance of Austria from Germany in 1866

---

[1] Pfannkuch at 1897 Party Congress, *Verhandlungen*, p.97. For a detailed account of the complicated controversies among the Polish Socialists, see J. P. Nettl, *Rosa Luxemburg* (London 1966), chs V and XIII. See also H.-U. Wehler, *Sozialdemokratie und Nationalstaat* (new ed., Göttingen 1970).

[2] By Wlastimil Tusan at the Copenhagen International Congress 1910. *Proc.* p.90.

and their virtual exclusion from Hungary in 1867. The establishment of a genuinely international Socialist movement in the
Monarchy offered the best hope both of reforming the Empire
and of providing for the future of the Germans within it. But
the difficulties were enormous; as Victor Adler told the Paris
International Congress in 1900, 'We in Austria have a little
International ourselves, we are the ones who know best the
difficulties which have to be overcome.'[1] Victor Adler and his
friends never gave up hope of overcoming the difficulties, but
they were to be disappointed. It was a paradox characteristic of
the most paradoxical of empires that the Socialists, whose political life was devoted to the most violent criticism of the monarchy ('There is no degree of disgust with Austria I have not
known,'[2] Victor Adler once said), should have been among those
most anxious to preserve it. 'We know that we shall have to live
with one another in this Austria, and that there is nothing else
to do but to find a way to prevent the collapse of Austria and to
enable its natives to live together.' These words were used by
a socialist leader[3] at the Party Congress at Brünn (Brno) in 1899,
the first congress at which the Party met as a *Gesamtpartei* composed of different national sections. A resolution was carried
recommending the establishment of a federal state based on
autonomous areas with the protection of minorities guaranteed
by law. But the Czechs were already worried about the pre-
dominance of the German language, even as the day-to-day *ad
hoc* language of Austria (*Verkehrsprache*), and, though for the
moment a compromise was accepted, a suspicion of German
intentions remained. The German-speaking leaders were in a
difficult position: in spite of the growing strength and self-confidence of the Czechs, they were inevitably the leading group in

---

[1] Adler, *Aufsätze*, VIII, p.67.
[2] '*Kein Grad des Ekels an Oesterreich ist mir fremd.*' *Aufsätze*, VIII, p.117.
[3] Josef Seliger; quoted in Arthur J. Kogan, 'The Social Democrats and the
Conflict of Nationalities in the Habsburg Monarchy' in *Journal of Modern
History*, vol. 21 (1949), p.207.

Austrian Social Democracy and it was easy to accuse them of trying to dominate the movement from Vienna. And there were plenty of German Socialists who would encourage this belief, even if what they said contained a grain of unpalatable truth, as when one of them, in the same debate, said: 'German will remain a language of culture and communication whether we like it or not and regardless of the likes and dislikes of our Czech comrades.'[1]

Yet for ten years a measure of unity was achieved. Social Democratic writers like Karl Renner and Otto Bauer published detailed studies of the national problem which, had the machinery for change existed, might have provided a basis of reorganization of the monarchy.[2] But even with the best will in the world it was difficult, in the mixed areas of Moravia for instance, to find a formula about such matters as the distribution between nationalities of rates and taxes, that could not be accused of favouring the Germans. In any case such discussions remained theoretical: the practical struggle was still for such rudimentary political rights as universal suffrage, and for these ends German and Czech socialists could co-operate. (The socialists of other nationalities were not yet sufficiently numerous for the problem of their relationship with the Germans to be acute; and, for the most part, their members did not live so closely side by side with the Germans as did the Czechs.) The demonstrations which preceded the granting of universal suffrage in 1907 were as much those of the Czechs in Prague as of the German Socialists in Vienna; and on this the aim of 'petty bourgeois nationalists' and Social Democrats was the same.

On everyday issues in the parliament German and Czech

[1] Prehausen (Salzburg); quoted in Kogan, p.210.
[2] See Karl Renner, *Das Selbstbestimmungsrecht der Nationen* (Vienna 1918); Otto Bauer, *Die Nationalitätenfrage und die Sozialdemokratie* (Vienna 1907). See also R. A. Kann, *The Multinational Empire*, 2 vols. (New York 1950) and Hans Mommsen, *Die Sozialdemokratie und die Nationalitätenfrage im Habsburgischen Vielvölkerstaat* (Vienna 1963).

Socialists could vote solidly together. It was in the trade unions that the real national strain was felt, for in Bohemia and Moravia workers of both nationalities side by side in the same factories inevitably felt the growing national tension. The Czech trade unionists began to demand separate unions on the analogy of the autonomous Socialist political organizations they had had since 1897; and the Germans retorted that it was absurd to substitute meaningless national divisions for real economic ones, since what Czechs and Germans had in common in this connection—the desire for better conditions from their employers—had nothing to do with national differences. But at a time when, as Adler himself put it, what was the matter with Austria was that 'the question of the names of railway stations had become one of principle of the most important kind',[1] the Czechs were unwilling to accept what looked like dictation from Vienna, however reasonably and persuasively Adler argued the case—and there may well have been local Socialist bosses who were less tolerant.

The question of how far the Austrian Social Democratic Party, with its German preponderance, could really lead a genuine international party was now squarely posed by the Czechs. And in 1910 the matter was raised by the Austrians at the Congress of the International at Copenhagen. It was a sign of the important role that the International and its Bureau had come to play in the affairs of the member parties that a dispute of this kind should be brought before it. It had also the disadvantage, familiar in other later international bodies, of submitting complex issues to the vote of delegates who had only the vaguest ideas about the circumstances of the case, and who voted according to an *a priori* doctrine. The Czechs, under Anton Nemeč, who himself had originally been returned to parliament for a Viennese constituency, in fact behaved with great modera-

---

[1] V. Adler, *Das Verhältnis zu den Bruderparteien in Oesterreich* in *Aufsätze*, VIII, p.90.

tion, and were genuinely anxious to preserve the unity of the Socialist movement in Austria. All they asked, in fact, was to be given another chance of settling the trade union question as a domestic one without interference from outside: and, indeed, it is likely that, for all Victor Adler's moderation, the Austrians were hoping to deal with the matter for good at Copenhagen by marshalling their Marxist allies (in this case especially Legien, the leader of the German trade unions, and Plekhanov) in support of their views. The Czechs' claim for separate unions was rejected by the International and the necessity for single unions upheld. This was the real test of the extent to which Austrian Social Democracy could genuinely embrace the various nationalities of the Empire. After Copenhagen a majority of the Czech socialists refused to accept its decision; the Czech socialists split and a new specifically Czech socialist party was established by the majority, although a minority of 'Centralists' remained loyal to the monarchy up to 1918. 'Do the Czech Social Democrats feel themselves to be the Czech group of the International or are they the Social Democratic group within the Czech parties?'[1] Victor Adler asked at the time of the breach. The answer was clear enough; and with it the 'little International' of Austrian Social Democracy had broken down.

The failure of the Austrian Social Democrats to preserve their *'Gesamtpartei'* is not only an instance of the difficulties of practical co-operation between members of different nationalities. It also showed that the International itself was unable to do much to influence the course of development followed by its member parties. Its success in uniting the French Socialists was not to be repeated. In fact, from time to time dissident groups tried to use the Bureau of the International to back their own views and force their rivals to conform, but normally without success. The British Labour Party presented a special problem; for could it be said to be a socialist party at all? Doubts were expressed at

[1] V. Adler, *Aufsätze*, VIII, p.88.

the International Congress of 1907, but a year later the orthodox Marxists, headed by Kautsky, failed to prevent its being
represented in the Bureau; and its rivals, the British Socialist
Party, (the descendants of the old Social Democratic Federation), were equally unsuccessful in persuading the Bureau to
order them to unite the British groups on terms that would make
the movement explicitly 'socialistic'—but the British Labour
Party anyway remained somewhat incomprehensible to most
European Socialists, and, like the American groups, lay outside
the main stream of the movement, sometimes rather consciously
and even regretfully. 'The accomplished leaders of the Continental Socialists,' Beatrice Webb noted in her diary on 8 March
1914, '–Vandervelde, Jaurès, Huysmans and the German Social
Democratic Party—dislike the disreputable dissensions of the
British Labour and Socialist Movement as shown in the mutual
abuse of the ILP and BSP, the "Liberalism" of the Labour
Members and the absence of any socialist policy. These continental leaders are bigger men than our leaders and the continental working-men are far more thorough-going in their
socialism.'[1] Again, the International failed to unite the Russian
Socialist Party; Bebel had offered his services as a mediator in
1905; nothing had come of the offer; but it was agreed that Bolsheviks and Mensheviks should each have a representative in the
Bureau of the International. The question was taken up again
on two subsequent occasions, so that in July 1914 a special sub-
committee was preparing to report its failure to the next International Congress—a failure largely due to Lenin's refusal to
accept any save his own terms: 'Lenin desires unity as a man
desires unity with a piece of bread; he swallows it'.[2]

---

[1] *Beatrice Webb's Diaries 1912–1924* ed. by Margaret Cole (London 1952),
p.20.
[2] The phrase is Plekhanov's. Bertram D. Wolfe, *Three Who Made a
Revolution* (New York 1948), p.611. The documents on the International's
attempts to unify the Russian Social Democrats are printed in Oliver Hess
Gankin and H. H. Fisher, *The Bolsheviks and the World War* (Stanford 1940)
Ch. I, sections A, C and F.

Yet individual failures to regulate the internal affairs of member parties were not enough to quell the hopes placed in the International. The belief remained that in a moment of real crisis differences would be forgotten and that the working class would take some dramatic united action expressive of its growing power. Unfortunately the discussion of what form that action should take was itself to lead to more difficulties. It was easy enough to lay down the aspects of the existing system which were particularly to be blamed—imperialism, militarism, chauvinism. Yet even here there was room for differences of opinion and distressing signs of disunity. While nearly all socialists seemed unanimous in condemning the Boer War, there were reports that some of the English had supported it, and there was an embarrassing moment at the International Congress of 1907 when Ledebour accused Robert Blatchford, one of the ablest propagandists of the early days of the British Labour movement, of making his daughter play 'Rule Britannia' on the piano to him every evening during the South African War. More seriously, there were some socialists who were beginning to justify certain types of imperialism themselves. There had always been people among the Dutch Socialists, for example, to say that the raising of the standard of living among backward peoples was an aim socialists could adopt, provided that the natives of colonial territories were not subjected to the exploitation of rival capitalist powers. But after the turn of the century there were some people prepared to go farther. One ex-Socialist militant, Augagneur, even became governor of Madagascar in 1905. The orthodox Marxists believed the doctrine later expounded by Lenin in his *Imperialism—The Highest Stage of Capitalism*, written in 1916: that capitalist states were driven into colonial expansion by their own economic nature. And they went on to say that this would lead to rivalries, and the rivalries to a war which in turn would destroy the whole system. Therefore many Socialists maintained at the Stuttgart

International Congress of 1907 when the colonial problem was discussed, for example, or at the SPD Party Congress of 1912 when there was a full scale theoretical debate on imperialism, that, as in so many other matters, they need do nothing more than be against the whole thing, and wait for the collapse of the bourgeoisie and triumph of the proletariat. However, representatives from those states that possessed both a colonial empire and an effective parliament—England or Holland, for instance—saw that the colonies were not so easily got rid of, and that socialists had a duty to improve the way in which they were governed. Even in 1907 Ramsay Macdonald had to point out to the delegates at Stuttgart that many of the English colonies were in fact self-governing; and he and others began to see that a socialist colonial policy would have to consist of something more than the condemnation of British rule in India which was a regular feature of international conferences.

Some of the German revisionists shared this view (though one of them, Dr David, was literally shouted down when he tried to vote against the majority of his colleagues at Stuttgart). By 1912, indeed, some of the intellectuals on the right of the German Party were drawing another conclusion from arguments about the economic necessity of colonies, and were even saying that Germany would be justified in entering the colonial struggle since it was only by possessing colonies that the German working class could maintain its standard of living. Their academic articles (in the revisionist *Sozialistische Monatshefte*) caused more stir outside Germany than at home. For in 1912 and 1913 Charles Andler, Professor of German at the Sorbonne, an old socialist and an expert on German thought, published a series of articles in which he drew attention to these and certain other disquieting trends in German Social Democracy.[1] He

---

[1] The articles are collected and reprinted together with Jaurès' replies in Charles Andler, *Le Socialisme impérialiste dans l'Allemagne contemporaine* (Paris 1918).

was at once plunged into a disagreeable personal controversy inside his own party, for Jean Jaurès rushed to the defence of the Germans with a virulence rare in his polemical writings, perhaps, one is tempted to think, because he now placed all his hopes of preserving peace in the strength and loyalty of the German Social Democratic Party and hated to hear anything that could shake the faith on which all his political action rested.

VI

THE BELLS OF BASLE

What could the members of the International hope to do to prevent war? From 1904 onwards this was inevitably the chief theme at their congresses. The political action that each party could take depended on the constitutional circumstances in each country (an obvious fact which in the enthusiasm of International Congresses was sometimes overlooked). Yet, even where there was a strong Socialist party in parliament, Socialists alone were not able to exercise much influence on the foreign policy of their Governments. Jaurès' incessant campaign against Delcassé's Moroccan policy ('*ce gnome malfaisant*' he called him) did not have any effect: Delcassé's fall in June 1905 was the result more of cabinet intrigues than parliamentary opposition. The German Socialists' opposition to the Government's Moroccan policy in this same crisis was more than ineffective; it was, as one or two people on the left of the Party pointed out, in fact half-hearted. Thus the constant motions of disapproval—of the great powers' intervention in China and Persia, of Austria's annexation of Bosnia-Herzegovina, of the Balkan wars—were expressions of feeling rather than instruments of political action. There were, however, sometimes significant differences in the feelings expressed. Jaurès, for example, was far more ready to attribute peaceful intentions to the Liberal Government in Britain than were the Germans (with the honourable exception of Eduard Bernstein) and thus, as he had always done, made distinctions between capitalist governments in a way the Germans were reluctant to do. But the one point on which all socialists could unite in feeling strongly was hatred of Russia.

Thus the revolution of 1905 was of enormous emotional importance, for not only did it raise hopes that even the severest of
despotisms could be overthrown or at least curbed if it started
an unpopular war; it also revived a belief in the efficacy of direct
popular action of a revolutionary kind. Was not, after all, the
mass strike the most effective way both of stopping war and of
winning power?

The Russian revolution of 1905 revived the flagging discussion about the nature of revolution and the tactics of seizing
power, not only within the Russian Socialist movement, where
the controversy between Bolsheviks and Mensheviks, started in
1903, was transferred to a situation where, for the first time in
Russia, there was a possibility of a legal, parliamentary social
democratic party on western lines. For the 1905 revolution not
only posed once again the question that divided Plekhanov from
Lenin about the speed with which the bourgeois revolution in
Russia could be accomplished and thus open the way for the
dictatorship of the proletariat, it also reminded socialists everywhere that revolutions of a violent kind might still be possible
without waiting for the overthrow of the existing system by the
inexorable working of the historical process. There were even
optimists who thought that the revolution might break out
elsewhere—even in Germany— *'het begint te rommelen . . . .'*
the Dutch Socialist Anton Pannekoek wrote, 'a strong revolutionary movement is starting among the German workers.'[1]
In fact, however, the events of 1905 tended to point the contrast
between the law-abiding, respectable, bourgeois nature of
Social Democracy in Germany and other western countries,
compared with a real revolutionary movement forced by circumstances into a desperate outbreak, as in Russia. The corres-
pondent of *Le Temps* wrote about the SPD's Congress at Jena:

'The peaceful disposition of the German Socialists has made

[1] R. Michels, *Die deutsche Sozialdemokratie im internationalen Verbande.*
(*Archiv für Sozialwissenschaft und Sozialpolitik* vol. 25, 1907), p.206.

a strange impression on the Russians who came in large numbers to attend the Congress as curious spectators. Boy and girl students, vibrant with revolutionary enthusiasm, seem a little put out by this bourgeois Congress of the German Socialists who have nevertheless provided the theoretical education of revolutionary Russia and who have too just sent 100,000 francs over the frontier to support those who are fighting and struggling.'[1]

Nevertheless, the situation in Germany, too, encouraged talk of direct action. There were rumours that the Government were thinking of restricting the franchise in order to curb the growth of Social Democracy, and the question of what could be done to prevent this was much discussed, particularly as a restriction of the franchise in the Kingdom of Saxony, which had virtually suppressed socialist representation, had been introduced in 1896 without any effective protest being made. Some members wanted to try the strike weapon to force an extension of the franchise in Prussia. Above all, there was a group of people on the left of the Party who believed that the general strike was the best way, not only to win reforms at home, but also to stop war. Accordingly, at the Jena Congress of 1905, there was a full-scale discussion of the mass political strike, opened by Bebel in a three hour speech of great rhetorical power reviewing the whole previous history of the movement in favour of the mass strike. Bebel was in fact a sufficiently experienced politician and organizer to see that the question involved the examination both of the limits of possible action by the Social Democratic Party and, more delicate still, its relations with the trade unions. The unions had shown quite clearly by their conduct of the May Day demonstrations that they had no faith in political gestures that did not bring any immediate benefits to their members. And, for all their electoral successes, the Social Democrats were not yet a majority, while not all workers belonged to socialist trade unions. Bebel, therefore, was obliged to make a speech that

[1] *Le Temps,* 21 September 1905, quoted in Michels, *Die deutsche Sozialdemokratie im internationalen Verbande,* p.164.

would not seem too discouraging, while recognizing the limits
on effective action imposed by the trade unionists. So, while his
speech contained striking phrases—'In the name of our martyrs
will you not for once go hungry for a few weeks to defend your
highest human rights?'[1]—and while he admitted that the mass
strike was sometimes a justifiable weapon, the final resolution
was a compromise that would give some comfort to the extre-
mists on the left—and Rosa Luxemburg had reminded the
Congress that there was a revolution going on in Russia, in a
fiery speech which caused Bebel to remark that he found himself involuntarily looking down at his boots to see whether they
were already wading through pools of blood[2]—and at the same
time left discreetly and consciously vague the question of just
what were the circumstances when it would be justifiable to
use it.

In fact even this went too far for the trade unions, who were
necessarily revisionist in practice, and reluctant to accept too
great a degree of direction from the political leaders of the
Party. During the next year private discussions between the
Party Executive Committee and Trade Union General Committee on the issue of the mass strike were going on. Then,
much to the annoyance of the union leaders, the Party published
an account of these talks, and so the whole discussion was
opened again at the Party Congress of 1906, with Bebel and
Karl Legien, the trade union leader, rather uneasily presenting
a common front against critics on right and left. Legien, who
was in 1920 at the moment of the Kapp Putsch to demonstrate
how effective strike action could be in certain political situations, was also quite clear about its limitations, and the unionists
had stated them at their annual congress at Cologne shortly
before. Legien told the Party that their control of industry was
very far from complete. To paralyse the state there would first

---

[1] *Verhandlungen* 1905, p.305.
[2] *Verhandlungen* 1905, p.336.

need to be a strike of the transport workers: and the railwaymen were not organized in a socialist union. A mass strike would be possible in the metal, wood and building trades and in part of the textile industry; food would be more difficult. Under these circumstances, Legien asked, what good could a political strike be? In the debate which followed Bebel's and Legien's speeches no new points were made: there was insistence on the necessity of unity and discipline on the one hand, while Rosa Luxemburg and Karl Liebknecht on the other urged the necessity of an imaginative and active policy if the Party was to increase its membership and strengthen its organization. And, indeed, one Party member present at these debates, Robert Michels, at this time one of the 'localistic anarcho-socialists' so hated by Legien, was to erect a whole sociology of the political party on the foundation of his experiences, and to make one of the profoundest analyses of the working of party politics of the twentieth century.[1]

The resolution that emerged in 1906 was characteristic of the German Social Democratic Party both in its pretentiousness and wordiness and in the careful compromises it concealed, committing nobody to anything. It asserted that there was no contradiction between the Jena resolution and the resolution passed by the trade unions at their congress (which there clearly was, or otherwise there would have been no need to bring the matter up), allowed for consultation between Party and unions should the Party executive decide a mass strike to be desirable, stated how necessary the unions were to the socialist movement but only if they were socialist: finally 'to ensure this unity of thought and action between the Party and the unions which is an indispensable requirement for the victorious progress of the proletarian class-struggle, it is absolutely necessary that the trade union movement should be filled with the spirit of social democracy. It is therefore the duty of every Party member to

[1] See especially R. Michels, *Les Partis Politiques* (Paris 1914).

THE BELLS OF BASLE

work in this direction.'[1] The drafting was Kautsky's; and the motion was carried by 386 votes to 5. It was a symbol both of the strength and the weakness of the Party, for by the very fact of its success as a disciplined mass party it was prevented from taking the bold revolutionary action possible to a minority group in an economically backward country. It was Lenin, not Bebel, who had drawn the right lessons from 1905.

Yet the German tactics were based on careful consideration of what was practicable. In countries where the Syndicalist movement was strong, especially France, the attitude to the general strike was less realistic. As Georges Sorel had seen, the myth of the general strike had an attraction of its own and could be used as an incitement to action even if there was no chance of its ever in fact coming about. Actually, industrial unrest was growing in France; and the unions were becoming more confident. For although there still were more people living in the country than in the towns and although of the million odd workers organized in unions only some 600,000 belonged to the militant CGT,[2] out of a total labour force of more than seven million, the workers could already give those shocks to sections of the economy, produce those short periods of paralysis which have remained their tactics, with increased, if never final, effectiveness, until the present. Thus in the years after 1907 a postal strike, a railway strike, and numerous others, shook the economy and frightened the bourgeoisie, though without producing many effective benefits for the working class. At the same time a section of the Syndicates, notably the metal workers under Alphonse Merrheim, were becoming more and more outspokenly revolutionary and impatient of any political activity whatever. Just as the German Socialists were sustained in a policy of inaction by their apocalyptic vision of the historically

[1] *Verhandlungen* 1906, p.305.
[2] See the comparative figures from various sources given in Drachkovitch, p.150.

inevitable triumph of the proletariat, so the Syndicalists in France, Spain and Italy were encouraged in a revolutionary policy by an equally apocalyptic vision of the inevitable success of the general strike. There is no doubt that Syndicalist doctrine, as systematized by Sorel, had a considerable appeal to romantic intellectuals for whom the rigid quasi-scientific and rationalist doctrines of the Marxists seemed too dry and dull. Even in England, Beatrice Webb noted, 'Syndicalism has taken the place of the old-fashioned Marxism. The angry youth, with bad complexion, frowning brow and weedy figure is nowadays a Syndicalist; the glib young workman whose tongue runs away with him today mouths the phrases of French Syndicalism instead of those of German Social Democracy.'[1]

The French Socialists were in a difficult position. They lacked the disciplinary apparatus of the Germans. Their relations with the CGT were not nearly so close as those of the German Socialists with the Free Trade Unions, and although Guesde would have liked a more centralized organization and a closer link with the Syndicates, the whole temper of the French working class movement was against such a scheme. The most that could be hoped for was, in Jaurès' words, 'a free co-operation . . . . without confusion or subordination or suspicion'.[2] But if that co-operation was to be effective some concessions had to be made to Syndicalist ideals of direct action. It was in the discussions about how to prevent war that the question of the general strike came up most frequently, and it produced some curious alignments within the Party. For Jaurès, whose dominant political aim was now increasingly the prevention of war, was prepared to join with the old Blanquist Vaillant in a policy expressed by the slogan '*Plutôt l'insurrection que la guerre*'. Indeed, the idea of a spontaneous popular demon-

---

[1] *Beatrice Webb's Diary*, 1 December 1912, p.7.
[2] Hubert Rouger, *La France Socialiste* (Paris 1912), I, p.237; quoted in Drachkovitch, p.80.

stration against war corresponded to the needs of his own
buoyant romantic optimism. From 1905 on, therefore, Jaurès
emerged as the protagonist of an active policy against war 'by
all means from parliamentary intervention, public agitation,
popular manifestations, to a general strike of the workers and
insurrection'.[1] This resolution was carried against the opposition both of Hervé and his followers who demanded, rhetori-
cally and unequivocally, that any declaration of war of any kind
should be followed by insurrection and a 'military strike', and
of Guesde who refused to advocate anything more than a refusal
to vote war credits, pending the day of inevitable socialist
victory. Jaurès, the 'reformist' in internal politics, found himself to the left of Guesde in international affairs. And, as before,
the conflict was soon transferred to the Second International as
a whole. As over the question of parliamentary activity at
Amsterdam in 1904, two rival conceptions confronted each
other at the International Congress at Stuttgart in 1907.

It was the first International Congress on German soil and
the German members who attended it, 289 in number, organized it efficiently and even lavishly: there were flowers in
abundance on the delegates' tables, and the proceedings began
with a version of the most famous of all German hymns, modi-
fied for the occasion to run '*Ein feste Burg ist unser Bund*'.[2] In
the circumstances, faced with the evidence of the German
Socialists' strength and prestige, in spite of their considerable
electoral defeat earlier in the year, Gustave Hervé showed considerable courage in launching a virulent attack on them. The
occasion was the debate on anti-militarism and war which had
been provoked by his agitation in France. As a member of the
commission discussing the problem that was, in the eyes of most
of the delegates, perhaps the most important on the agenda, he

[1] For the full text see *Troisième Congrès National. Compte Rendu analy-
tique* (Paris 1905), pp.214ff. Also A. Zévaès, *Le Parti Socialiste de 1904 à
1923*, pp.57–8.
[2] 'A stronghold sure is our League.'

not only proposed a motion, as at the previous congresses of the French Party, that any declaration of war should be met by revolt and a general strike, but he also took the opportunity of attacking the bureaucracy and *embourgeoisement* of the German Party, their reliance on 'the moral weight of their three million votes' and the fact that they had become a mere machine for counting votes and cash. As always, he overstressed his points, and the tone of his speech made it embarrassing, especially to the other French representatives; the hatred of Germany, which, after 1914, was to turn him into as hysterical a chauvinist as he had once been pacifist, was already a predominant motive with him. Yet, as in the criticism of Domela Nieuwenhuis, of which everyone was reminded, there was much truth in what he said— particularly in his picture of the German proletariat: 'I was excited at meeting personally German Social Democracy which I for years had only known, and dismissed with a shrug of the shoulders, from its quibbling hair-splitting quarrels about the exegesis of Karl Marx. Now I've seen the German proletarians in the streets of Stuttgart. My naïve illusions are destroyed, they are all good contented and satisfied bourgeois (*Spiess-bürger*).'[1]

The Germans, indeed, maintained that there was no need to discuss the question of action in the event of war any more. It had been on the agenda at all previous Congresses of the Inter-national: Nieuwenhuis' resolution, which was very like Hervé's, had been formally outvoted at Zürich in 1893; a resolution sponsored by Jaurès and Briand at Paris in 1900, calling for plans to be made for a general strike, had been thrown out. At Amsterdam the idea of the general strike had been accepted, but in such a form that it was clear that it need never become a serious and immediate practical issue. There were some grounds, therefore, for Bebel's contention that all that was needed was to reaffirm previous resolutions—and these had the

[1] *Proc.* 1907, Monday 19 August, p.85.

advantage that they did not require anybody actually to do
anything, whereas Hervé's proposals raised the awkward question of what in fact the socialist parties of the world (and in his
opening address Vandervelde had stressed that the movement
was now a world-wide one, 'on which the sun never set'), could
do, beyond stating that war was inherent in the nature of capitalist society and urging the substitution of militias for standing
armies.

None of the protagonists in the discussion really faced the
problem, but four different lines of possible action—or inaction—were suggested. Hervé's was the one extreme: Guesde's
was the other. For Guesde and a minority of the French delegation maintained that there was no need for any special treatment of the question and that all that was needed was to
continue as before until a Socialist victory, by removing the
root causes of war, would remove war itself. The German stand-
point was much the same, reiterating the need for the abolition
of standing armies, but at least committing Socialists in the
event of a threat of war 'to do all in their power by the use of
whatever measures seem most effective to stop war or, should
it break out, to work for its rapid conclusion'. Between Hervé's
romantic belief in the possibility of insurrection and mass
desertion and Guesde's and Bebel's carefully obscure expressions of conventional doctrines, two other proposals were
discussed.

One was supported by Jaurès and Vaillant and represented
the terms of the motion carried by the French Socialists at
Limoges the previous year. It was a product of Jaurès' desire
to retain the support of the French champions of direct action,
but it was also the expression both of his passionate concern
with the international situation and of his inextinguishable
optimism. Vaillant and Jaurès explicitly rejected Hervé's absolute pacifism: the working class of a nation attacked by another
had a duty to defend themselves. But, they implied, the intro-

duction of a militia system could stop the situation ever arising, while, if it unfortunately did arise, the International Bureau would be able to organize appropriate international action which would go as far as an insurrection or a general strike if necessary. As always, Jaurès was ready to emphasize any event, however small, which seemed to give ground for hope. It was intolerable for him to admit that nothing could be done to stop a war: 'It would be a sad thing if we could not say anything more than Bebel does, that we know of no specific means to stop strife and murder between nations; sad if the strongly increasing power of the German working class, of the international proletariat did not extend further.'[1]

It was not only the French, supported by some of the Italians, who attacked the inactivity of the SPD. Those with personal experience of the Russian revolution were anxious for a policy of action. Lenin, who was now aged thirty-seven, had, since leaving Russia in 1900, established himself as a brilliant journalist, and, by his quarrel with Plekhanov and the subsequent split in the Russian Social Democratic movement, had won a reputation outside Russian *emigré* circles and was rapidly to become a prominent member of the left-wing group in international socialist conferences. He had returned to Russia in time to witness the last days of the Petersburg Soviet, while Rosa Luxemburg had gone back to Poland to lead the Socialist movement there; she had been arrested and imprisoned for three months before she was released on grounds of health and allowed to return to Germany with, so it is said, the German Social Democratic Party standing bail for her.[2] Lenin and Rosa Luxemburg realized clearly what Engels had predicted and what Bebel and Kautsky saw but refused to face—that a European war was likely so to weaken the machinery of the capitalist state as to give socialists the opportunity to make a successful revo-

[1] *Proc.* 1907, p.89 (1st Commission Tuesday 20 August).
[2] See Frölich, p.139.

lution. And so Rosa Luxemburg, speaking for the Polish and
Russian delegations, urged that agitation, insurrection and
strikes on the outbreak of war should not only be aimed at ending the war but at the 'overthrow of class rule'. The lesson
which they had drawn from the Russian events of 1905 was not
that revolution at the end of an unpopular war would fail, but
simply that it must be better organized and led. 'What confusion! What a lack of determination and energy!' Rosa Luxemburg had exclaimed in prison. 'But let me be there, be there!
Heavens above! I'd wake them up, if I had to knock their heads
together first.'[1]

Both the proposals of Vaillant and Jaurès, and the amendment
put forward by Luxemburg and Lenin, were unwelcome to
Bebel. He realized how far the whole apparatus of the German
Party, which he personally had done so much to construct over
the past fifty years, was bound up with the structure of contemporary society: any violent attempt to destroy the latter
might well demolish the former too. It was a belief that was to
be of great importance in determining the action of Bebel's successors in 1914; and in 1918 it led to the German Socialists
themselves taking over the running of the existing bourgeois
state. At Stuttgart it was only hinted at in Bebel's response to
the demand that the SPD should commit itself to doing something definite in the event of a war: 'We cannot allow ourselves
to be driven to adopt methods of struggle which could be full
of grave consequences for life in the Party and even in certain
circumstances for the existence of the Party.' The German
Socialists were always impressed by the strength of the German
(and especially the Prussian) state; most of them realized clearly
the limits of action possible to them. They pointed out, for
example, how easily Hervé got away in France with agitation of

[1] Frölich, p.138. A slightly different version of the same sentiments occurs
in a letter to Luise Kautsky on 7 April 1906 (Rosa Luxemburg, *Letters to
Karl and Luise Kautsky from 1896 to 1918* ed. by Luise Kautsky, tr. by
Louis P. Lochner (New York 1925), p.117).

a considerably more extreme kind than that for which Karl
Liebknecht was awaiting trial: Bebel could tell the delegates that
no less than three of the editorial staff of the *Leipziger Volks-
zeitung* were in prison. And, indeed, the members of the Congress could see for themselves some of the difficulties experienced by their German comrades when one of their own number, a member of the British Social Democratic Federation,
Quelch, was expelled by the government of Württemberg, in
whose territory the conference was meeting, because he had
said at one of the earlier sessions that the Hague Conference
was a 'thieves' supper' and this had been interpreted to mean
that he had called the Czar and the other sovereigns represented
at the Hague 'thieves and robbers'.[1]

Out of these conflicting opinions and suggestions a compromise resolution was drafted, as so often. It was felt that the
whole point of a resolution about action in the event of war was
that it should be a unanimous expression of socialist opinion,
and so a sub-committee of fourteen was appointed to produce
something on which everyone could agree. This sub-committee
included Bebel and Vollmar, Jaurès and Guesde, Victor Adler
and Rosa Luxemburg, and it met in private. What in fact
emerged was a very long and involved resolution which contained something for everybody while committing nobody to
anything.[2] From the proposals of the orthodox Marxists like
Guesde and Bebel came the statement that war was inherent in
the capitalist system and would only disappear with its removal,
but in the meantime Socialists were to press in parliament for
reduction of armaments and abolition of standing armies, while
the International was rather vaguely to try and co-ordinate all
these efforts. Then there was a great puff of Jaurèsian optimism:
examples of effective international socialist co-operation were
cited. And finally in the case of a threat of an outbreak of war,

[1] *Proc.* 1907, Thursday 22 August, p.32.
[2] The text of the Stuttgart resolution is printed in the Appendix, p.206.

'it is the duty of the working classes and their parliamentary representatives in the countries taking part, fortified by the unifying activity of the International Bureau, to do everything to prevent the outbreak of war by whatever means seem to them most effective, which naturally differ with the intensification of the class war and of the general political situation'—a formulation that carefully avoided any specific commitment to a general strike or insurrection, while not excluding it. The last sentence of the whole motion was the contribution of Rosa Luxemburg and Lenin and gave the resolution a revolutionary twist which was presumably accepted because no one except its sponsors took it seriously: 'Should war break out in spite of all this, it is their duty to intercede for its speedy end, and to strive with all their power to make use of the violent economic and political crisis brought about by the war to rouse the people, and thereby to hasten the abolition of capitalist class rule.'

The resolution was adopted unanimously and with enthusiasm by the full Congress, Hervé even jumping on the table and holding up both his hands. The Stuttgart resolution was to be the basis of socialist action against war, and the pleasure with which it was greeted obscured the imprecision of its terms. The list of occasions on which international Socialists had actively collaborated to lessen international tension looked impressive, but did not really amount to much. The meetings between English and French trade unionists after Fashoda took place when the crisis had already been resolved by diplomatic means: the parliamentary action of the French and German Socialists in the Moroccan affair had little direct effect on the resolution of the crisis. Demonstrations by Austrian and Italian Socialists in Trieste showed the genuine desire of the Austrian Social Democrats to transcend national differences; there is no reason to suppose that they were taken very seriously by either the Austrian or Italian governments. The demonstrations in Sweden to prevent an attack on Norway were only part of a general desire to achieve separation of the two countries by peaceful means; and it was in fact a plebiscite sponsored by the government that ended the union peacefully and constitutionally. The only example of really effective action remained the 1905 revolution in Russia.

There were still people whom the Stuttgart resolution failed to satisfy and who suspected that parliamentary action by parties which were, after all, a minority, would prove disastrously inadequate unless it was backed up by mass extra-parliamentary pressure. Consequently, in 1910, at the next International Congress, Vaillant was joined by a new and unexpected supporter of direct action—James Keir Hardie, the first ILP Member of Parliament and a veteran of the British Labour movement, who was certainly not a representative of the revolutionary left wing. Whereas at Stuttgart most Socialists had envisaged a war coming over a colonial issue like Fashoda or Morocco, by 1910 their ideas had changed. They had been reminded by the Austrian annexation of Bosnia in 1908 that war might start in the Balkans, and, above all, the naval rivalry between England and Germany filled them with alarm as increasingly huge sums were being spent to construct the new Dreadnoughts, thus intensifying the armaments race, increasing the danger of war and imposing, so it was thought, a burden both on the working class and the national economy as a whole that would soon prove intolerable and contribute to the impending collapse of bourgeois society.

The debates at Copenhagen were less interesting and less spirited than previously: as one reads the account of the proceedings one has the impression that most of the protagonists are thoroughly tired of the subject and have certainly nothing new to add. Bebel, indeed, did not find it possible to attend as both his daughter and grandson were ill. What does emerge, perhaps, is the increasing tension between socialists of various nationalities (another committee was simultaneously discussing the question of the Czech trade unions): the Serb delegate

accused the Austrian Social Democrats of not protesting with
sufficient vigour against the annexation of Bosnia; and the
Germans were openly suspicious of the British. This suspicion
arose from a lack of knowledge of the whole political situation in
England, where the Labour Party in Parliament was in general
supporting the Liberal Government in the most radical series
of social reforms yet seen in Britain. But since by voting in
favour of expenditure on social legislation they simultaneously
voted for rearmament, because the budget was presented as a
single bill, they were much attacked by the Germans for voting
in favour of military credits, a situation that the Germans had
up till then been able to avoid since each block of credits was the
subject of a separate vote in the Reichstag, though it was a
dilemma with which they were soon to be confronted. The misunderstandings between German Social Democracy and the
British Labour Party were moreover increased by the fact that
two of the most widely known names in the British Labour
movement were now openly preaching preparation for defence
against a German attack—Robert Blatchford and H. M. Hyndman, perhaps the best known figure abroad, since he was one of
the few British leaders ready to talk the Marxist language.

The German irritation with the British Labour movement
showed itself at another point in the conference when Adolf
Cohen, a member of the German metalworkers' union, made a
bitter attack on the British trade unions for their lack of international solidarity, since they had only contributed a trifling
sum in support of the Swedish unions who had called a major
strike the previous year. Anderson of the ILP rather half-
heartedly explained the English unions' attitude on the grounds
that they were only just beginning to be influenced by socialism;
so that Cohen retorted: 'We hear with some astonishment the
phrase that the idea of socialism is just now beginning to make
headway in England and that the English have learnt a lot at
this Congress. They've been participating in international

workers' and trade unions' congresses for a long time and we've often heard these remarks. Therefore somebody ought to tell us once and for all whether all representatives of the English trade unions are really in earnest about the necessary reforms . . . .'[1] With remarks like these being made at other points in the Congress it is not surprising that the discussions on militarism contained some sharp exchanges between Ledebour and Keir Hardie on the subject of British Labour's attitude. Indeed, they did not get much beyond this; and it was with relief that the delegates voted in favour of a proposal by the professional mediator, Vandervelde, to refer the Vaillant-Keir Hardie amendment urging the general strike for consideration by the International Bureau and for discussion at the next Congress. The notion of the general strike was finally shelved.

There were good reasons for this: and the German objections to the mass strike were, as we have seen, well grounded. Both the Germans and Austrians were aware how little they were able to achieve by direct action against their governments and armies. As Dr Renner remarked ruefully, in the committee on militarism at Copenhagen: 'The Austrians and Germans (*Reichsdeutsche*) come from the countries where militarism is strongest and therefore have the sad advantage of being experts on the question.'[2] Where effective action against military power was most likely to be required, that very power made it impossible for the effective action to be taken. Two things emerged from the Stuttgart and Copenhagen Congresses: one a feeling of international solidarity that transcended the particular difficulties which the congresses had failed to solve or glossed over with ingeniously drafted formulae. The other was a tendency to treat the Bureau of the International as if it had real power to take and enforce decisions on member parties, in spite of the lack of any evidence that it had. At Copenhagen the task of co-

[1] *Proc.* 1910, Saturday 3 September, p.55.
[2] *Proc.* 1910, Friday 2 September, p.39.

ordinating international Socialist action in face of a threat of war, which at Stuttgart had been vaguely laid on the International as a whole, was explicitly given to the Bureau: 'To execute those measures the Congress charges the Bureau in the face of threatening danger of war to take the necessary steps to bring about agreement between the workers' parties of the countries concerned in order to protect them from the war.' It was a terrible responsibility.

2.

'The German working class has an increasingly positive and strong will. It is marching by the light of an idea towards a new social order: but it knows that it can only go there by stages. Through its co-operatives and unions it wants to become an immediate force. And it wants to transform political institutions, infuse them with democracy in order to make the guarantees of peace more sure and bring about social evolution more freely. In the solid mass of German socialism an ever freer, more lively and more ardent spirit is circulating. And the strongest conviction I have brought back from the Congress of Copenhagen and my rapid trip in Germany is that neither Europe nor Germany itself forms an impenetrable block of conservatism and militarism: that a less crushing European order is possible and that it would be enough to hasten a magnificent and healthy evolution all over Europe if a great republican people like France, instead of dragging itself through the equivocations and the wretched chicaneries of a policy without ideas, were to affirm clearly and vigorously a policy of full democracy, social progress, international arbitration and certain peace.'[1]

This was the impression which Jaurès brought back from Copenhagen: and it was one which was shared by most Socialist leaders abroad. All that was needed to save Europe was for the other Socialist parties to display the vigour, discipline and efficiency of the German Social Democratic Party. The position of German Social Democracy, its power and prestige were

[1] *La Dépêche de Toulouse*, 14 September 1910. Jaurès, *Pour La Paix. Oeuvres*, VII, pp.204–5.

greater than ever: the existence of over four million German Socialists seemed the strongest guarantee of peace in Europe.

Indeed, German Socialism seemed to be about to win new triumphs, to enter a new phase. In the general election of 1912 the Socialists won 110 seats and four and a quarter million votes. One German elector in three was voting Socialist. Yet, while the German Social Democratic Party was the great hope and strength of the Second International, the International was by no means the main interest of the German Social Democratic Party. The party programme on which their victorious election campaign was based, like all such documents, contains little reference to anything except those domestic reforms with which the ordinary voter was most concerned: and they were reforms that were most necessary in Imperial Germany—revision of the Prussian electoral system, introduction of genuine parliamentary government with a Chancellor responsible to the Reichstag, liberalizing of the administration, and so on. There was a demand for the introduction of a popular militia system to ease and equalize the burden of conscription, and a criticism of the armament policy of the government because it involved increased taxation, but it was inevitably as a party interested in domestic reforms and not in foreign policy that the Social Democrats fought the election. As Bebel had once said, 'The heart of the people turns towards us because we take up the cause of their daily needs.'[1]

Moreover, there was perhaps a change in the temper and interests of the party. The old generation of leaders was passing away. Bebel died in August 1913, and Jaurès wrote:

'If the German Socialist Party were still in its formative period the death of Bebel would not only be a sad loss but also a grave peril. But it is so strongly organized, it rests on such a broad basis and on such solid traditions of method that it cannot be undermined by the disappearance of the truly admirable man who contributed so largely

---

[1] Quoted by Winnig at 1913 Party Congress. *Verhandlungen*, p.480.

to its growth . . . . Bebel's influence rested on the authority of an absolute disinterestedness, on the strength of a vehement and resolute temperament and on the clear-sighted wisdom of a precise and powerful mind which knew how to formulate the opportune solution in moments of crisis . . . . It is not without emotion, I admit, that I saw the letter giving his last wishes . . . . He felt himself under the threat of sudden death . . . . he was preoccupied with lessening the full shock to his daughter. And at the moment when he was living, so to speak, at the heart of death, his calm and serene words called for the union of France and Germany in democracy, peace and a common search for justice. It is a noble end and a moving presage of the better days which will come for Europe, for this high confidence will not be disappointed.'[1]

The younger Social Democratic leaders were very different from their predecessors. They had grown up in the political machine instead of creating it; they had become accustomed, especially in the State Diets, to a day-to-day political life which was revisionist in practice, if not in theory; they were increasingly ready to compromise with the existing régime. Some of them, notably Eduard David and Gustav Noske, had already begun to give limited approval to the Government's naval policy. As an old man Noske was to recall his irritation with 'the number of foreigners mostly from Poland and Russia'[2] who had the impertinence to act as schoolmasters, (perhaps he really meant schoolmistresses), to the German working class; and from 1907 on he advocated support for the military budget in the interests of national defence, although as yet he was in a small minority in the Party. The Social Democrats had won some of their seats in the 1912 elections by means of a discreet electoral alliance, in some constituencies, for the second ballot, with the independent liberals (*Fortschrittliche Volkspartei*). And in 1913 came an even greater test both of their power and of their mood.

---

[1] *La Dépêche de Toulouse*, 22 August 1913; *Oeuvres*, IX, pp.293–5.
[2] Gustav Noske, *Erlebtes aus Aufstieg und Niedergang einer Demokratie* (Offenbach-am-Main, 1947), p.27.

It was a moment when the German Government were proposing fresh military increases but were also looking round for fresh means of financing them. Accordingly they proposed that the new expenditure should be covered by new direct taxes on income and property. This was a fiscal reform that had long been on the Socialist Party programme, and indeed, in the spring of 1913 the French and German Socialist parliamentary groups had issued a joint manifesto urging that the costs of armaments should not be borne by the working class. The members of the Socialist Party in the Reichstag were therefore in a difficult position. Should they vote against the military increases and in favour of the new taxes that were to give the money for the new military programme? Or should they reject the taxes for which they had been clamouring because they disapproved of the ends which they were to serve?

The problem was a confusing and difficult one, and the parliamentary party was deeply divided. For more than six hours they debated hotly how they should vote, and eventually decided by a narrow majority (fifty-two to thirty-seven with seven abstentions) to support the proposed new taxes. The arguments on both sides were sound. On the one hand the slogan 'Not a man and not a penny to this system' had been one which the party had long proclaimed and now seemed to be abandoning, with the implication that the existing military policy was being not only condoned but furthered. On the other hand, the military increases were certain to be voted anyway, so why should the Socialists not take the opportunity to win an important fiscal reform? Moreover, on the issue of the income tax the 110 Socialist votes could have a decisive influence. The Conservatives, representing those most likely to be affected by the new taxes, would oppose the bill: if they were joined by the Socialists the bill might be rejected. And the Government might then dissolve the Reichstag, leaving the Social Democrats the difficulty of justifying to the voters their action in joining with the Con-

servatives to throw out a measure that was avowedly part of
their own programme. It is not surprising that in the Social
Democratic Party opinions were confused or that people
changed their views back and forth and ended up in unexpected
company. But the taxes were voted, and the parliamentary
party received a vote of confidence by 336 votes to 140 votes
when the matter was discussed at the Party Conference a few
months later; and there was the surprising sight of Karl Liebknecht voting with the majority. Yet the people on the left who,
since 1903, had been worried by the effects of the very successes
of the Party, were now growing increasingly dismayed by the
extent to which actions such as voting for the new taxation
proposals were involving them with the existing régime. One
aspect of this anxiety was summed up by a speaker at the 1913
Party Congress: 'It has been represented to us here that it is a
great success for the party that the Government has at last demanded direct taxes for militarism. We must not get a wrong
idea of the party's strength. We have not seen the much extolled
size and power of the party being able to stop the passage of the
most monstrous military proposals—even in this Reichstag with
its 110 Social Democrats.'[1] The party was, in fact, equally
powerless, under the existing system, to achieve any other major
reforms. Accordingly, at the 1913 Congress, a group of left-wing
members, among whom Rosa Luxemburg was the most
prominent, again raised the problem of direct action and the
political mass strike, particularly to win a revision of the Prussian suffrage system. The arguments, and indeed the protagonists, were by now familiar. Bebel was dead, but the new party
bosses, notably Philipp Scheidemann, repeated his arguments
and emphasized the achievements of the party machine. But
perhaps a new note of impatience was creeping into the discussions—impatience with their critics on the part of the Party
leadership, and impatience with the stagnation of the official

[1] Stadthagen at 1913 Congress. *Verhandlungen,* p.477.

Party line on the part of the left. And, as before, there was no doubt of the result of the vote. In this particular discussion the exponents of direct action could point to the most recent of the remarkable Belgian achievements—the general strike of 1913 which had finally won universal suffrage. In fact, the Belgian Socialists' success was the result of their disregard of the tactical rules laid down at International Congresses; for their mass agitation on the streets was coupled with an alliance with the Liberals in parliament who shared their aim. Some of the Germans at the 1913 Party Congress, indeed, were so angry at the Belgian success that they tried to minimize it, and alleged that the result of the great strike was a fall in trade union membership—an assertion that was at once indignantly and formally denied by the Belgians.

However, what happened in Belgium could have little effect on the problem of peace and war with which some Socialist leaders, and especially Jaurès, were now preoccupied above all else. He was conducting a vigorous campaign inside and outside parliament to prevent the introduction of a law extending the period of military service from two to three years. In this he was no more successful than the Germans had been in preventing military increases, and the 'Three Years Law' was passed in 1913, while Jaurès was bitterly attacked by the whole nationalist press as a pro-German traitor. Moreover, while the Germans were rejecting the general strike as a political weapon, both the French Socialists and the trade unions were asserting its value as a weapon against militarism and war. The CGT had often asserted its faith in the insurrectional general strike against war, and would doubtless have done so again at its congress in September 1914 if this had not been overtaken by events. In November 1912 an extraordinary congress had asserted that 'if through folly or from calculation the country . . . were to plunge into the hazard of war (*une aventure guerrière*) and reject our opposition and our warnings, the duty of every worker is to refuse to answer the call-up order and ... to carry on the struggle against his only adversaries—the capitalists.'[1] In December 1912, a 24-hour general strike was called as a rehearsal for the great day.

The French Socialist Party was somewhat more cautious. However, at a special congress on 16 July 1914, summoned to prepare the brief for the delegates who were to represent the French party at the congress of the International due to meet in Vienna late in August, the Party resolved 'Among all the means available to forestall and prevent war and to force governments to have recourse to arbitration, the Congress considers as particularly effective the workers' general strike organized simultaneously and internationally in all the countries concerned....'[2] The police spy reporting the discussion was nevertheless of the opinion that the government had nothing really to worry about from this show of militant anti-militarism; and, indeed, it seems that Jaurès, in supporting this motion, was anxious to maintain a show of solidarity with the CGT and to preserve and strengthen the fragile links between the party and the unions. He envisaged—as indeed the resolution makes clear, if read carefully—that the strike against war would be called before war had actually started and would be used to put pressure on the government to accept arbitration.[3] Still, to the opponents of the Socialists there appeared to be little difference between Jaurès' idea of the general strike and the insurrectionary refusal to obey the mobilization orders preached by the syndicalists.

The weaknesses of all these impressive resolutions are obvious, and the Germans at least avoided their lack of realism. First, both in the SFIO and the CGT there were strong minori-

[1] *Compte rendu du congrès de Paris*, quoted in Zévaès, *Le Parti Socialiste de 1904 à 1923* (Paris 1923), p.102.

[2] Quoted in Annie Kriegel, 'Patrie ou Revolution: le mouvement ouvrier français devant la guerre (juillet–aout 1914)', *Revue d'Histoire Economique et Sóciale*, vol. xliii no. 3, 1965, p.369.

[3] For a discussion of Jaurès' attitude see Annie Kriegel, *Le Pain et les roses* (Paris 1968), pp.107–24.

ties opposed to the general strike against war—Guesde and his followers in their political movement, and the moderates in the trade unions who looked for immediate benefits—and, if the Sorelian myth of the general strike was to operate successfully, it must produce a unanimous and simultaneous *élan* in which nobody felt any inhibitions. Secondly, only a minority of the population was organized either in local political parties or in syndicates: in 1914 the SFIO had 72,765 members, won 1,398,000 votes and was represented by 103 deputies; the CGT had 600,000 members out of a total of just over 1,000,000 organized workers.[1] Even had they been unanimous they were only a minority in a population of just over forty million. The militant Syndicalist leaders were themselves perhaps the chief victims of the myth of the general strike.

It was inevitable that international Socialist solidarity should come to mean solidarity between the Socialist parties of France and Germany. None of the other great powers had Socialist parties of such importance, whose voices could be heard in parliament and whose agitation affected hundreds of thousands of voters. Moreover, the secular hostility between the two countries gave a particular emotional quality to the fraternizing between French and German Socialists. Each party, for instance, claimed that it alone was capable of solving the question of Alsace-Lorraine. The German Socialists would use their influence to gain real autonomy for the two provinces; (it is noteworthy that right up to the end of the war there was no talk of ceding Alsace-Lorraine to France; the furthest the German Socialists were prepared to go by 1918 was to propose a plebiscite). The French Socialists repeated again and again their determination not to fall victims to nationalist propaganda about the lost provinces, while expressing their confidence in the ability of the German Socialists to improve their lot as a neces-

[1] Drachkovitch, pp.80, 150, where the figures and resources of the French Socialist Party and trade union movement are carefully examined.

sary condition of a real Franco-German *rapprochement*. Indeed, it was in France and Germany, alone among the great powers, that there was a serious possibility of Socialists influencing their governments; yet the failure to prevent the German military increases of 1913 or the extension of the period of military service in France was only the latest in a series of events which showed how small the possibility in fact was. Neither Jaurès' statesmanlike speeches in the Chamber nor the annual resolutions of the SPD Party Congresses had been taken very seriously by their governments. Nevertheless, both governments were worried by the size and activity of the two parties and were anxious about their reactions in the case of war. The French Ministry of the Interior had drawn up a list—the notorious *Carnet B*—of militant Syndicalists and Socialists who were to be arrested immediately in the event of war. The Germans, too, were worried by the increased strength of the Socialists, and the government was already in touch with individual Social Democrats who they thought would be susceptible to patriotic appeals; Noske had been invited to visit a battleship; Südekum, at least by July 1914, was in touch with the Imperial Chancellor's office.

It was the French and German Socialists alone whose attitude might seriously check a government intent on war. In the other two great empires of Europe which might be expected to become involved in war—Austria and Russia—the Socialists were unlikely to be able to do anything effective. 'The workers of Austria and Russia declare loudly that they are not willing to allow themselves to be hurled against each other',[1] but there was very little they could do to stop it. The Italian Socialists failed to stop the seizure of Tripoli in 1911, in spite of widespread strikes and demonstrations; a lonely Socialist in Bulgaria, bravely standing out against the torrent of patriotic feeling in the autumn of 1912, could not hope to prevent the war with

---

[1] Jaurès in *L'Humanité*, 10 November 1912. *Oeuvres*, IX, p.175.

Turkey. As if from a need for reassurance, the Socialists of the small countries turned towards the Germans and French and to the International. Visits of leading Socialists to other countries multiplied, and there were frequent demonstrations of Franco-German solidarity, with meetings and encouraging speeches from visiting leaders from the other country. Fraternal delegates affirmed their solidarity at the party congresses of other Socialist parties. Scheidemann came, for instance, and spoke in Paris, and his speech, translated by the Alsatian Socialist Salomon Grumbach, an indefatigable worker for Franco-German understanding, aroused great enthusiasm, especially when he proclaimed 'We will never fire on you',[1] (though on this occasion there was not the additional attraction of Mlle. Kolber, 'l'éminente cantatrice allemande' who had appeared at the meeting held earlier in the year to celebrate the German electoral successes).

Jaurès in particular was active in this respect. He himself liked Germany; he had a genuine admiration for the people of Kant and Hegel, Goethe and Schopenhauer; he enjoyed the warmth and *Biederkeit* with which he was received; he admired the achievements of German Social Democracy. He spoke German, and, indeed, on a visit to Berlin in 1912 astonished his audience by his power to improvise a speech in German when, at the last minute, the authorities had forbidden him to speak in French. He was quick to reply to any criticism of the German Socialists, as in his controversy with Andler, and was always ready to give them the benefit of the doubt if their motives were questioned. Above all, in spite of the repeated accusations that he was a pro-German traitor, he persisted in believing that only by solidarity between French and German Socialists could war be prevented; and he was, in fact, to overestimate their power and even, perhaps, their good will. As in other directions his optimism was inextinguishable. Just as he

[1] A. Zévaès, *Le Parti Socialiste de 1904 à 1923*, p.81.

had dismissed one of the basic problems of the egalitarian society by the belief that 'there are surely people who have a vocation to be dustmen', so he hoped something would turn up to prevent war, in spite of the repeated rejection of his and Vaillant's proposals for specific measures.

The outbreak of the First Balkan War in the late summer of 1912 naturally caused great alarm, not only to socialists. The bureau of the International met in Brussels on 28 October to decide what action ought to be taken, in an atmosphere more critical even than that at the time of the Moroccan crisis in the previous year. In the summer of 1911, indeed, the action of the Bureau had been outstripped by events. On 28 July Huysmans, its secretary, had tried to get Adler's support for an immediate meeting of the Bureau in accordance with the Copenhagen resolution, but the Germans were reluctant to go to the trouble of travelling to Brussels and Adler replied, not without reason, though mainly because he did not want to go against Bebel's wishes, that a meeting would be 'either too late or too soon',[1] and Huysmans had accepted this position. This time, however, Adler was personally concerned. The next International Congress was due to meet in Vienna in the summer of 1913; but with Austria likely to be involved in trouble in the Balkans it was uncertain whether this would be possible. Both Adler, therefore, conscious of the difficulties with which the Austrian Socialists were at any moment likely to be confronted, and Jaurès, who was demanding 'immediate, passionate, effective international action',[2] pressed for the immediate summoning of an International Congress, while Bebel, prevented from attending by bronchitis and by his daughter's breakdown, was gloomily prophesying a European war within the next year.[3] The Bureau, with the co-operation of the Swiss federal and

[1] Adler, *Briefwechsel*, p.537.
[2] *L'Humanité*, 14 October 1912. *Oeuvres*, VIII, p.148.
[3] Letter to Victor Adler, 6 October 1912. Adler, *Briefwechsel*, p.550.

cantonal authorities, was accordingly able to arrange for an emergency congress to meet at Basle.

On Sunday, 24 November, 555 representatives from twenty-three different Socialist parties duly assembled, (the Serbs were absent, saying that they were too busy with the war to come). Bebel—it was to be his last international appearance—arrived at the *Burgvogtei* where the opening meeting was held, with Greulich, a veteran of the Swiss Socialist movement, in the chair, and as the *Sängerbund Vorwärts* struck up a Hymn to Freedom, the other leaders of the International came in together—Adler, Kautsky, Anseele, Jaurès, Camille Huysmans, the secretary of the Bureau. (Vandervelde was ill and unable to come.) England was represented by Keir Hardie, and nearly all the other leaders of the international Socialist movement were there.

For a moment the congress stood in silence to commemorate their dead leaders—Liebknecht, de Paepe, Varlin and the Swiss Bürkli and Becker. Then after greetings from the cantonal authorities, Edouard Anseele made a bold statement of Socialist demands, interspersed with storms of applause:

'The proletariat, which from today henceforth must be recognized as the herald of world peace, demands peace in the Balkans, republican autonomy for the Balkan peoples, the abandonment of alliances and diplomatic intrigues which carry with them the seed of every war. Austria-Hungary must not try to rob the Balkan peoples of the fruit of their victories, and, if Russia attacks, the Russian proletariat itself will arise and support it (the international proletariat) enthusiastically and admiringly. For France and Germany the hour of reconciliation has struck. There is to be no more war between Germany and France,' (there was particularly excited applause at this point) . . . . 'Great Britain and Germany should arm but not in a race to build warships for a war that will bleed them white, but arm to overcome misery and oppression . . . . The International is strong enough to speak in this tone of command to those in power and if necessary to follow up their words with deeds. War on war, peace for the world, hurrah for the workers' International!'

This speech struck the keynote for the rest of the conference: optimism, confidence—and vagueness about the means by which the desirable ends enumerated were to be achieved. On that Sunday afternoon the mood became even more exalted and the setting more impressive. Led by children in white singing socialist songs, the delegates marched through the streets to the cathedral which had been obligingly put at their disposal, where they were greeted with the sound of bells and organ music. Once inside, speaker after speaker got up to paint the horrors of war and affirm the strength of the proletariat—Sakasoff, the Bulgarian, who had been the only member of the Sobranje to protest against the war and who had just arrived from the Macedonian front, Hugo Haase, who was to succeed Bebel as the leader of the SPD parliamentary group, Keir Hardie, who claimed that the congress represented fifteen million Socialist voters and forty-five million members of the working class, Greulich, who asserted that the four and a quarter million Socialist votes in Germany were a splendid guarantee of international peace. Victor Adler alone, perhaps, expressed a certain hesitation and, for all his general confidence, struck a note of doubt: 'It unfortunately does not depend on us Social Democrats whether there is a war or not.'[1]

But the speech which closed the day's proceedings and which remained in the memory of the delegates was that of Jean Jaurès. The occasion was indeed one likely to inspire him to one of his best pieces of rhetoric. The cause was one about which he was deeply concerned: it was an occasion for one of those large liberal, humane and sentimental appeals at which he excelled. For, indeed, as he said, there was a hope 'that we shall not stand alone in this struggle. Here in Basle the Christians have opened their cathedral to us.' In fact, he said very little of substance; but he ended with one of the most celebrated pieces of oratory of a whole generation:

[1] *Proc.*, p.17.

'In this very church I heard just now as it were a call to general reconciliation—the sound of the bells that welcomed us. It reminded me of the motto which Schiller set at the head of his wonderful Song of the Bell: *Vivos voco:* I summon the living to defend themselves against the monster appearing on the horizon. I mourn the innumerable dead lying out there to the east, the stench of whom reaches us like a remorse; I will break the thunderbolts of war which are threatening in the clouds.'

The religious note of the afternoon's proceedings, which were attended by a huge audience, was emphasized again as the organ played Bach,[1] and the congregation sang
'*Denn die Völker wollen Frieden*
Frieden jedes Menschenherz.'
The next day's proceedings were a little less exalting and a little, a very little, more practical, and consisted in the unanimous adoption of the motion drafted by the Bureau, which repeated the Stuttgart and Copenhagen resolutions and added to them certain explicit statements of Socialist policy on specific issues: the Balkan Socialists should work for reconciliation, the Austro-Hungarians must be prevented from attacking Serbia, Austria-Hungary must keep off Albania. But 'the most important task in the action of the International falls to the working class of Germany, France and England' while Socialists must agitate for a naval agreement between Germany and England 'since the Congress regards as the greatest danger for the peace of Europe the artificially nourished opposition between Great Britain and the German Empire'.[2] (It seems likely that it was Jaurès who had insisted on stressing this point, for he had been maintaining it in speeches and articles for several years previously.) The speeches in support of the resolution added little; and the ones that added least were the ones that were most

[1] The official report describes the piece played as the 'C minor mass', so it is not quite clear what the organist thought appropriate to so remarkable an occasion.
[2] *Proc.*, pp.25–6.

applauded, like those of Keir Hardie, and of Klara Zetkin speaking for the Socialist women. Haase limited himself to the cautious promise: 'We will exert the maximum of our strength, by using the methods which our situation and our political and trade union organization permit, to secure what we all wish to secure, world peace and our future;'[1] and the Dutch delegate Troelstra expressed the hopes which the small nations placed in the International: 'The proletariat of the small countries stands with its possessions and its blood at the disposal of the International for anything it decides in order to banish war.'[2]

The proceedings closed in the same religious strain as the ceremonies of the previous day. The aged and revered Bebel speaking 'as an atheist' thanked the Church authorities for the use of the cathedral and went on to say 'I am frankly of the opinion that if the Christian Saviour were to reappear today and see the many Christian communities, the hundreds and millions who today call themselves Christians but are so in name alone, he would not stand in their ranks but in our army'. And Greulich, when finally closing the proceedings, not only referred to Bach's B Minor Mass but even, though with an apologetic 'Don't be alarmed', quoted from the Roman Catholic liturgy to express the socialist hope: 'Exspecto resurrectionem mortuorum et vitam venturam saeculis.'[3]

The Basle Congress marks the high point of the International's optimistic self-confidence; and it reveals how far socialism had become almost a religious movement in feeling, and how much blind faith was placed in the actual existence of the International. On this occasion, at least, war over the Balkans seemed to have been averted; and throughout the autumn of 1912 massive demonstrations against war had been held in the major capitals of Europe and seemed to assert the power of the working class to stop war. The optimism generated at Basle only faded in July 1914. Up to the last minute con-

[1] *Proc.*, p.30.　　　　[2] *Proc.*, p.33.　　　　[3] *Proc.*, p.42.

fidence in the possibilities of international action against war
was encouraged by the speeches and writings of Socialist leaders,
the constant exchange of visits and courtesies, and by such
demonstrations as the Congress at Berne in 1913 where members of the French and German parliaments, liberals as well as
socialists, met to proclaim their desire for friendship, and which
they were to repeat at Basle in the spring of the following year.
Above all Jaurès' optimism was unshaken and the hopes he
placed in the German Socialists undiminished. 'Don't worry,'
he said to a friend in the spring of 1914, 'the Socialists will do
their duty', and, 'Four million German Socialists will rise like
one man and execute the Kaiser if he wants to start a war.'[1] The
crisis of 1914 found the Socialists of Europe with the bells of
Basle still ringing in their ears.

[1] Lair, *Jaurès et l'Allemagne*, p.221.

VII

SUMMER 1914

The crisis of July 1914 came with startling and shattering sud-
denness on a Europe oddly unprepared for dealing with it. For
although there had been constant talk of war for the past ten
years, each crisis had in fact been survived without the expected
débâcle, while in the last year there had, perhaps, even been
some lessening of the tension. And the news of the assassination
of the Archduke Francis Ferdinand on 28 June, though shocking, was not entirely surprising. The assassination of royal
persons or of heads of states was not uncommon; within living
memory an Emperor of Russia, the Empress of Austria, three
Presidents of the United States, a President of the French
Republic and a King of Italy had all been murdered, to say
nothing of the King and Queen of Serbia, the King of Portugal,
several Russian Archdukes and other minor princes, or of many
unsuccessful attempts. After the first shock had passed most
people in Europe, the members of the Socialist parties among
them, sighed with relief, and turned to the more pressing and
interesting problems of domestic politics and scandal.

The Austro-Hungarian Government, in fact, had been completely successful in lulling any suspicions that might have been
entertained, simply by allowing more than three weeks to elapse
between the murder of the Archduke and the dispatch of their
ultimatum to Serbia. In the meantime the Social Democratic
press of Europe, though continuing to express a general anxiety
about possible trouble in the Balkans, did not show any sign of
expecting an immediate and disastrous crisis. The French
Socialists voted in the Chamber against the special credits

demanded to pay for the visit of the President and Prime Minister to St. Petersburg (they left on 15 July), for fear that they might enter into unspecified secret agreements Otherwise, Socialist pronouncements on the international situation followed the accepted pattern; and the leaders of the International were able to leave for their vacations—Kautsky to Rome, Ebert to the island of Rügen, Victor Adler to Bad Nauheim, Scheidemann to climb in the Alps. Even Lenin had gone to the Carpathians for his wife's health. Jaurès, after the conclusion of the annual Party Congress which met in Paris on 14, 15 and 16 July, remained in Paris (he very rarely took a holiday) until the 24th when he went to the South to take part in a by-election campaign in Lyons, and there he received the news of the Austrian ultimatum.

The publication of the ultimatum showed that the Austrian government were determined on war: but it was not yet clear whether this would be more than a local war or not. In Austria itself the Socialists were already beginning to experience what a war would mean; a press censorship was already in operation, and as early as 22 July—before the presentation of the ultimatum to Serbia—articles against militarism had been cut out of the Socialist newspapers. Moreover, in Vienna and the German speaking cities at least, the idea of a war with Serbia was not at all unpopular: 'The flood gates were opened, and the entire people and press clamoured impatiently for immediate and condign punishment of the hated Serbian race.'[1] It was not long before the Austrian Socialists began to discover that it was impossible to resist the flood. The German Social Democratic leaders at once came out unequivocally against the Austrian policy and methods. On 25 July *Vorwärts* declared that the Austrian Government was bent on war and that it had been

---

[1] Sir M. de Bunsen, British Ambassador in Vienna, to Sir E. Grey, 1 September 1914 (G. P. Gooch and Harold Temperley, *British Documents on the origins of the War* (London 1926), XI, p.357).

goaded on by the chauvinist press in Germany, while 'un-
questionably Herr von Bethmann-Hollweg has himself promised Herr Berchtold to stand behind him'.[1] And at the same
time the Executive issued an appeal on the lines foreseen at
Stuttgart and Copenhagen:

'No drop of a German soldier's blood must be sacrificed to the
Austrian despots' lust for power, to imperialist commercial interests.
Comrades, we call upon you to express immediately in mass-meetings
the unshakable will for peace of the class-conscious proletariat . . . .
The ruling classes, who in peace-time oppress you, despise you,
exploit you, want to use you as cannon fodder. Everywhere the cry
must ring in the despots' ears: "We want no war! Down with war!
Long live international brotherhood." '[2]

Jaurès, when he received the news of the Austrian ultimatum,
at once saw the terrifying consequences; and his electioneering
speech at Vaise, near Lyons, was in fact a solemn warning of the
perils of the situation:

'Ah, citizens, I do not want to stress the dark colours of the picture,
I don't want to say that the diplomatic breach between Austria and
Serbia, the news of which we received half-an-hour ago, necessarily
means that a war between Austria and Serbia is going to break out,
and I am not saying that if war breaks out between Serbia and Austria the conflict will necessarily extend to the rest of Europe, but I
also say that we have at this moment against us, against peace,
against human life, terrible odds, in the face of which the proletarians
of Europe must make every effort at solidarity of which they are
capable . . . . We are perhaps at this moment on the eve of the day
when Austria hurls herself on the Serbs, and then, with Austria and
Germany hurling themselves on the Serbs and the Russians,
Europe is in flames. The world is in flames . . . . Citizens, if the
storms breaks all of us socialists will take care to escape as soon as
possible from the crime which our governors will have committed,
and meanwhile, if anything remains to us, if any time remains to us,

[1] *Vorwärts*, 25 July 1914, quoted in Edwyn Bevan, *German Social Democracy during the War* (London 1918), p.6.
[2] *Vorwärts*, 25 July 1914.

we will redouble our efforts to prevent the catastrophe. Our German comrades in the *Vorwärts* are already rising in indignation against the Austrian note, and I believe that our Socialist Bureau has been summoned. I should be ashamed of myself, citizens, if there were one among you who could think that I am trying to use the drama of events for an electoral victory, however precious. But I have the right to tell you that it is our duty, the duty of all of you, not to let slip a single opportunity to show that you belong to that international Socialist party which at this moment, as the storm breaks, represents the only promise of a possibility of peace or of the re-establishment of peace.'[1]

The alarmed Socialist leaders rapidly began to return to their respective capitals, while the Bureau of the International was summoned to meet on 29 July in Brussels (and the delegates were to have some difficulty in travelling there by railways already cluttered up with military traffic). So far the ceaseless agitation prescribed by the International and called for by the Party leaders went on as planned. The Party press continued to attack militarism and secret diplomacy, at least in those countries where freedom of expression was still allowed them: mass meetings were held all over Germany between 26 and 30 July, and on the eve of his departure for Brussels, Jaurès drafted a manifesto calling for more mass meetings in France.

The French Syndicalist leaders were also openly opposing participation in a war, in accordance with the often repeated resolutions of their conferences. 'Workers must answer any declaration of war by a revolutionary general strike,' their newspaper, *La Bataille Syndicaliste*, wrote on 26 July. Jouhaux, the secretary of the CGT, was in Brussels on that and the following day as fraternal delegate to the congress of the Belgian trade unions, and Karl Legien, who had the equivalent post in the German socialist trade unions, was also there. They had five minutes' conversation, and as neither spoke the other's language, it is not surprising that little was said—nor that it is

[1] *L'Avenir Socialiste*, No. 384, August 1914. Jaurès, *Oeuvres*, IX, pp.382-6.

uncertain what that little was. Jouhaux seems to have been extremely anxious to discover what the German trade unions would do to stop a war, and declared that the French were ready to call a general strike if the Germans would do the same; Legien remained prudently silent.[1]

Yet, in spite of the increasing gravity of the situation, members of the International found it hard to believe that a war would actually occur: Ebert, for example, said to a friend on 27 July: 'They look too much on the black side. I told them so in reply to their last letter asking me to return . . . . Frau Ebert is doubtful, but I'm sure it's nonsense. There will be no war.'[2] Jaurès was, as always, ready to find a glimmer of hope in Grey's proposals to mediate. And even after the meeting of the Bureau of the International on the 29th, Bruce Glasier, one of the British delegates, was still hopeful: 'But although the dread peril of a general eruption of war in Europe was the main subject of the deliberations, no one, not even the German representatives, seemed apprehensive of an actual rupture between the great powers taking place until at least the full resources of diplomacy had been exhausted.'[3]

Actually, the meeting of the International in Brussels on 29 July must have been a depressing occasion, although it met in a building that was a visible symbol of the progress of socialism—the new wing of the *Maison du Peuple* which had recently been opened by Anatole France. However, nearly all the leaders of the movement were there: Vandervelde, the president, Jaurès, Victor Adler (who was accompanied by his son Friedrich, the secretary of the Austrian Party), Rosa Luxemburg, Keir Hardie, Hugo Haase, Angelica Balabanova, the indomitable Russian who had won (and was to retain for nearly

[1] *La Bataille Syndicaliste*, 26 September 1914. A. Rosmer, *Le mouvement ouvrier pendant la guerre* (Paris 1936), pp.136, 159–68. Dolléans, II, p.218.
[2] Scheidemann, *Memoirs of a Social Democrat* (Eng. ed. London 1929), I, p.192.
[3] W. Stewart, *James Keir Hardie* (New ed. London 1925), p.356.

half a century) a leading position in the Italian Socialist movement, where she was then closely associated with the rising young Socialist agitator Benito Mussolini, and representatives from the Dutch, Danish, Swiss and Spanish parties. Lenin was not there and only sent a very minor member of the Bolshevik Party, while Russia was also represented by the Menshevik Axelrod and the Social Revolutionary Rubanovitch, and Trotsky was in fact in Brussels at the time for the negotiations with the Bureau about unifying the Russian Socialist parties, which had taken place unsuccessfully a fortnight before. As at Basle two years earlier, it was not possible for a delegate of the tiny Serbian party to come.[1] Victor Adler was the first to speak, and he was extremely depressed, as well he might be, for all he could report was the impotence of the Austrian Socialists to do anything except allow things to take their course: mobilization had already begun and martial law was in operation; the Socialists were already helpless. Adler himself was a very sick man; during the four remaining years of his life he was constantly struggling with pain and the threat of death. He was appalled at the thought of war, like all the Social Democratic leaders, and had not expected that the Austrians would in fact start it. At the same time he was aware of the mood of the German working class in Vienna, as well as of their comparative political weakness. 'It is better to be wrong with the working class than to be right against them,'[2] he once said; and in the crisis of July 1914 he felt obliged to follow the temper of the Vienna crowds. Victor Adler's confession was supported by the admissions of Nemeč and Burian for the Czech Socialist party. Bruce Glasier

---

[1] The main sources for this meeting are Vandervelde, *Jaurès* (Paris 1929), pp.5–6; *Friedrich Adler vor dem Ausnahmegericht* (Berlin 1919), pp.16–17; A. Balabanova, *My Life as a Rebel* (New York 1938), pp.114–8; P. G. La Chesnais: *The Socialist Party in the Reichstag and the declaration of War* (London 1915), pp.37–43; A. Zévaès, *Jean Jaurès* (Paris 1951). The official record has now been published by Georges Haupt in *Socialism and the Great War* (Oxford 1972), Appendix, pp.250–65.

[2] Otto Bauer, Introduction to Adler, *Aufsätze*, VI, p.xxx.

burst out with a sharp protest against the Austrians, but Adler
was able to muster enough spirit to make a mocking and
crushing reply.

The long discussion, which went on for most of the day on
29 July, soon fell, however, into a more familiar pattern. The
main practical decision to be taken was what to do about the
forthcoming International Congress, due to meet at Vienna
late in August. Vienna was clearly out of the question as a
meeting-place; but the French offered to act as hosts in Paris. It
was, moreover, obviously desirable that the Congress should
meet before September, and, after some discussion in which one
of the English delegates pointed out how difficult it would be to
get a full attendance at short notice and suggested that the
original date should be retained, it was agreed that the congress
should be summoned for 9 August. The first item on the
agenda was to be 'the War and the Proletariat', and the other
topics due for discussion, such as imperialism and alcoholism,
were to be relegated to second place. As often before, since no
immediate practical action suggested itself, it was decided to
arrange for further discussion. None of the delegates could
know that on the next afternoon the Czar would finally sign the
order for Russian general mobilization, and that there would be
no time for talking any more.

In the evening there was a great mass-meeting in the *Cirque
Royale*. Thousands of Belgian workers came in from the sub-
urbs and neighbouring cities and crowded into the largest hall
in Brussels to hear the famous leaders of the movement on
which their hopes of peace now rested. Yet this last huge
demonstration of the International was perhaps less convincing
than on previous similar occasions. Victor Adler did not attend,
to his son's bitter disappointment, and Jaurès had a bad head-
ache. In spite of this Jaurès' short speech, as so often, was the
most effective and the most applauded, while his appearance
with his arm around Haase's shoulders was symbolically reas-

suring. But whereas Hugo Haase could only criticize the German Government and praise the German proletariat's will for peace, Jaurès was able to give unequivocal support to the policy of the French Government:

'As for us French Socialists, our duty is simple: we do not need to impose on our Government a peaceful policy. They are practising one. I, who have never hesitated to draw down on my head the hatred of our chauvinists by my obstinate and unfailing will for a Franco-German rapprochement, have the right to say that at this moment the French Government wants peace and is working for the maintenance of peace. The French Government is the best ally in the cause of peace of that admirable English Government which has taken the initiative in conciliation.'

And then he concluded with a warning and a characteristic hope:

'If in the mechanical chain of circumstances and in the intoxication of the first battles our masters did succeed in dragging the masses along with them, then, as typhus finishes off the work of the shells, as death and destitution strike, men returned to sobriety will turn on the rulers of Germany, France, Russia and Italy and ask them what reasons they can produce for all these corpses. And then Revolution unleashed would tell them "Begone and ask pardon of God and men!" But if we avoid the storm, then I hope that the nations will not forget, and that they will say: We must stop this spectre rising from its grave every six months to terrify the world. Human beings of all countries, this is the work of peace and justice we have to accomplish!'[1]

The next morning the delegates left for home. Jaurès' spirits seem to have risen again. He had not lost his belief in conciliation and seems to have hoped that President Wilson might be able to act as mediator. Vandervelde tells a typical story that as they were saying goodbye, Jaurès said 'It will be like Agadir. There will be ups and downs. But it is impossible that things won't turn out all right. I've got two hours before catching

---

[1] Jaurès, *Oeuvres*, IX, pp.395–6.

the train. Let's go to the Museum and see your Flemish primitives.'[1] 'Les choses ne peuvent ne pas s'arranger!': it could be the motto of those two centuries of belief in human progress which were being brought to a close with the end of the old Europe.

2.

In Germany the Government had already begun to be concerned about the reactions of the Social Democrats. As early as 26 July, Hugo Haase had been asked to call at the Prussian Ministry of the Interior, and, accompanied by Otto Braun, he went there and found the Chancellor Bethmann-Hollweg himself. Bethmann attempted to outline what he thought it would be legitimate to say at the mass-meetings which he understood the Socialists were going to hold. He stressed that Germany would stand by her ally Austria, and refused to listen to the Socialists' arguments that they would not consider Germany bound to help Austria except in a defensive war; and this the present war against Serbia was not. Nothing else seems to have happened at this meeting, though the Socialists also received a warning that in the event of war a 'state of siege' was likely to be imposed and the freedom of the press curtailed. For the moment, then, the Socialist agitation against war continued unabated. Scheidemann, the most active member of the Executive returned to Berlin on the 27th, though Ebert refused to interrupt his holiday till the 29th; and the Executive began to take precautions to preserve the party machine in the event of a war. On 30 July about lunch-time there appeared in a Berlin newspaper a report that mobilization had been decided on; it was a premature rumour and was immediately denied, (the actual decree of general mobilization was issued two days later), but the Socialists at once decided to send Ebert, the president of the Party Executive, and Braun, the Party Treasurer, to Zürich, so that some at least of their responsible leaders should

[1] Vandervelde, *Jaurès*, p.6.

be in safety in the event of a general suppression of the Party. In fact, Bethmann-Hollweg drew another conclusion from his meeting with Haase and Braun on the 26th. In the later stages of the crisis it is clear that his diplomacy was directed less at preventing war than in making it appear, if not to history, at least to the Social Democratic Party, that it was the Russians who had attacked Germany. Moreover, he had already been privately in touch with some of the more 'reliable' Socialist leaders on the right wing of the Party. He was able to reassure the Prussian Ministry of State on 30 July that there was nothing 'particular to fear from Social Democracy or from the leadership of the Social Democratic Party, as he believed he could conclude from transactions with Reichstag Delegate Südekum. There would be no talk of a general strike or of sabotage.'[1]

Jaurès, too, was in touch with his government, but it was he who took the initiative. He had long been worried by the possibility that France might be dragged by her alliance with Russia into a war that would be only of interest to the Czar. Poincaré, the President, and Viviani, the Prime Minister, had just been visiting St. Petersburg (they left on their return journey by sea on the 24th, and communication with them had been difficult) so there was some real cause for anxiety that they might have been encouraging the Russian Government in a reckless policy. Some of the Socialist leaders had an opportunity of expressing this view in an interview with Bienvenu-Martin, the acting Foreign Secretary, on 28 July. The President and Prime Minister landed at Dunkirk early on the 29th, as the members of the International Bureau were assembling in Brussels: Jaurès got back from Brussels on the next day, anxious to see the Prime Minister. The situation was growing worse: and Jaurès, who was in the Chamber on 31 July, received there the bad news of

---

[1] *Outbreak of the World War*. German Documents collected by Karl Kautsky and edited by Max Montgelas and Walter Schücking. Translated by the Carnegie Endowment for International Peace (New York 1924), p.382.

the Russian mobilization, and in the late afternoon, of the German reaction—a declaration of a 'state of imminent danger of war' (*Kriegsgefahrzustand*). The German word was ominous; but Jaurès, still trusting that the situation might really be less grave than it appeared to be, sent out for a larger dictionary in the hope of reading some slightly less alarming meaning into the cumbrous term.

As soon as he returned from Brussels, Jaurès had seen Viviani for a brief interview, and as he left, he is reported to have said 'You know, if we were in their place, I don't know what more we could do to preserve peace.'[1] However, on the next day when he was in the Chamber, he saw Abel Ferry, the Under-Secretary for Foreign Affairs, and according to Ferry's later account,[2] accused the government of being dupes of the Russians. It is hard to know what in fact passed between them as nobody else was present. One of Jaurès' friends subsequently claimed that Ferry asked Jaurès what he would do if war came, and Jaurès replied that he would continue his agitation for peace, to which Ferry replied: 'You won't dare to as you would be shot at the first street corner.'[3]

After leaving Ferry's office Jaurès went to the editorial office of *L'Humanité* to discuss policy with his colleagues and then went on with some of his friends to have supper in a nearby café. In spite of the tension and anxiety of the moment he engaged in a humdrum conversation with some socialist journalists at the next table and admired the photograph of the small daughter of one of them. Suddenly a shot was fired; and in the midst of the uproar that followed Jaurès' friends realized that he had been killed. The murderer was a hysterical young man

[1] Reported by the Socialist deputy for the Haute-Garonne, Bedouce, in *Le Populaire du Centre* 3 August 1915. See Annie Kriegel, 'Jaurès en Juillet 1914', *Le Pain et les roses*, p.108.
[2] Abel Ferry, *Carnets secrets* (Paris 1957), pp.26–7.
[3] See A. Zévaès, *Jean Jaurès*; Charles Rappoport, *Jean Jaurès* (Paris 1916) and Annie Kriegel, 'Jaurès en Juillet 1914' for the various contradictory accounts of these conversations.

called Raoul Villain, who really believed what he had read in the *Action Française* and other nationalist papers about Jaurès' treachery. He seems to have had no associates and to have acted in the isolation of a neurotic's world: there is no evidence to support the rumours which soon became current to the effect that the assassination had been sponsored by the Government or even by the Russian Ambassador, Izvolsky.[1] The French Socialists were left without a chief and the International without its most buoyant leader at a moment when the international crisis was at its height.

The members of the French Socialist Party, both leaders and rank and file, were stunned and bewildered by this blow. The Government were anxious about popular reactions to the murder of Jaurès, and Viviani issued an appeal for calm: 'In the serious circumstances through which our country is passing, the government counts on the patriotism of the working class and the whole population to maintain calm and not to add to the emotion of the public by agitation which would throw the capital into disorder,'[2] and President Poincaré sent a warm letter of personal sympathy to Mme Jaurès. On the next day the notices announcing general mobilization were posted. And on 4 August Jaurès' funeral was attended by a crowd already thinned out by the departure of the reservists. And Viviani over his tomb called, successfully, for national unity: 'The mighty orator, if he could rise trembling with passion, would not say anything else.'[3]

The crowds in the streets of Vienna were enthusiastic for war against Serbia. In France even militant trade unionists were loyally obeying their call-up notices, either from fear of the consequences or, in most cases, from a genuine and overriding desire to preserve their homes from the Boche. And in Germany the mood of the Socialist party was beginning to change. As it

[1] See L. Albertini, *Le Origini della Guerra del 1914* (Milan 1943) vol. III, pp.83-7.
[2] Zévaès, *Jaurès*, p.257; Rappoport, *Jaurès*, p.95.
[3] Zévaès, p.259.

became clear that the Russians were going to enter the war in support of Serbia, the old traditional fear of the barbarous Slav hordes began to revive: and it was a fear on which the Government was able to play. On 30 July there was already a division of opinion on the editorial board of *Vorwärts* about the line the paper should adopt. Friedrich Stampfer, the chief editor, remembering what Engels and Bebel had said about the Russians, thought that this was the moment to say that if attacked by Russia 'we will not have our women and children sacrificed to the brutality of the cossacks'.[1] He was opposed by Heinrich Ströbel, who did not wish to do anything that might minimize the Party's agitation in favour of peace; and for the moment the paper did not modify its line, although some of the provincial papers printed anti-Russian articles next morning.

However, as the situation grew still worse, and the *Kriegsgefahrzustand* became general mobilization, the discussion of the party's attitude to the emergency could not be postponed. The Executive met on 31 July, and later in the day was joined by the committee of the parliamentary party: they were still expecting repressive measures and discussed plans for preserving the party machinery. Haase had by now returned from Brussels and was able to report on the discussions there. Above all, with mobilization expected hourly, and an emergency session of the Reichstag in prospect, the party had to decide what attitude they would adopt to the voting of the war credits in parliament. It was the beginning of three days of argument and emotion; and the rifts in the party were becoming serious and painful. One of the most embarrassing things, which would have been avoided had Bebel still been alive, was that the leader of the parliamentary party, Hugo Haase, was one of the minority in favour of voting against any war credits. And so Scheidemann, who had already decided that rejection of the war credits would be both dangerous and undesirable, determined to postpone a

---

[1] Scheidemann, *Memoirs of a Social Democrat* (London 1929), I, p.189.

decision until a meeting of the full parliamentary party could be summoned and he should have time to consult with his friends. No decision on this vital question was therefore taken at this stage. It was, however, decided to send Hermann Müller, a member of the Executive, to Brussels and then on to Paris with Camille Huysmans, the secretary of the International, to make a last attempt to co-ordinate international action between the two Socialist parties most directly concerned.

Hermann Müller set off immediately, and arrived in Brussels early the next morning.[1] He went straight to Camille Huysmans' house where he received the news of Jaurès' murder which had been telephoned to Huysmans the previous evening. However, Müller decided to continue his journey, and he and Huysmans set off by motor car for Paris accompanied by a young Belgian Socialist, Henri de Man, who was to act as interpreter. They arrived in a city where mobilization was already in progress and where the signs of impending war were all about them, and went straight off to the Palais-Bourbon to meet the leading Socialist deputies, for whom Renaudel and Marcel Sembat seem to have done most of the talking. (Guesde and Vaillant were unable to be there.) Müller was kindly received and the motives for his journey appreciated,[2] but the moment was a difficult one and the French had hardly had time to recover from the shock of Jaurès' death. The conversations with Müller went on for several hours on that sultry summer night, first at the Chamber and then at the offices of *L'Humanité*.

[1] Müller's report to the executive is printed in Scheidemann, *Der Zusammenbruch* (Berlin 1921), pp.12–18. Henri de Man has given three accounts: *L'Humanité*, 4 March 1915, *The Remaking of a Mind* (New York 1919), pp.36–45, *Cavalier Seul* (Geneva 1948), pp. 81–82. These agree in substance although there are small points of discrepancy. Renaudel gave a brief account in *L'Humanité*, 26 February 1916 (reprinted in La Chesnais App. 1). A short account by Huysmans is printed in Karl Grünberg, *Die Internationale und der Weltkrieg*, 1. (*Archiv für die Geschichte des Sozialismus und der Arbeiterbewegung* Vol. VI, 1916, p.225).

[2] It is necessary to stress this, since the German Socialist Südekum pretended after the war had started that Müller had been received with hostility.

Müller explained that the German Party thought it important to try to reach some agreement about the policy to be adopted towards the voting of the war credits, so that each party would have some idea how the other might act. Actually, he was in a difficult position since the German parliamentary group had not yet decided what to do. He was careful, therefore, to say that he could only give his personal opinion about what his colleagues might do. According to his own account, he said that there was a strong current against voting for the war credits, that there had been some discussion about abstaining (which was what Bebel and Liebknecht had done in 1870), but that part of the Party was ready to support the Government and vote in favour. This was a perfectly correct account of the state of mind of the German Party at the moment of his departure; and it seems likely that he personally thought it improbable that the Party would go so far as to vote *for* the credits. At one point he used the phrase 'I think it out of the question that we should vote for the war credits' ('Dass man für die Kriegskredite stimmt, das halte ich für ausgeschlossen'), though he maintained later that he only meant this to apply to a situation in which a common policy had been adopted by both the French and the German parties. In any case, he stressed that whatever decision was eventually taken, the Party would act unanimously. It soon emerged in the discussion that no one among the French leaders considered for a moment that the French might vote against credits required for a war in which France clearly would be the victim of German aggression. It was a surprise to Müller to see the situation in this light, and he affirmed the orthodox German view that it was Russia who was the danger and that the French should be preventing the 'pan-Slav war Party' in St Petersburg from starting the war.

The inconclusive discussion showed how impossible it was to co-ordinate international action in a situation of such complication and danger, and the talks ended with a pious hope that both parties should see whether it might be possible to reach agreement on abstention in the vote on the war credits, with both Müller and the French emphasizing that they were not in fact undertaking to follow this course.

Müller left at once, in the early hours of 2 August. He was next to see Paris in 1919 when he came as one of the German representatives to sign the Treaty of Versailles. Germany had just declared war on Russia and, as the war fever rose, hope of peace diminished. Müller himself began to feel the effects of war; he had refused the offer of a French passport and he was arrested twice and accused of being a spy. It was only after he had stated (untruthfully) that he had started out to attend Jaurès' funeral, and had turned back, that he was allowed to cross the Belgian frontier on foot. However, he eventually made his way back by train via Brussels to Berlin, where he arrived in the late afternoon on 3 August. He went straight from the station to the Reichstag building where the parliamentary party was meeting. The Party leaders and the Socialist members of the Reichstag had been in almost constant session since the previous morning.

When the Party Executive met on the morning of 2 August, it was already known that the Reichstag was to meet on the 4th to vote the war credits. The discussions among the Socialist leaders were prolonged and agonizing; indeed at one moment Richard Fischer burst into tears. Haase and Ledebour vigorously opposed the voting of the credits with some support from Kautsky, who for a time was in favour of abstention, and by mid-afternoon no agreement had been reached except that it was impossible for a party as large as the SPD to abstain in this critical vote. The meeting was adjourned until nine in the evening, and in the meanwhile Scheidemann and his friends met in the garden of a suburban villa (it is in an atmosphere of oppressive summer heat that all these discussions must be envisaged), to draw up a common declaration of policy. Yet when the

Executive Committee met again in the evening, the only result was three more hours of fruitless discussion and disagreement before the Party leaders dispersed for an uneasy night. When Scheidemann and Haase got home they found an invitation from the Chancellor, Bethmann-Hollweg, to an interview at noon on the next day. In the morning there was a full meeting of the parliamentary party: but further discussion was postponed until after Haase, Scheidemann and Molkenbuhr came back from the Chancellor's palace. However, Scheidemann was encouraged by the mood of his fellow deputies; and one or two even of the radical wing assured him they would vote for the war credits. When Haase and his two companions got to the Wilhelmstrasse they found the leaders of the other parties in the Reichstag assembled there. Presently Bethmann-Hollweg came in, tired and grey, his high stiff collar limp with sweat, and, after greeting them, he read the speech which he was proposing to make in the Reichstag on the following day. It seemed to be taken for granted that the credits for which he was going to ask would be voted unanimously, and the Social Democrats, somewhat embarrassed, had to admit that their party had not yet made up its mind. The situation was all the more awkward since Haase and Scheidemann held opposing views on the matter, and were beginning to get on each other's nerves. The meeting ended with a characteristic discussion as to whether the Socialists would be ready to shout 'Hurray for the Kaiser!' at the end of the next day's session in the Reichstag, and the equally characteristic suggestion that they would be ready to shout 'Hurray for Kaiser, People and Fatherland'.[1]

After Haase and the other two Socialist deputies had returned to their colleagues and the discussion was resumed, Müller (who was himself not a member of the Reichstag, but was on the

[1] Scheidemann, *Der Zusammenbruch*, p.12. This book contains extracts from Scheidemann's diaries. Scheidemann added some details in his *Memoirs of a Social Democrat* (Eng. Ed. 1929), I, pp.185–99. See also Grünberg, II (*Archiv für die Geschichte des Sozialismus*, vol. VII).

Party Executive) appeared and was at once asked to report on his trip. The account was bound to be discouraging showing as it did the breakdown of international links and the growing sense of isolation. Late in the evening a vote took place after a number of speeches on both sides; of the ninety-two deputies present only fourteen (including Haase himself, Ledebour and Karl Liebknecht) were in favour of opposing the war credits. The next day Haase sacrificed his own beliefs to the solidarity of the party, just as Jaurès had done in 1904, and on 4 August declared in the Reichstag the Socialist support for the prosecution of the war.

'We are confronted by an hour big with fate. The consequences of the Imperialist policy, by which an epoch of competitive armaments was brought in and the antagonisms between the nations accentuated, have broken upon Europe like a deluge. The responsibility for this rests upon those who followed this policy: we disclaim it. Social Democracy has fought this ominous development with all its strength and right up to the last moment it was worked for the preservation of peace by means of powerful demonstrations in all countries and especially in intimate agreement with our French brothers. Its efforts have been in vain. For our people and its peaceful development, much, if not everything, is at stake in the event of the victory of Russian despotism which has stained itself with the blood of the best of its own people. Our task is to ward off this danger, to safeguard the culture and the independence of our own country . . . .'[1]

Those who had successfully urged this course felt themselves unable to do otherwise: they believed genuinely, as Bebel had done, in their duty to resist what was represented as a Russian attack, and they did not notice what was happening in the West, nor do they even seem to have been very upset by the breach of Belgian neutrality announced by Bethmann-Hollweg in the course of his speech in the Reichstag. As Müller had learnt in

---

[1] E. Bernstein, *Die Internationale der Arbeiter-Klasse und der Europäische Krieg* (Tübingen 1916), pp.20–21; Bevan, pp.20–1; W. E. Walling, *Socialism and the War* (New York 1915), p.143; Grunberg, I, p.448.

Paris, while the French Socialists were voting war credits to resist the Germans, the German Social Democrats were voting to defend themselves against the Russians. But above all, as in Austria, there was the feeling that any other action would be a betrayal of the interests and intentions of the rank and file.

One of the back-bench members expressed this clearly in a letter to a friend:

'On 3 August Dittmann and I travelled from Dortmund to Berlin to attend the party meeting on that day, at which the question of voting the war-credits was to be decided . . . . I shall never forget the crowded incidents of those days. I saw reservists join the columns and go forth singing Social Democrat songs! Some Socialist reservists I knew said to me: "We are going to the front with an easy mind because we know the Party will look after us if we are wounded, and that the Party will take care of our families if we don't come home." Just before the train started for Berlin, a group of reservists at the station said to me: "König, you're going to Berlin, to the Reichstag: think of us there: see to it that we have all we need: don't be stingy in voting money." In the train I told Dittmann what a deep impression all this had made upon me. Dittmann confessed that things had happened to him, too, which affected him in the same way. For hours, as the train carried us towards Berlin, we discussed the whole situation, what our attitude should be to national defence, whether the party would vote the credits. We came to the final conclusion that the Party was absolutely bound to vote the credits, that, if any difference of opinion came up in the meeting, that was the line we should have to take. Dittmann wound up by saying: "The Party could not act otherwise. It would rouse a storm of indignation among men at the front and people at home against the Social Democratic Party if it did. The Socialist organization would be swept clean away by popular resentment." '[1]

It was in Germany that this decision of the Social Democrats

[1] *Vossische Zeitung*, 5 May 1916. Printed in Bevan p.15. Cf. also the similar experiences recorded in Konrad Haenisch, *Die deutsche Sozialdemokratie in und nach dem Weltkriege* (Berlin 1919), p.20.

to support the war was most striking. This, the most powerful Socialist party in the world, had hitherto publicly dissociated itself from the German state. (Indeed, at the last prorogation of the Reichstag, the Socialist deputies, instead of leaving the hall before the traditional cheers for the Kaiser, had remained there ostentatiously refusing to rise to their feet, and some of the Prussian conservatives were pressing for their prosecution.) And, in turn, the German state had on several occasions publicly disowned the Socialists—'fellows without a country' (*Vaterlandslose Gesellen*) the Kaiser had called them in a much quoted phrase. So the unanimous voting of the war credits by the Socialists in the Reichstag (only one, Fritz Kunert, slipped out of the Chamber before the vote and tried to claim credit for this later when the war was losing popularity), and the unanimous tone of resigned patriotism in the socialist press were both surprising and welcome, for at last the German working class seemed to be integrated into the German community and one of the main stresses in German society thus temporarily appeased. There had not yet been time to count the cost.

In no other Socialist party was the struggle about whether to support the war or not so prolonged or so important. The French Socialists, in spite of the confusion and depression produced by Jaurès' death, do not seem to have hesitated a moment. Even before the German declaration of war on France on 3 August, there were only a very few who were not ready to vote war credits: and after that they were unanimous, so that the parliamentary group unquestioningly voted the credits on 4 August—the afternoon of Jaurès' funeral. Indeed Jaurès himself had publicly praised the will for peace of the Government: and his whole teaching had implied that it was legitimate to support the Government when the country was attacked and invaded. It was only later, when the movement against war had revived after 1916, that the militants on the left tried to claim that Jaurès would have been on their side had he lived. For the ordinary party member the situation was none the less painful, and the pressure, social and emotional, to which he was subjected, was strong.[1] For although the Government on 30 July took the decision not to arrest the militant socialists, syndicalists and anarchists listed on the *Carnet B*, the penalty for desertion was death.

'I have only one reproach to make to myself . . . .,' a French Syndicalist wrote later, 'and it is that I, an anti-patriot and anti-militarist, left with my comrades on the fourth day of mobilization. I did not have the strength of character not to go, although I did not recognize frontiers or fatherland. I was afraid, it's true, of the gallows. I was afraid . . . . But at the front, thinking of my family, scratching the names of my wife and son on the bottom of the trench I said "How is it possible that I, anti-patriot, anti-militarist, who acknowledged only the International, come to be attacking my companions in misery and perhaps shall die for my enemies against my own cause and my own interests?" '[2]

The Austrian Social Democrats, too, voted for the war credits. Although their paper had disclaimed all responsibility for the ultimatum to Serbia and declared their international solidarity with 'the class-conscious workers of the whole world and not least with the Social Democrats of Serbia',[3] yet when the moment came they felt they could not stand aside. 'I know we must vote for it (the war credits). I just don't know how I opened my mouth to say so,' Adler said. And then he sketched the whole dilemma of Austrian and, indeed, international Social Democracy. 'An incomprehensible German to have done anything else. An incomprehensible Social Democrat to have done it without being racked with pain, without a hard struggle with himself and with all his feelings.'[4]

[1] The atmosphere has been vividly recaptured in Roger Martin du Gard's novel *L'Eté 1914* (Paris 1936).
[2] Dolléans, II, p.221 n.
[3] Quoted in Bernstein, *Die Internationale*, p.14.
[4] O. Bauer, Introduction to Adler, *Aufsätze*, VI, p. xxix.

In fact, the attitude of the Austrian Social Democrats was one implicit in their attitude to the national question. Even with the best will in the world they had always been a German party, and a German party they were to remain. They had regretted the separation of Austria from Germany in 1866; they were to be the first to demand an *Anschluss* with Germany in 1918. So it is not surprising to find their paper, the *Arbeiterzeitung*, publishing on 5 August a notorious leading article called *The Day of the German Nation*, and praising the action of the German Social Democratic Party. The Czech Social Democrats were non-committal; but the Poles in the Monarchy came out in more enthusiastic support of the war against Czarism than anyone else, proclaiming 'this struggle to be their highest duty'.[1] The Austrian Socialists' support for the war, in any case, was bound to be somewhat academic: for, the war credits once voted, the parliament was adjourned and did not meet again until 1917, when all was crumbling and there were more powerful forces opposing the war than the Socialists could muster.

Elsewhere the pattern was the same: an irresistible tide sweeping men off to the war with only a few standing against it.

'It was a strange London on Sunday,' Beatrice Webb noted on the following Tuesday, 'crowded with excursionists to London and baulked would-be travellers to the continent, all in a state of suppressed uneasiness and excitement. We sauntered through the crowd to Trafalgar Square where Labour, socialist, pacifist demonstrators—with a few trade union flags—were gesticulating from the steps of the monuments to a mixed crowd of admirers, hooligan warmongers and merely curious holiday-makers. It was an undignified and futile exhibition, this singing of the Red Flag and passing of well-worn radical resolutions in favour of universal peace.'[2]

But for England, standing outside the European social democratic world, the crisis was as much one of the liberal as of the

[1] Grünberg, I, p.479.
[2] *Beatrice Webb's Diaries, 1912-1924*, p.25.

socialist conscience; and five members of the Liberal Government resigned rather than be party to the war. The Labour Party for the most part supported the war, with only a few individuals opposing it. Hyndman had already become strongly anti-German and became an active patriotic propagandist. And among the conscientious objectors perhaps as many were inspired by a religious pacifism as by a socialist dogma. For Keir Hardie, the figure in the British Labour movement most prominent at International Congresses, the situation took on the aspect of a personal drama: 'I understand what Christ suffered in Gethsemane as well as any man living.'[1] (One can see why some people found him a conceited man.) His political part in fact had been played: and he died a year later, old and broken.

In two of the belligerent countries alone did the socialist representatives make the hopeless but courageous gestures of voting against the credits demanded for the war—Serbia and Russia. In Serbia the two Socialist deputies, while condemning the Austrian ultimatum, condemned equally Serbian nationalism and the power politics and secret diplomacy of the great powers. In the Russian Duma, too, Bolsheviks and Mensheviks (fourteen altogether), united temporarily with the eleven members of Kerensky's Labour Party in abstaining from the vote and disclaiming all responsibility for the war; and soon the Social Democrats began working for a revolution, in spite of an appeal from Vandervelde, calling on them to support the allied cause. ('I know and share your sentiments with regard to Czarism', he wrote to the Menshevik leader, Tchkeidze, on 11 August, 'But I am asking you—and our poor Jaurès, if he were still alive, would certainly ask you too—to take a general view of the situation of social democracy in Europe.'[2]) Outside Russia Plekhanov and the veteran Anarchist Kropotkin, who had prac-

[1] Stewart, *Keir Hardie*, p.365.
[2] Vandervelde, *Souvenirs d'un militant socialiste* (Paris 1934), pp.185–6.

tical experience of the benefits of British and French liberal institutions, supported the allied cause. But Lenin's position was clear and unequivocal. At the outbreak of the war he was in Galicia and was arrested as a potential spy. He was only released when Victor Adler had personally assured the Minister of the Interior that Lenin was a fanatical enemy of Czarism. (These acts of socialist solidarity and personal kindness were soon omitted from the official Communist accounts of the period.) Again with Adler's help, he made his way to Switzerland in September and at once began to preach revolution and a new International: 'Overwhelmed by opportunism the Second International has died. Down with opportunism and long live the Third International . . . .!'[1]

3.

As soon as the French, German and Austrian Socialists had voted in favour of the war credits the Second International in effect ceased to exist. And just as the Stuttgart and Copenhagen resolutions had come to nothing with the cessation of the 'war on war', so the Amsterdam resolution that forbade co-operation with bourgeois parties and the entry of Socialists into bourgeois governments was equally rapidly abandoned.

Vandervelde was the first leading Socialist to join his country's government. Indeed, for him and his colleagues there was no problem, for they could with justice disclaim all responsibility for a war in which nobody had expected Belgium to be involved. When German troops appeared on Belgian soil the consciences of the Belgian Socialists were clear and Vandervelde immediately accepted an invitation to become a member of the Government. In Germany a *Burgfrieden* was proclaimed, in France a *Union sacrée*. German Socialists suddenly found themselves invited to army headquarters; one Socialist deputy, Ludwig Frank, was among the early casualties. And although they still

[1] Lenin, *Collected Works* (New York 1930), XVIII, p.89.

refused to attend court functions (there is a story that the Kaiser erroneously thought that Scheidemann was at his reception of parliamentary leaders after the declaration of war and said to a bewildered member of the Conservatives: 'I am particularly glad to see *you* here, Herr Scheidemann'), they played an active and co-operative part in the war effort. In France, within a month of the outbreak of war, and in the critical moments of initial military defeat, Guesde and Marcel Sembat had become members of the 'Government of National Defence': 'The national unity, which at the beginning of the war once more revealed itself and comforted our hearts, must display all its power. The entire nation must rise for the defence of its soil and its liberty in one of those outbursts of heroism which always repeat themselves in similar hours of our history . . . . We are struggling that the world, freed from the shifting oppression of Imperialism and from the atrocities of war, may finally enjoy peace in respecting the rights of all. The Socialist ministers will communicate this conviction to the whole Government. With it they will animate its work. They will share it with the heroic army, where the flower of the nation fights today. And, by persevering effort and forceful enthusiasm, they will at the same time assure the safety of the country and the progress of humanity.'[1] And Edouard Vaillant who, like Keir Hardie, was to die the following year, threw himself into support of the war. 'How can your members work by the side of Briand and Millerand?' he was asked by a journalist. 'We must only judge them by their actions now and in the future,' he replied. 'In the interests of the country at large we cannot, at this critical moment, consider their actions in the past.'[2] The arguments once used by Millerand were now adopted by those formerly his

---

[1] Declaration of the Socialist Parliamentary Group, the Permanent Administrative Commission and the Administrative Council of *L'Humanité*. Quoted in H. W. Humphrey, *International Socialism and the War* (London 1915), pp.83–4.
[2] Humphrey, pp.81–2.

most bitter opponents. Guesde's prophecy of 1900 was fulfilled: 'With an Italian Millerand, a German Millerand, an English Millerand there would be no International possible any more.'[1]

[1] See p.97 above.

EPILOGUE

Once the war had started and the majority of socialists in nearly all the belligerent countries had rallied to policies of national defence, it was hard to see what was left of the ideals and hopes of the International. Nevertheless, internationalism was so deeply rooted in the socialist tradition that efforts were made on both sides to show that the movement was still an international one. The International Socialist Bureau continued to exist under the guidance of Camille Huysmans, who organized its removal from Brussels to The Hague, in the hope that it could continue to operate from neutral territory. Vandervelde, the president of the Bureau, like most of the Belgian socialists, was far from neutral and was convinced of the justice of the Allied cause and of the wrong done to his country by the German invasion. Huysmans tried, not without success, to maintain a semblance of neutrality and some freedom of movement, and concentrated on keeping the International Bureau in being. Consequently he resented any proposals by the socialists in the neutral countries which seemed to take the initiative out of his hands.

While the British, French and Belgian socialists were establishing links with each other, and while the relations between the German and Austrian Social Democrats continued, as before the war, to be very close, both groups were active in attempts to influence socialist opinion in the neutral countries. The Germans sent emissaries to put their case to the neutrals: Scheidemann went to the Netherlands, Südekum to Italy and Roumania, while the Russian-born journalist, Alexander Help-

hand, who had made his name as a theorist on the left wing of
the German party under the pseudonym of Parvus, and who
was to continue active in clandestine international activity
throughout the war, was busy in Constantinople conducting
anti-Russian propaganda in Bulgaria and Roumania and putting forward to the German authorities plans for revolutionary
subversion in Russia itself. For these propagandists, the war
remained primarily one against Russian autocracy, just as the
Allied socialists emphasized the liberal and democratic nature of
the French and British states and the oppressive and militarist
character of the Kaiser's Germany.

In the first months of the war, too, the socialists in the
neutral countries hoped to do more than resist passively the
propaganda of the belligerent socialist parties. As long as Italy
remained out of the war, the position of the Italian socialists
was crucial, but within three months they were bitterly divided.
By November 1914, Benito Mussolini, the editor of the socialist
newspaper *Avanti!* and one of the most effective socialist
journalists and agitators, who had been in the forefront of the
opposition to the Italian attack on Libya in 1911, had decided
to come out in favour of Italian intervention on the side of
France and Britain. Within a few months he and his followers
had broken with his party and he became, with some discreet
financial support from the French, one of the leaders of the
popular campaign which brought Italy into the war in May
1915.

However, in 1914 the majority of the Italian socialists opposed the war and remained faithful to their undertakings as
members of the International. In the winter of 1914–15 they
were able to join with the Swiss socialists in an attempt—viewed
with some distrust by Huysmans and the official leaders of the
International—to revive the links between the parties severed
by the war. The leading figures on the Swiss side were Hermann
Greulich, a representative of the older generation of moderate

reformists in the Swiss trade unions, and Robert Grimm, a devious and subtle politician who not only believed in the necessity and possibility of international socialist action to end the war, but also believed that, at a time when the pressures of militarism in the belligerent countries prevented the socialists there from carrying on the class struggle, it was the duty of the militants in the neutral countries to keep the revolutionary tradition alive.

An Italian-Swiss socialist meeting at Lugano at the end of September 1914 showed the limits of the action open to the neutrals, since all that the conference was able to do was to ask the Swiss socialist leaders to urge the International Socialist Bureau to take some initiative, at least in summoning a meeting of neutral socialists.[1] Once the Italians were at war, the possibility of a neutral initiative was diminished still further, and the Swiss socialists had to limit themselves to acting as go-betweens, and to providing physical points of contact between those socialists on both sides who, from 1915 on, were in open opposition to the war. As far as the Italian socialists were concerned, once war was declared, they did not openly oppose it but were in the awkward situation of neither resisting nor supporting it, a policy which was expressed in the slogan '*nè aderire, nè sabotare*'.[2] It was a policy which, while it did credit to the intellectual consistency of the Italian socialist leaders, served to alienate the party from the Italian state, with disastrous results in the post-war years.

In other belligerent countries, it was in 1915 that a current of opposition to the war began to be visible in the working-class movement. We are only at the beginning of the detailed research which is required to give us any insight into popular reactions to the war or which will enable us to analyse how much active

[1] See Yves Collart, *Le Parti Socialiste Suisse et l'Internationale 1914–1915* (Geneva 1969), p.126.

[2] See Leo Valiani, *Il Partito Socialista Italiano nel periodo della Neutralità 1914–1915* (Milan 1963).

opposition, as opposed to passive grumbling, there was to a war the length and destructiveness of which none of the governments who had embarked on it had foreseen. On the surface, however, a few voices were raised publicly to call for an end to the slaughter, and a very small minority, of whom Lenin was the most consistent, repeated the call to turn the war into a civil war and to use the opportunity to start the revolution.

The apparent unanimity among the Social Democratic members of the German Reichstag was first broken by Karl Liebknecht, who, in December 1914, voted against a renewal of the war credits. In March 1915, he was joined by one more socialist deputy, and thirty-one of his colleagues abstained. During the next eighteen months the split in the party grew, and the parliamentary leader, Hugo Haase, who in August, 1914 had only voted in favour of war credits out of solidarity with the rest of the party and against his own instincts, finally broke the party unity in March 1916 and was formally expelled. In April 1917 the breach was formalized and an Independent Social Democratic Party came into being. At the same time, outside parliament, isolated opposition to the war grew: Rosa Luxemburg, who had been imprisoned in February 1915, and Karl Liebknecht, first conscripted and then imprisoned, wrote a series of pamphlets published under the pseudonym of Junius reasserting the necessity for the unremitting conduct of the class war instead of support for a nationalist and capitalist struggle. This group, known first as the *Gruppe Internationale* and then as the Spartacus group (after the famous slave revolutionary of Roman times), together with some revolutionary cells among the industrial shop-stewards, provided an active left-wing to the Independent Socialist movement and went further than their insistence on ending the war and negotiating peace. The divisions in the German Social Democratic movement became so deep that they were never wholly healed.

In France, it was in the syndicalist movement and among a

few sections of the socialist party—mostly those remote from
the battle front and the occupied territories—that the first
opposition to the war and to the *Union Sacrée* began to be
expressed. Among the syndicalists, the metal workers were the
most important representatives of this trend; and Alphonse
Merrheim, the secretary of the metal workers' union, the
Syndicat des Métaux, became its main spokesman, together
with the veteran syndicalist leader from the south of France,
Pierre Monatte, who in December 1914 resigned from the
national committee of the CGT because of its refusal to respond
positively to an invitation from the Scandinavian socialist
parties to send a representative to a conference of neutral
socialists in Copenhagen. These were protests which aimed at
an end to the war rather than at social revolution, and, as yet, in
1915, they found little support, though they were the basis for
a growing movement as the war dragged on.

In Austria, it was not until the autumn of 1916 that there was
an open breach in the solidarity of the socialists and a startling
and dramatic protest against the government and against the
socialist leaders' acceptance of its policies. The secretary of the
Austrian Social Democratic party, Friedrich Adler, the son of
its venerated founder, soon found himself in bitter opposition
to the policy of support for the war, a policy of which his
father, though in rapidly failing health, was the chief advocate.
As the war dragged on into its third year he became convinced
that the only possibility of giving expression to his views, in a
country where the press was censored and parliament per-
manently prorogued, was to commit an act of such startling
violence that, at least in the courtroom he would have an
opportunity, while making his defence, to attack the entire
system. Accordingly, after careful reflection, he decided to
assassinate the Austrian Prime Minister, Count Stürgkh.
Stürgkh lunched every day at the same restaurant in Vienna,
and it was easy enough for Fritz Adler, a nervous, donnish

figure with a stoop and a long moustache, to find a table from which the Prime Minister would be within pistol range. After ordering a meal of several courses, so as not to arouse suspicion by lingering too long over empty plates, and waiting until he was sure that there was nobody near Stürgkh who might be accidentally wounded, he walked quickly across to the Prime Minister's table. 'Count Stürgkh?', he asked, to be quite certain there was no mistake, and shot him dead.

It was an act which had surprisingly few consequences: Fritz Adler was given the opportunity to make his political appeal during the trial, and was allowed remarkable latitude to do so, with only a few protests from the judge telling him not 'to speak out of the window'. He rejected angrily his father's suggestion that the act was the result of the mental instability inherited from his mother's family. But the proceedings were overtaken by events to which the socialist opposition contributed little. While Adler was still in prison the revolution of October 1918 broke out, the multinational empire fell apart under the strain of military defeat and the defection of its subject nationalities. Adler was liberated from prison and found himself the hero of the Viennese revolutionaries, to live for over forty years trying rather ineffectually to heal the breaches in the post-war international socialist movement.

All the socialists and syndicalists who protested against the continuance of the war thought of themselves as carrying on the tradition of the International and were anxious to re-establish links with socialists abroad, including those in enemy countries, in spite of the difficulties of making personal contact in wartime and in spite of the lack of information available about comparable movements elsewhere. The congress of the Scandinavian and Dutch socialists in Copenhagen, even if it was not able to re-establish any links between socialists on the opposing sides, at least began a discussion of war aims and the possible conditions for a negotiated peace; and such ideas were not without their effect on the development of thinking about a post-war settlement, especially in the United States. An international congress of socialist women was organized in Berne in March 1915, by Klara Zetkin, a supporter of the anti-war minority in the German party, and it provided the first occasion on which socialists from England, Germany and France could meet one another, even without the official sanction of their respective parties, and even if their numbers were very small. It was as a gesture rather than a practical step that this meeting had any importance, especially as it was very little noticed in the press; and the same is true of an international conference of socialist youth movements held a week later (the first venture at organization of the German Willi Münzenberg, later to be the famous and mysterious leader of the Young Communists in the 1920s and 1930s), at which no representatives from the Allied countries were present.

More significant, though in its historical perspective rather than in its immediate achievements, was the conference organized, again with the Swiss as hosts, at Zimmerwald from 5 to 8 September 1915. The Zimmerwald Conference has its place in revolutionary history, for it has subsequently been claimed to mark the moment to which the origins of the Third International can be traced. Indeed, the presence of Lenin, who lived in Zürich from the outbreak of the war until his return to Russia in April 1917, expressing the views which he had continuously maintained since the Stuttgart Congress of the International in 1907, certainly makes it in some sense a link between the old International and the Communist movement. In fact, at the time it seemed a small affair and attracted little attention: less than forty delegates, several of them representing only themselves, and several of them, like Lenin and Zinoviev, already living in isolated exile in Switzerland, assembled in a modest Swiss pension, the Kurhaus Beau-Séjour. There is a certain truth in Trotsky's comment: 'The delegates themselves

joked over the fact that half a century after the foundation of the
First International, it was still possible to seat all the internationalists in four coaches. But they were not sceptical. The
thread of history often breaks—then a new knot must be tied.
This is what we were doing at Zimmerwald.'[1]

It was in fact hard for those delegates not already in Switzerland to attend at all. The Italian socialist Morgari had visited
Paris and had tried to persuade Vandervelde, as president of the
International, and the French socialist leaders to take the lead in
summoning a conference, but had met with a total refusal. As
a result it was the Italian socialists and the indefatigable Robert
Grimm who organized the meeting. Neither the French nor the
German parties were officially represented, and the British
delegates, from the Independent Labour Party and the British
Socialist Party, were refused passports by the British government. A group of Russian émigrés, Martov, Axelrod and
Trotsky himself, were able to come from Paris, where Trotsky
was collaborating with the Menshevik Martov in editing an
obscure Russian revolutionary daily newspaper—an activity
which was to lead to his expulsion from France a year later and
to a move to New York. Alphonse Merrheim and a left-wing
socialist, Bourderon, were the only French representatives. The
German group, bringing greetings from the imprisoned Karl
Liebknecht, and knowing that Klara Zetkin had just been
arrested for her activities in connection with the socialist
women's conference earlier in the year, were led by Ledebour,
who was bitterly attacked by Lenin for not adopting a more
openly revolutionary line.

The discussions soon revealed the lines of division within the
minority movement, with Lenin representing a minority within
the minority, when he repeated his call for a new International
and for the conversion of the war into a revolutionary civil war.
Most of the delegates, however, were concerned above all to

[1] Leon Trotsky, *My Life* (London 1930), p.214.

find ways of putting an end to the slaughter, and for them the main point of the congress was the re-establishment of links with other socialists in the hope of restoring some measure of international socialist co-operation for the purpose of ending the war rather than of bringing about immediate revolution. A declaration by the French and German representatives under-lined their intention to denounce the *Union Sacrée* and the *Burgfrieden*, and 'while remaining firmly attached to the class struggle which served as a basis for the constitution of the socialist international', to 'struggle among our fellow-citizens against this terrible calamity and for the end of the hostilities which have dishonoured humanity.'[1] The sentiments of Zim-merwald were not very far removed from those of Stuttgart or Basle.

The under-current of criticism of the war continued to swell during 1916 and contributed to the political crisis which con-fronted all the belligerent governments between the autumn of 1916 and the autumn of 1917. The activities of the Zimmerwald movement therefore tended to be overshadowed by more wide-spread evidence of unrest. However, the attempt to establish new links between the various socialist parties continued: an Italian–Swiss committee, with Robert Grimm as secretary, kept the movement going and received messages of adherence from groups in the neutral countries and isolated minority organiza-tions in the belligerent states. Of the major socialist parties, the Italians were alone in declaring their support for the Zimmer-wald line. It was clear that the split in the old International which Zimmerwald had marked was going to increase in size and continue more and more to divide the international socialist movement.

Grimm and the other members of the committee in Switzer-land decided that events were moving so fast that it would be

---

[1] Alfred Rosmer, *Le Mouvement ouvrier pendant la guerre: I. de l'union sacrée à Zimmerwald* (Paris 1936), p.378.

advisable to hold another conference within a few months of the first; and in April 1916, under conditions of some secrecy, a further meeting was held at Kienthal, in the Swiss Alps. It was even harder than in the previous year for delegates to get there: Trotsky could not obtain a passport or visa; Merrheim and Bourderon were refused permission to leave France, as the government had been attacked when it had become known that they had actually met Germans on neutral soil in the previous year. Three French socialist deputies succeeded in attending, but they were thought not to be representative of the main opposition groups in France. None of the better known members of the German left could come. While, of the forty-five representatives from nine countries who were present, more were now prepared to support Lenin and the Left than at Zimmerwald, the majority were still not ready to vote for a complete break with the majority of socialists and with the old International. Once again, the emphasis was on organizing pressure on governments to end the war and on the socialist leaders to vote against war credits; and once again the participants had difficulty in obtaining adequate press coverage for their resolutions.

During 1916 and 1917 the governments of all the states at war began to be aware both of the necessity of retaining the support of the organized working-class movement and of the danger which vigorous working-class action might present to the war effort. There were impressive strikes in Germany in March and April 1917, and a series of mutinies in the French army following the disastrous failure and heavy casualties of the spring offensive of 1917; but the movement of revolt was largely one against the economic hardships of war and against the iniquities in the distribution of the ever scarcer supplies of food, or, in the case of the French mutinies, against the apparently pointless slaughter on the western front, rather than in favour of the social revolution for which Lenin and the Zim-

merwald Left were calling. As a result, the demands of liberals
and socialists for a just peace and an end to the war seemed
almost indistinguishable, while the possibilities of specifically
socialist international action still seemed rather remote.

The event which changed the situation and the whole history
of the international socialist movement was the Russian Revolution. The February Revolution of 1917 and the fact that, from
May, supporters of the Zimmerwald movement were in the
Russian government, forced the Allies to think seriously about
the nature of their war aims in the hope of keeping the Russians
in the war while, at the same time, the entry of the United
States into the war and President Wilson's insistence that
America was fighting for a new international order, revived
discussion of possible peace terms. In October 1917, the Bolshevik revolution transformed the position of Lenin and the
Bolsheviks, so that instead of being a minority within a minority
of the international socialist movement, they were able, within
the next two years, as leaders of a victorious if still beleaguered
revolutionary government, to carry out Lenin's long-maintained
intention and found a Third International.

It was in 1917 that the future of the Second International was
decided, because it was in this year that the revolutionary
challenge from the left really became serious and because many
of the beliefs about international relations which socialists had
propagated for many years were now accepted by all liberals
who were working for 'a peace without annexations and
indemnities'. As President Wilson was calling for a new
international order based on open covenants openly arrived at,
disarmament, arbitration and the self-determination of peoples,
many of the ideals of the International seemed to have found a
non-socialist champion, anxious to meet the threat of revolution
by the adoption of some revolutionary ideas himself.[1] Finally, it

[1] See Arno J. Mayer, *Wilson versus Lenin. Political Origins of the New
Diplomacy 1917–1918* (New Haven 1959).

was in 1917 that, under pressure from the socialist rank and file
in many countries, and in the hope of meeting the Russian
provisional government's desire for peace, a last unsuccessful
attempt at an international socialist congress was made.[1]

The initiative came from the Russians, and for a short time it
looked as though Huysmans and the International Socialist
Bureau might reluctantly take up the idea so as to avoid being
outflanked by the Left. However, it soon became clear that
neither Vandervelde and the Belgians nor many of the leading
French and British socialists would be willing to sit at a conference table with the German majority socialists, at least until
they had come out openly against their government and against
the war. As a result, the Russian government tried to organize
a conference at Stockholm in association with the Dutch and
Scandinavian socialist parties, and especially with the Swedish
socialist leader, Hjalmar Branting, whose sympathies with the
Allies were well known and who therefore carried considerable
weight with the French and British. Although there was in the
spring of 1917 considerable enthusiasm for the idea among the
rank and file of the socialist movement, so that the leaders of
the French socialist party were forced to abandon their hostility
of the congress, nothing in fact came of it. The date was postponed several times, and finally the congress was never held.
This was mainly because the French and British governments
remained firmly opposed to the proposal. The French government, at the insistence of the army leaders, preoccupied with
the crisis in the morale of the French troops, refused to grant
passports to the socialists wishing to attend, while in Britain the
government's hostility was made all the more convincing by the
fact that a powerful working-class group, the Seamen's Union,
refused to allow Ramsay Macdonald, the pacifist leader of the

[1] See Hildamarie Meynell, 'The conference of Stockholm', *International
Review of Social History*, Vol. V (1960), pp.1–25, 202–25, and Marc Ferro,
The Russian Revolution of February 1917 (London 1972), pp.234–52.

Independent Labour Party, to embark on the ship that was to have taken him to Stockholm.

The situation was further complicated by the divisions on the left of the socialist movement. While the Russian provisional government placed its hopes in the Stockholm conference, Lenin and the 'Zimmerwald Left' were opposed to the idea of any co-operation with the pro-government socialists in Germany, France or Britain and continued to call for a complete break with the past and for the foundation of a new revolutionary Third International. The cause of the Left, however, was not helped by the rumours—which were true, as evidence which was only published some forty years later has shown—that Robert Grimm, the Swiss secretary of the Zimmerwald committee had been in touch with German officials, not just in order to make possible the journey of Lenin back to Russia in April 1917, but also in order to provide a channel through which German secret service funds had reached the Bolsheviks and other Russian opposition groups.

Thus the proposals for an international socialist congress at Stockholm, rather than marking a resuscitation of the Second International and a re-establishment of organized links between the socialist parties only served to emphasize the complex divisions in the socialist world. If the Second International had died in July 1914, it was interred at Stockholm in 1917.

2.

By 1917 the international solidarity of the socialist world was broken. Although the Second International was revived after the war under the name of the Labour and Socialist International, it never acquired the influence or prestige of its predecessor. The attempts made in the early 1920s, notably by Friedrich Adler, to reunite the Socialist and Communist Internationals in what was soon nicknamed the 'Two-and-a-Half International', broke down, as the enmity between socialists and communists grew. The Third International remained, until its dissolution in 1943 (a gesture by the Soviet Union towards inter-allied solidarity in the Second World War), an effective means of imposing the policies of the Soviet Union on the communist parties outside Russia, but it based itself on a total rejection of the old International, the history of which was regarded as evidence for the failure of social democracy and a justification for the discipline and ruthlessness of the communist movement.

From 1918 onwards the social democrats were going to have to fight on two fronts; and their critics could maintain that their parties had become indistinguishable from bourgeois parties, their leaders no different from bourgeois politicians, their officials indistinguishable from bourgeois civil servants. By the middle of the twentieth century the reformists had gained control; and it was significant that in 1958 the Social Democratic Party in the German Federal Republic dropped all Marxist doctrine from its programme. Yet the experiences of socialists in the great days of the Second International had been unforgettable ones which had left their mark on socialist thought and above all on political organization. Political life in Europe was never to be the same again.

The parties in the International, and especially the great German-speaking parties in Germany and Austria had come to embrace more and more of the life of their members, while the Marxist doctrine as interpreted by the great theorists of the Second International, Plekhanov, Kautsky and the rest, produced answers to every problem. And for the ordinary party member there were innumerable little pamphlets stating the crude truths of dialectical materialism in simple language. Membership of a Socialist party was for many Europeans much the same as membership of a church, and a church whose own laws would ensure its triumph.

A description by Joseph Buttinger of his own early years

in the Austrian Social Democratic Party gives an idea of the range of the party's activities and the flavour of the socialist world:

> 'Spurred on by the socialist press, he furiously participated in the "cultural endeavours of the working class" by attending every evening lecture, never missing a rehearsal of the Socialist Glee Club, partaking in every excursion of the party's "Friends of Nature" and even becoming a socialist folk dancer and amateur actor. From the Workers' Co-operative he acquired his first toothbrush, and from the Workers' Library he borrowed his first book, *The Origin of Private Property, the Family and the State* by Friedrich Engels. As a "matter of principle" he now changed his shirt once a week . . . .'[1]

It is obvious how useful and attractive this kind of all-embracing organization could be in a period of rapid economic expansion and violent industrial competition.

In England some of the nonconformist churches had from time to time done something to lessen the rigours of the industrial revolution and provide the industrial worker with a centre of interest and a focus for his social life. On the Continent, or at least in the Catholic countries, the Church, despite the good intentions of a few social reformers, was irrevocably on the side of the established order. Thus the Socialist movement was vigorously anti-clerical, and it was the declaration of a Social Democrat's faith to label himself as '*Konfessionslos*' (no religion) when he had to fill in an official form or to register himself for military service. Here again Social Democracy took the place of a church, with the professional politicians and agitators as its Jesuits (a fact which Bismarck recognized when drafting his anti-socialist legislation, where the professional agitators were liable to the same penalties as the Jesuits had

---

[1] Joseph Buttinger, *In the Twilight of Socialism* (New York 1954), p.389. Cf. also Guenther Roth, *The Social Democrats in Imperial Germany* (Totowa, N.J. 1963).

been during the *Kulturkampf* a few years earlier).

Such a movement, which went far beyond the bounds of what is normally considered the function of a political party, could produce examples of touching devotion and self-sacrifice, and it soon developed its own code of morals. It was to have its fanatics and its puritans as well as its heretics and its schismatics. Many socialists followed an austere ideal of personal behaviour which made them eschew all luxury that might raise them above the level of the ordinary worker.[1] Marriage was often despised as a bourgeois institution, but 'free love' took the form of life-long fidelity to a 'loyal companion for life'. Some socialists were earnest teetotallers; a few became vegetarians. This high-minded devotion to a common cause and to fellow human beings, though it could lead to a priggish intolerance, could also be one of the most attractive aspects of socialist life and do much to compensate for the arid doctrines and unscrupulous political behaviour of some of the movement's leaders. These are not exclusively socialist virtues; and they have survived within the socialist movement after the Marxism with which they were associated has lost its power—in the communal settlements of Israel, for example, which owe so much to the Russian Menshevik tradition and have an ancestry that goes back beyond Marx to the dreams of earlier utopian socialists.

The truth is that in practice Marxist social democracy was tempered by liberal ideals; and this gave it both its strength and its weakness. The slogans which the Danish Socialists thought suitable to decorate the hall at Copenhagen where the International held its congress in 1910, remind us how much of an older tradition had survived the Marxist efforts at *Gleichschaltung*:

> Labour is the source of wealth.
> We build on solidarity.

[1] The present writer remembers entertaining a foreign trade unionist whose comment on seeing the menu in a London restaurant was: '*Feines Essen hab' ich nicht gern.*'

Knowledge is strength.

Religion is a private matter.

Removal of class differences.

No private monopolies.

The Will of the People is the highest law.

Universal equal suffrage.

A maximum working day of eight hours.

Disarmament means peace.

One and the same law for women and men.

Liberty, Equality, Fraternity.

The trouble with these eclectic slogans was that they had been so often repeated that they had little to do with practical politics. Rosa Luxemburg saw this danger and bitterly attacked Jaurès for his faith in the incantatory power of such phrases.

'The melodies Jaurès still sings', she wrote, 'remind me of the good old arias of Verdi: once in sunny Italy they were on the lips of every happy, dark-eyed urchin like the promise of a people's spring, and now we hear them still, but ground out with horrible monotony on barrel-organs: *Tempi passati!* And the organ-grinder stares into space with an air of detached boredom as he grinds; the same songs, but the spirit has gone.'[1]

Yet Rosa Luxemburg herself was more deeply imbued with liberal principles than she ever admitted. She believed in 1918 that a revolution could only be made on the basis of a spontaneous rising of the working class, and would have found intolerable the compulsion and terror which the Bolsheviks were obliged continuously to use in order to make their revolution and maintain themselves in power; and just before her death she was complaining about Lenin's attempt to dictate to the new International. 'The proletarian revolution needs for its purposes no terror, it hates and abominates murder . . . ,' she wrote. 'It is no desperate attempt of a minority to fashion the world after its own ideal, but the action of the great mass of the

[1] Frölich, p.223.

millions of the people which is called to carry out the mission of history, to transform historical necessity into reality.'[1]

Had she lived she would have had to face more urgently and more practically than ever before the dilemma inherent in her position. On the one hand the Bolsheviks gave an example of a successful revolution under conditions never foreseen by Marx, while the German Social Democratic Party had failed to over-throw the structure of German society. On the other hand, it gradually became clear that the Russians had achieved their success only by discarding most of the liberal presuppositions which had become part of the international social democratic tradition. Many Socialists in Europe were ready, however reluctantly, to follow their example: the Communist parties owed their attraction to the Russian success. Each failure of Social Democracy, notably those of 1933 and 1934, gave new strength to Communist arguments.

> 'Our fatal unconfidence attempted a bridge
> Between revolution and the already providing
> World . . . .'[2]

When that bridge broke it was felt by many that the only hope lay in the strictness and ruthlessness of the Communist dis-cipline, backed by the strength of the Soviet Union. Many were later to regret their choice; disillusioned with Marxist Com-munism, they became in our day the most fanatical of the pro-fessional anti-Communists, just as the people educated in Jesuit schools had become the most determined anti-clericals a generation earlier.

Those Social Democrats who were unable to throw away their beliefs in humanity, liberty and democracy were in a more difficult position, especially where, as in France or Italy, they were faced with rich men unwilling to give up any of their

---

[1] *Bericht über den Gründungsparteitag der Kommunistischen Partei Deutsch-lands* (*Spartakusbund*), pp.49–56, quoted by E. H. Carr, *The Bolshevik Revolution 1917–1923* (London 1953), III, p.105.

[2] Stephen Spender, *Vienna* (London 1934), p.27.

privileges. The fortunate socialists were those in countries like Britain or Sweden where the course of practical reform was unimpeded by a general all-embracing theory about the nature of history and society. It is a great deal easier to think about old age pensions or a national health service if one is not obsessed by the idea of 'carrying out the mission of history' or 'transforming historical necessity into reality'. On the other hand, it is very hard to work for the overthrow of existing society if one is stopping by the way to improve the drainage system or the transport service.

The members of the European Socialist movement between 1880 and the Second World War were constantly faced with situations where they might have asked themselves whether Marxism and democracy were compatible, and whether Marxism provided a suitable basis for practical political action. Too often they were content simply to reaffirm Marxist dogmas without testing their validity; and, where they achieved political success, it was often in spite of, rather than because of, their assertions of doctrine. For it is doubtful whether a general all-embracing dogmatic theory of history and the nature of man can ever serve as a proper basis for political action in a society which believes in parliamentary government and personal liberty.

THE STUTTGART
RESOLUTION

MILITARISM AND INTERNATIONAL CONFLICTS

'The Congress confirms the resolutions of previous International Congresses against militarism and imperialism and declares anew that the fight against militarism cannot be separated from the socialist class war as a whole.

'Wars between capitalist states are as a rule the result of their rivalry for world markets, as every state is not only concerned in consolidating its own market, but also in conquering new markets, in which process the subjugation of foreign lands and peoples plays a major part. Further, these wars arise out of the never-ending armament race of militarism, which is one of the chief implements of bourgeois class-rule and of the economic and political enslavement of the working classes.

'Wars are encouraged by the prejudices of one nation against another, systematically purveyed among the civilized nations in the interest of the ruling classes, so as to divert the mass of the proletariat from the tasks of its own class, as well as from the duty of international class solidarity.

'Wars are therefore inherent in the nature of capitalism; they will only cease when capitalist economy is abolished, or when the magnitude of the sacrifice of human beings and money, necessitated by the technical development of warfare, and popular disgust with armaments, lead to the abolition of this system.

'That is why the working classes, which have primarily to furnish the soldiers and make the greatest material sacrifices, are natural enemies of war, which is opposed to their aim: the creation of an economic system based on socialist foundations, which will make a reality of the solidarity of nations.

'The Congress holds, therefore, that it is the duty of the working classes, and especially their representatives in parliaments, recognizing the class character of bourgeois society and the motive for the preservation of the opposition beween nations, to fight with all their strength against naval and military armament, and to refuse to supply the means for it, as well as to labour for the education of working class youth in the spirit of the brotherhood of nations and of socialism, and to see that it is filled with class consciousness.

'The Congress sees in the democratic organization of the army, in the popular militia instead of the standing army, an essential guarantee for the prevention of aggressive wars, and for facilitating the removal of differences between nations.

'The International is not able to lay down the exact form of working-class action against militarism at the right place and time, as this naturally differs in different countries. But its duty is to strengthen and co-ordinate the endeavours of the working classes against the war as much as possible.

'In fact since the International Congress in Brussels the proletariat, through its untiring fight against militarism by the refusal to supply means for military armament, and through its endeavours to make military organization democratic, has used the most various forms of action, with increasing vigour and success, to prevent the breaking out of wars or to make an end to them, as well as making use of the upheaval of society caused by the war for the purpose of freeing the working classes: for example, the agreement between English and French trade unions after the Fashoda incident to ensure peace and to re-establish friendly relations between England and France; the intervention of the Social Democratic parties in the German and French parliaments during the Morocco crisis; the announcements, prepared by French and German Socialists for the same purpose; the joint action of Austrian and Italian Socialists, who met in Trieste to prevent a conflict between the two states; further the emphatic intervention of the socialist trade unions in Sweden to prevent an attack on Norway; finally the heroic, self-sacrificing fight of the socialist workers and peasants in Russia and Poland in opposition to the Czarist-inspired war, to stop the war and to make use of the country's crisis for the liberation of the working classes.

'All these endeavours testify to the growing strength of the proletariat and to its power to ensure peace through decisive intervention; the action of the working classes will be the more successful the more their minds are prepared by suitable action, and the more they are encouraged and united by the International.

'The Congress is convinced that pressure by the proletariat could achieve the blessings of international disarmament through serious use of courts of arbitration instead of the pitiful machinations of governments. This would make it possible to use the enormous expenditure of money and strength which is swallowed by military armaments and war, for cultural purposes.

'In the case of a threat of an outbreak of war, it is the duty of the working classes and their parliamentary representatives in the countries taking part, fortified by the unifying activity of the International Bureau, to do everything to prevent the outbreak of war by whatever means seem to them most effective, which naturally differ with the intensification of the class war and of the general political situation.

'Should war break out in spite of all this, it is their duty to intercede for its speedy end, and to strive with all their power to make use of the violent economic and political crisis brought about by the war to rouse the people, and thereby to hasten the abolition of capitalist class rule.'

SELECT BIBLIOGRAPHY

ADLER, VICTOR, *Aufsätze, Reden und Briefe* (9 vols) (Vienna 1929).

—— *Briefwechsel mit August Bebel und Karl Kautsky* (ed. Friedrich Adler) (Vienna 1954).

ANDLER, CHARLES, *Le Socialisme impérialiste dans L'Allemagne contemporaine* (Paris 1918).

—— *La Décomposition politique du socialisme allemand 1914–1919* (Paris 1919).

—— *Vie de Lucien Herr* (Paris 1932).

BALABANOVA, ANGELICA, *Memoirs of a Zimmerwaldian* (Leningrad 1925).

—— *My life as a Rebel* (London 1938).

BAUER, OTTO, *Die Nationalitätenfrage und die Sozialdemokratie* (Vienna 1907).

BEBEL, AUGUST, *Aus meinem Leben* (3 vols) (new ed. Berlin 1946).

—— *Briefwechsel mit Friedrich Engels* (The Hague 1965).

BEER, MAX, *Fifty Years of International Socialism* (London 1935).

BERLAU, A. JOSEPH, *The German Social Democratic Party 1914–1921* (New York 1949).

BERNSTEIN, EDUARD, *Die Internationale der Arbeiterklasse und der Europäische Krieg* (Tubingen 1916).

—— *Die Vorraussetzungen des Sozialismus* (1899. English translation, 1901).

—— *My Years of Exile* (translated by Bernard Miall) (London 1920).

BEVAN, EDWYN, *German Social Democracy during the War* (London 1918).

BLUM, LÉON, *Les Congrès ouvriers et socialistes français* (2 vols) (Paris 1901).

—— *Jaurès* (Paris 1933).

—— *Souvenirs sur L'Affaire* (Paris 1935).

—— *L'Oeuvre de Léon Blum 1891–1905* (Paris 1954).

BOTHEREAU, ROBERT, *Histoire du Syndicalisme français* (Paris 1947).

BRANDIS, K., *Die deutsche Sozialdemokratie bis zum Fall des Sozialistengesetzes* (Leipzig 1931).

BRAUN, LILY, *Memoiren einer Sozialistin. I. Lehrjahre II. Kampfjahre* (Munich 1909).

BRAUNTHAL, JULIUS, *History of the International Vol. I 1864 to 1914* (London 1966).

—— *Victor und Friedrich Adler* (Vienna 1965).

BRETON, J. L., *L'Unité Socialiste* (Paris 1911).

BRUGEL, LUDWIG, *Geschichte der oesterreichischen Sozialdemokratie* (5 vols) (Vienna 1925).

BUREAU SOCIALISTE INTERNATIONAL, *Comptes rendus, manifestes et circulaires Vol. I 1900–1907* (Paris—The Hague 1969), ed. G. Haupt.

CARR, E. H., *The Bolshevik Revolution 1917–1923* (3 vols) (London 1950–3).

CHARNAY, M., *Les Allemanistes* (Paris 1911).

COLE, G. D. H., *British Working Class Politics 1832–1914* (London 1941).

—— *A History of Socialist Thought (Vol. II Marxism and Anarchism 1850–1890. Vol. III The Second International)* (London 1954–6).

COMPÈRE MOREL, J., *Grande Dictionaire socialiste* (Paris 1924).

—— *Jules Guesde* (Paris 1937).

DA COSTA, C., *Les Blanquistes* (Paris 1912).

DAVID, EDUARD, *Die Sozialdemokratie im Weltkrieg* (Berlin 1915).

DEUTSCHER, I., *The Prophet Armed. Trotsky 1879–1921* (Oxford 1954).

DOLLÉANS, E., *Histoire du Mouvement Ouvrier* (3 vols) (Paris 1946–53).

DOLLÉANS, E. and CROZIER, M., *Mouvements ouvriers et socialistes—Chronologie et Bibliographie* (Paris 1950).

DOMMANGET, M., *Histoire du Premier Mai* (Paris 1953).

DRACHKOVITCH, M. M., *Les socialismes français et allemand et le problème de la guerre 1870–1914* (Geneva 1953).

—— *De Karl Marx à Léon Blum* (Geneva 1954).

—— (ed.) *The Revolutionary Internationals 1864–1943* (Stanford 1966).

EISNER, KURT, *Wilhelm Liebknecht* (Berlin 1900).

ERMERS, MAX, *Victor Adler: Aufstieg und Grösse einer sozialistischen Partei* (Vienna and Leipzig 1932).

FAINSOD, MERLE, *International Socialism and the World War* (Cambridge, Mass., 1935).

FOLLOWS, J. W., *Antecedents of the International Labour Organization* (Oxford 1951).

FRÖLICH, PAUL, *Rosa Luxemburg* (London 1940).

GANKIN, OLIVER HESS and FISHER, H. H., *The Bolsheviks and The World War* (Stanford 1940).

GAY, PETER, *The Dilemma of Democratic Socialism* (New York 1952).

GOLDBERG, HARVEY, *The Life of Jean Jaurès* (Madison 1962).

GRADNAUER, G., *Wahlkampf!* (Dresden 1911).

GRUNBERG, KARL, *Die Internationale und der Weltkrieg* (2 vols) (Leipzig 1916).

HAASE, ERNST, *Hugo Haase, sein Leben und Wirken* (Berlin 1930).

HAENISCH, KONRAD, *Die deutsche Sozialdemokratie in und nach dem Weltkriege* (Berlin 1919).

HALÉVY, E., *Histoire du Socialisme européen* (Paris 1948).

HAMPDEN JACKSON, J., *Jean Jaurès* (London 1943).

HAUPT, GEORGES, *La Deuxième Internationale 1880–1914. Essai bibliographique* (Paris 1964).

—— *Programm und Wirklichkeit* (Neuwied 1970).

—— *Socialism and the Great War* (Oxford 1972).

HEIDEGGER, HERMANN, *Die deutsche Sozialdemokratie und der nationale Staat* (Göttingen 1956).

HILTON YOUNG, W., *The Italian Left* (London 1949).

HOCHDORF, MAX, *August Bebel* (Berlin 1932).

HUBERT-ROUGER, *La France socialiste* (3 vols) (Paris 1912–21).

HUMBERT, S., *Les Possibilistes* (Paris 1911).

HUMPHREY, A. W., *International Socialism and the War* (London 1915).

HUYSMANS, CAMILLE, *The Policy of the International* (London 1916).

HYNDMAN, H. M., *Record of an Adventurous Life* (London 1911).

—— *Further Reminiscences* (London 1912).

JAURÈS, JEAN, *Oeuvres* (ed. Max Bonnafous, 9 vols) (Paris 1932–9).

—— *Les Preuves* (Paris 1898).

JOLL, JAMES, *The Anarchists* (London 1964).

KAMPFFMEYER, PAUL, *Georg von Vollmar* (Munich 1930).

KANN, ROBERT A., *The Multinational Empire* (2 vols) (New York 1950).

KAUTSKY, KARL, *Der Weg zur Macht* (Berlin 1909).

—— *Taktische Stromungen in der deutschen Sozialdemokratie* (Berlin 1911).

—— *Die Internationalität und der Krieg* (Berlin 1915).

—— *Vergangenheit und Zukunft der Internationale* (Vienna 1920).

—— *Die Sozialisierung der Landwirtschaft* (Berlin 1921).

—— *Sozialisten und Krieg* (Prague 1937).

KEIL, WILHELM, *Erlebnisse eines Sozialdemokraten* (Stuttgart 1947).

KLÜHS, FRANZ, *August Bebel* (Berlin 1923).

KRIEGEL, ANNIE, *Le Pain et les roses* (Paris 1968).

LAIR, MAURICE, *Jaurès et l'Allemagne* (Paris 1935).

LANDAUER, CARL, *European Socialism* (Berkeley 1959).

LASKINE, EDMOND, *L'Internationale et le Pangermanisme* (Paris 1916).

LAZITCH, BRANKO, *Lénine et la IIIe Internationale* (Neuchâtel 1951).

LA CHESNAIS, P. G., *The Socialist Party in the Reichstag and the Declaration of War* (London 1915).

LENZ, J., *Rise and Fall of the Second International* (New York 1932).

LÉVY-BRUHL, L., *Jaurès* (Paris 1924).

LICHTHEIM, GEORGE, *Marxism* (London 1961).

LIEBKNECHT, WILHELM, *Briefwechsel mit Karl Marx und Friedrich Engels* (The Hague 1963).

LORWIN, LEWIS L., *Labour and Internationalism* (New York 1929).

LOUIS, PAUL, *Histoire du Mouvement Syndical en France 1789–1910* (Paris 1920).

—— *Histoire du Socialisme en France* (Paris 1946).

—— *Cent-cinquante Ans de pensée socialiste* (2 vols) (Paris 1947–53).

MAITRON, JEAN, *Histoire du Mouvement Anarchiste en France* (Paris 1951).

DE MAN, HENRI, *The Remaking of a Mind* (New York 1919).

—— *Au delà du Marxisme* (Brussels 1925, Paris 1928).

—— *Cavalier Seul* (Geneva 1948).

MAYER, GUSTAV, *Friedrich Engels* (2 vols) (The Hague 1934).

MEDA, FILIPPO, *Il socialismo politico in Italia* (Milan 1924).

MEHRING, F., *Geschichte der deutschen Sozialdemokratie* (Stuttgart 1897).

MICHELS, R., *Les Partis politiques* (French ed.) (Paris 1914).

—— 'Die deutsche Sozialdemokratie im internationalen Verbande' (*Archiv für Sozialwissenschaft und Sozialpolitik*,
vol. XXV, I Heft, 1907).

—— 'August Bebel' (*Ibid.*, vol. XXXVII, 1913).

MILHAUD, EDGAR, *La démocratie socialiste allemande* (Paris
1903).

MOMMSEN, HANS, *Die Sozialdemokratie und die Nationäli-
tatenfrage im Vielvölkerstaat* (Vienna 1963).

NETTL, J. P., *Rosa Luxemburg* (2 vols) (London 1966).

NIEUWENHUIS, D., *Van Christen tot Anarchist* (Amsterdam
1911).

NOLAND, AARON, *The Founding of the French Socialist Party*
(Cambridge, Mass., 1956).

NOSKE, GUSTAV, *Erlebtes aus Aufstieg und Niedergang einer
Demokratie* (Offenbach-am-Main 1947).

ORRY, ALBERT, *Les Socialistes Indépendants* (Paris 1911).

PARTI OUVRIER FRANÇAIS, *Aux travailleurs de France—11
ans d'histoire socialiste* (Paris 1901).

PELLOUTIER, F., *Histoire des Bourses du Travail* (Paris 1921).

PERTICONE, GIACOMO, *Le Tre Internazionali* (Rome 1944).

PLEKHANOV, G. V., *La Socialdemocratie et la Guerre* (Paris
1916).

PRICE, JOHN, *The International Labour Movement* (London
1945).

PROLO, JACQUES, *Les Anarchistes* (Paris 1912).

RAPPOPORT, CHARLES, *Le Socialisme et la Guerre* (Paris
1915).

—— *Jean Jaurès* (Paris 1916).

RENNER, KARL, *Das Selbstbestimmungsrecht der Nationen*
(Vienna 1918).

RIKLI, ERIKA, *Der Revisionismus* (Zürich 1936).

ROSMER, ALFRED, *Le Mouvement ouvrier pendant la guerre; I.
De l'union sacré à Zimmerwald* (Paris 1936).

RUSSELL, BERTRAND, *German Social Democracy* (London 1896).

SCHEIDEMANN, PHILIPP, *Der Zusammenbruch* (Berlin 1921).

—— *Memoirs* (English ed., 2 vols, 1929).

SCHORSKE, CARL, *German Social Democracy 1905–1914* (Cambridge, Mass., 1955).

SERGENT, A. and HARMEL, C., *Histoire de l'Anarchie* (Paris 1949).

SEVERING, CARL, *Mein Lebensweg* Vol. I (Cologne 1950).

SHADWELL, A., *The Socialist Movement 1824–1924* (2 vols) (London 1925).

STAFFORD, DAVID, *From Anarchism to Reformism: A study of the political activities of Paul Brousse* (London 1971).

STEWART, WILLIAM, *James Keir Hardie* (new ed. London 1925).

SUAREZ, GEORGES, *Briand: Sa vie, son oeuvre avec son journal et de nombreux documents inédits* (6 vols) (Paris 1932–52).

TSCHIFFELY, A. F., *Don Roberto* (London 1937).

TSUZUKI, CHUSHICHI, *H. M. Hyndman and British Socialism* (Oxford 1961).

—— *The Life of Eleanor Marx* (Oxford 1967).

TURATI, FILIPPO and KULISCHIOFF, ANNA, *Carteggio* (Milan 1949–1959).

VALIANI, LEO, *Histoire du Socialisme au XXe siècle* (Paris 1948).

—— 'Dalla prima alla seconda Internazionale' (*Movimento Operaio* Vol. VI No. 2, March–April 1954).

VAN DER ESCH, PATRICIA, *La Deuxième Internationale 1889–1923* (Paris 1957).

VAN DER SLICE, AUSTIN, *International Labor, Diplomacy and Peace 1914–1919* (University of Pennsylvania 1941).

VANDERVELDE, EMILE, *La Belgique envahie et le socialisme international* (Paris 1917).

—— *Jaurès* (Paris 1919).

—— *Souvenirs d'un militant socialiste* (Paris 1934).

—— *Le cinquantenaire du POB* (Brussels 1936).

VENTURI, FRANCO, *Jean Jaurès e altri storici della Rivoluzione francese* (Turin 1948).

VOLLMAR, G. VON, *Ueber die nächstan Aufgaben der deutschen Sozialdemokratie* (Munich 1891).

WALLING, W. E., *The Socialists and the War* (New York 1915).

WALLING, W. E. et al., *The Socialism of Today* (New York 1916).

WEBB, BEATRICE, *Beatrice Webb's Diaries, 1912–1924* (ed. by Margaret Cole) (London 1952).

WEHLER, H.-U., *Sozialdemokratie und Nationalstaat* (new ed. Göttingen 1971).

WEINSTEIN, HAROLD R., *Jean Jaurès. A Study of Patriotism in the French Socialist Movement* (New York 1936).

WILLARD, CLAUDE, *Le Mouvement socialiste en France 1893–1905: Les Guesdistes* (Paris 1965).

WITTWER, WALTER, *Streit um Schicksalsfragen: Die deutsche Sozialdemokratie zu Krieg und Vaterlandsverteidigung* (East Berlin 1964).

WOLFE, BERTRAM D., *Three who made a Revolution* (New York 1948).

ZÉVAÈS, ALEXANDRE, *Le Socialisme en 1912* (Paris 1912).

—— *Notes et souvenirs d'un militant* (Paris 1913).

—— *La Faillite de l'Internationale* (Paris 1917).

—— *Le Parti socialiste de 1904 à 1923* (Paris 1923).

—— *Jules Guesde* (Paris 1929).

—— *De l'introduction du Marxisme en France* (Paris 1947).

—— *Histoire du Socialisme et du communisme en France* (Paris 1947).

—— *Jean Jaurès* (Paris 1951).

INDEX

Czech Social Democratic Party, 36,
72, 119–23, 166
DAVID, Eduard, 126, 147
DEBUSSY, Claude, 79
DELCASSÉ, Théophile, 128
DELESCLUZE, Charles, 27
DITTMANN, Wilhelm, 179
Dresden,
SPD Congress 1903, 101
Dresden Resolution, 102–3
Dreyfus Affair, The, 16, 76, 83–7,
95, 100, 104
DUMAS, Alexandre, 62
DUPUY, 82

EBERT, Fritz, 162, 165, 169
Egalité, L', 26–7
Eisenach Congress 1869, 9
ENGELS, Friedrich, 11, 27, 31–2,
34, 52, 54, 58, 62, 73, 81, 92–3,
109, 173
and Paris Congress 1889, 31–2, 34
at Zürich 1893, 73
on effects of European war, 109
Erfurt, SPD Congress 1891, 7, 64

Fabian Society, 22, 72, 92
Fashoda, 141, 142
Fédération des Bourses de Travail,
60–1
*Fédération des Travailleurs Social-
istes de France* (Possibilists), 15,
78
Fédération Jurassienne, 25
*Fédération Nationale des Syndicats
Ouvriers de France*, 41, 60
FERRI, Enrico, 95, 105
FERRY, Abel, 171
'First International', see Inter-
national Working Men's Asso-
ciation
FISCHER, Richard, 176
Flemish Socialist Party, 26
FOURIER, F. C. M., 14, 27, 72
Fourmies, Fusillade at, 50, 81
France, 3–5, 12–18, 24, 30, 41, 44,
49–50, 57–8, 61–2, 76–7, 79,
86, 89, 95–6, 99–101, 106,
115–16, 133–5, 139, 145, 150–3,

164, 170–2, 180–1, 185, 190–1,
196, 198
growth of Socialism, 12–17
factory legislation, 44, 77
May Day, 49–50
attempt to unite Socialists, 96–8,
106
industrial unrest, 133
extension of military service,
150–1
FRANCE, Anatole, 165
FRANCIS FERDINAND, Archduke,
161
FRANK, Ludwig, 184
Free Trade Unions (in Germany),
14, 66, 69, 123, 130–3, 143, 145,
164–5

GALLIFET, General, 86
GAMBETTA, Léon, 80
German Social Democratic Party,
see *Sozialdemokratische Partei
Deutschlands*
Germany, 4–6, 8–10, 12, 18, 21, 24,
26–7, 44–5, 47, 51–2, 69, 73,
76–7, 79, 87, 92, 97, 108, 110,
112, 114, 115, 118, 126, 129–30,
138, 142, 145–50, 152–4, 156,
158, 163, 168, 169–70, 172–3,
176, 190, 193, 196, 200
Anti-Socialist Laws, 10–11, 24, 27
social legislation, 11, 44–5
May Day, 51–2
national problems, 116–19
see also Free Trade Unions,
*Sozialdemokratische Partei Deut-
schlands*
GIOLITTI, Giovanni, 89
GLASIER, Bruce, 165
Gotha Congress 1875, 7
Great Britain, 2, 21–2, 28–9, 37–8,
42, 44, 71, 74–5, 123–4, 126,
134, 142–4, 156, 158, 182–3,
187, 193, 194, 198–9
growth of Socialism, 21–2, 37–8,
42
factory legislation, 28–9, 44
Trade Unions, 28–9, 71, 134,
142–4